Angels & Earthworms

BOOKLING
PRESS

BOOKLING PRESS

Angels and Earthworms: An Unexpected Journey to Joy, Love, and Miralces
by Lorriane Segal
© 2022 Lorraine Segal

The beginning of Chapter 15 originally appeared in a slightly different form as "Healing a Broken Heart" in the anthology, *Stand Up, Speak Out Against Workplace Bullying.*

"You Say Hello, I Say Adios" in Chapter 8, originally appeared as a blog post on the Conflict Remedy website.

Excerpt from "Wishful Thinking: A Seekers ABC" by Frederick Buechner (Harper Rowe 1973) in Chapter 14 granted by permission.

Author's note: The Town and College of Carquenas are a fictional stand-in for the place I worked for twenty years.

Angels & Earthworms

an unexpected journey to joy, love, and miracles

A MEMOIR

Lorraine Segal

BOOKLING
PRESS

To my beloved wife Linda,
one of the greatest miracles of my life.

A long time ago, I read about a study of the brain and memory. Researchers discovered that we don't remember what actually happened. Instead, we tell ourselves a story about what happened, and that story is what we encode and remember. *These are my stories.*

"But, Ahbi, I don't want to keep making so many mistakes over and over. I wanted to be an angel of light!" I lamented.

Ahbi, my therapist, pinned me with her gaze. "Then what would you do here on the planet with all the rest of us earthworms?"

Contents

Chapter One

Welcome to Downey, Future Unlimited

When you entered the town of Downey in the 1950s, you saw a sign shaped like a futuristic lozenge that read, "*Welcome to Downey. Future Unlimited.*"

This was a joke even back then, because Downey was mostly a series of strip malls, parking lots, and tract homes. In this part of the greater Los Angeles area, Pico Rivera, Bellflower, Lakewood, Inglewood, Bell Gardens, Glendale, Norwalk, Paramount, and Downey were all only freeway exits off the Santa Ana freeway and later the Interstate 405, with no unoccupied land in between. There was no space for an expansive future.

Downey had few claims to fame. The third McDonald's restaurant in the world, a drive-in, opened on August 18, 1953 in Downey at Lakewood Boulevard and Florence Avenue. I remember as a very little girl getting takeout food there. And Downey had an office of the John Birch Society, the notorious ultra-conservative organization filled with wild conspiracy theories that predated the Tea Party movement and Q-Anon. The only time I ever heard Downey mentioned on the TV was an ad for Bob Spreen Cadillac that played over and over.

Their slogan was, "*Where the freeways meet — in Downey.*"

When I was very little, the narrow-thinking and extremely conservative politics and religious views didn't impact my life in any direct way. My family and our house and backyard were my whole world. I wasn't athletic, but I loved to be outside. I made up endless outdoor games and fantasies, joined by my sister when she was old enough. Play involved running around making lots of noise, gathering endless piles of leaves under the constantly shedding Brazilian pepper tree, digging holes to find buried treasure, or later burying treasures for a time capsule or for explorers to find, as well as picking flowers. We weren't allowed to pick the lovely purple geranium flowers, but we could pick as many small white ones as we wanted from the Jade green succulents that lined one side of the driveway. There was an incinerator out in back of the garage, which I found mysterious and interesting.

My only bad experience in the backyard was once stepping on a trail of big red fire ants. Their bites were like red-hot pokers on the bottom of my bare foot.

As we grew older, my world expanded to include our block, and I have some sweet memories of playing with neighborhood children our ages. Judy and DeeDee lived across the street and had an apricot tree in their backyard. They were in charge of when and how many we could eat, but they did share.

Not all the children were friendly. Mike who lived down the street was a bully, the same age as me. I never knew how to deal with him very well, but one day he started taunting and pushing my sister. I was too furious to be afraid.

I got right in his face and told him, "You leave my little sister alone!"

He tried to hit me and instead of running away, I hit him back and grappled with him a little as we both fell down. He was scared and startled, a coward like most bullies, and stood up and ran away. He never bothered either of us again.

Growing up in Downey and later in the San Fernando Valley in the '50s and '60s, the smog was horrific, but no one talked about the health dangers. When I was little, the smog was so thick that you could see it. I remember multiple times coming home from school with my chest and lungs aching and burning so painfully from the smog that I had to lie down.

Between that and my father's smoking, it is no wonder my lungs were vulnerable.

I heard a story, probably apocryphal, about the body of a woman being found in a canyon in L.A. She had no ID, but they knew she wasn't a native Southern Californian because when they did an autopsy to find cause of death: her lung tissue was too pink for her to have been there very long!

I remember being diapered as a very young child, probably two, and using a step stool to climb up into my crib. It is odd to have such a vivid memory as an adult. And I remember when I was three years old and my little sister was born. My Aunt Rose had come to stay and we stopped to buy flowers, red tulips I think, although I didn't know that name then, to bring to the hospital to my mom. My aunt wasn't happy about it, but I insisted that she buy a yellow tulip, so I had my own distinct flower to give to my mother. Then, I held my little sister on a pillow!

I wasn't always the best sister. She was always following me around, and I found it tiresome, even though she adored me. But we did make up many games to play together indoors as well as outside. We both loved *The Chronicles of Narnia*, and started having shared dreams in which we went through the wardrobe and had our own adventures. I usually woke up earlier in the dream than she did, and we had a daily "debrief" for a while. I would start telling what I remembered from the dream, and she would tell me what happened after I "left."

I also had my own small magic alternative world that I dreamed about. Our house in Downey had an old-fashioned metal furnace with a triangular angled grate that put out heat in both the living room and in the hall right outside my bedroom. You could kind of see into the space between and it was odd looking. I had dreams that talking animals, a fox and a cat, lived down there and I could magically go down and play with them. I remember a slide was involved!

Cowboys and Other Heroes of My Childhood

I had my own child-perceptions of what my family and Downey and 1950s culture, including TV, were like. TV was a significant influence on my childhood. In the 1950s, TV was very different from the shows they have on now. There were only a few channels, and the dominant genre was cowboy stories. I remember watching *The Rifleman, Rawhide, Have Gun — Will Travel, Gunsmoke, Maverick,* and *Bonanza.* I had a crush on Joe on *Bonanza.* I still remember the theme songs of many of these shows. Some of them I memorized without understanding the meaning of all the words. (*A knight without armor in a savage land. Paladin, Paladin. Where do you roam?*)

In all these shows, the cowboys were the heroes, sometimes clever, sometimes simply brave. I knew nothing about indigenous people. A favorite game when I was very little in my neighborhood was cowboys and Indians. I had a precious possession, a toy cowboy pistol with an ivory (plastic) handle.

One time we were strategizing about how to "ambush" the other team, and I suggested something I'd seen on TV, "We could hit them over the head with the butt of the gun."

A child who was a couple of years older than me said, "No way! That could really hurt him!"

I was bewildered and said, "Really?"

There didn't seem to be any consequences to doing that on the TV show, but I accepted his word for it. I was too little to really understand the difference between TV and real life.

Two of my other two favorite shows were *Robin Hood* and *Zorro*. I was very taken with Robin Hood and his merry band of men along with Maid Marian and the life they lived in the woods. It seems like they had a good altruistic purpose and a lot of fun.

But I think Zorro was my absolute favorite. There was something about his double identity and the dashing figure he cut. With his sword, his mask, and his cape rippling in the wind as he rode his beautiful stallion, he completely captured my imagination. My sister and I made up our own stories with adventures involving Zorro. We had plastic toy horses. I had a palomino and she a black stallion; and we had little dolls with bendable joints that could ride on the horses. We used those for our Zorro stories. My sister was an adventurer with Zorro, while I assumed all the "pretty girl" roles as we called the love interests. I always loved pretty clothes and femme stuff.

I also loved Superman, "*Is it a bird, is it a plane, no — it's Superman!*"

I imagined that I had a ballet tutu and that I could fly with him, combining two of my favorite fantasies, being a ballerina and flying.

My favorite cartoon show when I was very young was Mighty Mouse, "*Here he comes to save the day.*" I loved the idea that this tiny being had super powers and was more powerful than the bigger people around him.

In all these shows, men were the heroes and women secondary, and action was the path to courage. There was nothing about inner journeys or transformations.

A bit later, Shari Lewis, the puppeteer and ventriloquist, came along and I absolutely adored one of her puppets, Lamb Chop. Mr. Rogers was after my time, but we had *Romper Room* and in my part of Southern California, Sheriff John, who was a pretty benevolent figure. I loved *The Rocky and Bullwinkle Show*, though I didn't "get" all of their sly, subversive humor.

Although we usually ate at home, occasionally, we did go out to eat. My favorite restaurant was a German one. I enjoyed the food, roast beef in a sweet sauce with raisins, hot potato salad, and a sweet baked beans side dish. But my favorite part was that the walls of the restaurant were covered with cuckoo clocks.

I lived for the moment when the little cuckoo birds would come out on the hour and say "Cuckoo! Cuckoo!"

The restaurant also sold very well-made animal puppets and toy stuffed animals. Every once in a while, our parents let us choose a hand puppet. We had a cat, a little dog, and an owl. My sister and I had hours of fun playing with them.

Once for a school project, my father helped me build a little set, and I used the cat puppet and the owl puppet to do a dramatic hand puppet rendition of the poem "The Owl and the Pussycat" by Edward Lear.

The Romance of the Silver Surfboard

In sixth grade, romance entered my child world. Blonde surfer Neil and red-haired, freckled Carol Sue were two popular "cool" kids in the school. Neil asked Carol Sue to go steady and gave her a small silver surfboard on a chain to signify their love. This was a scandal, and kids and adults took sides. Carol Sue would walk around the playground, linking arms with a number of other girls who championed her. But adults were concerned that they were too young, and some kids found it shocking too. I was on the outside anyway and didn't quite get what the fuss was all about.

Later that year, another student, Larry, invited me to go on a "date" with him to the school carnival. I bluntly said, "No!" because I was already going with Lois. Poor Larry, it didn't even occur to me that I might have hurt his feelings.

The Beatles also entered my consciousness at this time. One girl brought fan cards with pictures of them. Their hair looked so long and wild and odd! We had never seen anything like it. The boys we knew were still getting crewcuts, or, daringly, longer hair slicked back with one piece falling into their eyes, like Neil. When I look at early Beatles pictures now, they look clean-cut and mainstream, but they were rebels for sure back then.

Childhood Difficulties and Traumas

Except for the images and ideas that I found in fantasy books, my childhood was completely devoid of Spirit. I felt lost at times, though I didn't know what was missing or why I didn't fit in at school. But I paid attention to what was happening around me, which helped me reframe and forgive later. The elements of political awareness and an awareness of injustice, of wanting to lift up the world, to help myself and others, all started in childhood.

My parents, Henry and Fran, loved me deeply, as much as and in the ways they knew how. They wanted to be good parents. They put time and energy and money and intention into it. The fact that they did it with mixed success, despite all their efforts, and gave me a lot of miserable messages about myself and how to live wasn't because of malice, but because they had appalling gaps in their own knowledge about life, in their own ability to love themselves and others, and in how to connect with Source.

They were children of the Great Depression, children of immigrants, descendants of Jews who fled pogroms (campaigns of genocide in Russia) and other expressions of anti-Semitism. They both had grown up culturally Jewish, little of which they transmitted to me.

Though it wasn't their intention, and there was no physical or sexual abuse in my childhood, there was what I've come to see as emotional abuse and micromanaging.

My mother, Fran, wouldn't let me leave the house to go to school without fussing and fussing over my hair and clothes. I wasn't allowed to choose my own clothes or comb my own hair.

I had long wavy hair, which I wore in braids. Fran cut my bangs for me, generally unevenly, so my bangs always had a slight unintentional slant, and for some reason she parted my hair on the side, so one braid always looked thicker than the other.

Every day, she would lay out the clothes that she wanted me to wear. Back then, little girls were not allowed to wear pants or shorts to school, so it was always dresses or skirts. Some of them were new, but many were hand-me-downs from my two cousins, Laurel and Elaine, who were both five years older than me. Some of the hand-me-down dresses had to be shortened and they would have very wide hems, which looked weird when I twirled. Since they both lived in much colder climates, Laurel in New York and Elaine in Minneapolis, there were also itchy wool skirts that were far too heavy for Southern California, but which I sometimes had to wear.

Every morning, after I put on the clothes my mother had chosen, she would braid my hair and then fuss over how I looked. She seemed very concerned and worried and she would often fuss for a very long time trying to get me to look the way she wanted. Sometimes she even made me change clothes. The message I received was that the way I looked wasn't good enough and my hair and my clothes were only marginally acceptable even after a great deal of fixing and fussing.

This feeling has persisted to this day. If I'm not grounded and centered, I still sometimes try on multiple outfits and fuss with my own hair and accessories from that worried place of not being okay or good enough. If I'm really stressed about going to an event, until very recently, I would end up with a bed piled with outfits that I'd tried on and rejected.

Trying to Pass

I understand now that this came at least in part from my mother's experience of anti-Semitism as a young working adult in Minnesota. I believe she felt she had to hide and pass and never felt good enough either. But during the prolonged period I experienced this as a child, it really fueled my feeling that somehow, I wasn't okay. That love and acceptance were conditional on my being perfect and I never measured up for more than a moment. I don't ever remember feeling completely loved just as I was, when I was growing up. And my mother put her excess energy into worrying about everything — our health, our school work, toxins in food, how I looked.

After years of laying out my outfit and giving me no say at all, one day Fran suddenly announced I was supposed to choose my own clothes. She didn't do what I witnessed my sister-in-law do with her daughter: give the little girl two outfits to choose from and ask her to pick which one she liked better. No, she went from being completely in charge and giving me absolutely no choice at all, to demanding I choose from a whole closet full of clothes without any guidance or process at all.

"You pick what to wear today," she said unexpectedly.

I flipped out and threw a temper tantrum. "No!" I screamed. "I don't know what to pick! I can't do it!"

I had no idea how to choose. And I was scared, sure that whatever I picked wouldn't be good enough or would be unacceptable. I had absorbed the false belief that I couldn't function in the world by myself without my mother's control, and that on my own I was never ever good enough.

With lips pursed in disapproval, she finally chose some clothes for me.

I don't think my mother had any friends to talk to when I was a child, because when I was eleven she started venting to me about the family grudges and resentments she had been holding her whole life. At the time, I was flattered and felt very grown up, but hearing her intense bitterness about all the slights or disrespect from in-laws and cousins, and her oldest brother, and my father's sister Rose, the vivid detail and deep resentments and anger she harbored for years were not at all a good model for how to deal with conflicts or differences. I, unfortunately, became rather good at holding grudges myself and had to work hard to unlearn that behavior later.

My mother thought she had the right to micromanage other people's lives as well as ours. She had told me many times how selfish she thought my Aunt Rose was. Rose was my father's sister who wasn't married and taught Sociology at Boston University.

Once we went to visit her at her summer home on Cape Cod. My aunt hated paper plates, but my mother absolutely insisted we use them. Her reasoning was, "It's your house and you're cooking, so I'm the one who will have to do the dishes, and I don't want to, so let's use paper plates." Respecting my aunt's wishes, even in her own house, was not part of Fran's thinking. My aunt and my mother had a monumental battle about it, while my father sat there silently, with a sick look on his face, and my sister and I were a captive audience.

My Mom Was a Terrible, Horrible Cook

Part of Fran's misery at doing housework was that she wasn't very good at it and didn't want to do it. She gave every appearance of feeling trapped and unfulfilled as a housewife. She spoke fondly of her previous career as a teacher. But post-World War II, endless propaganda was about the importance of the wife staying home with the children. June Cleaver was the model. And working, having a career, was particularly unacceptable for a mother of small children.

Fran had a lot to do, but hated all of it. My father would call her from work with an ever-lengthening list of errands he wanted her to run; and her frustration would mount with every item. And my poor mom was a truly horrible cook. I rarely had any decent food until I left home. She hated cooking but was stuck with making nutritious meals for us every night. Some of the culinary disasters included: Chef Boyardee canned spaghetti with green peppers added, grocery store-roasted chicken with generic curry powder added to the cut-up chicken, salads that consisted solely of iceberg lettuce and canola oil. I hated sardines with eyes and little bones. And there was the odd ham dish, yes, we ate ham, with some kind of ketchup sauce; and frozen fish sticks with overcooked frozen thin-sliced green beans. There were a few decent dishes — salmon patties, stuffed hamburgers, boiled beef and white beans.

Once in a while, my father made Baba Ghanoush, a Sephardic or Middle Eastern dish, with eggplant broiled over an open burner and mashed without the skin. I don't know where he learned to make it, but it was delicious. He also made Matzoh Brei with broken-up square sheets of matzoh (unleavened bread), and scrambled with eggs. Once in a very great while we had Kreplach, which were like Jewish ravioli.

But there was almost no spice or flavoring in anything. When I was little, we had whole wheat bread, but then my mother read an article about Strontium 90 in the wheat, and we never had whole grain bread again. We did have decent rye bread for a while.

And my mother in her anxiety to clean up at home, had a habit of snatching the dishes away before we had really finished eating, which was not conducive to a calm enjoyable meal. I knew nothing about blessing food before we ate either.

One hot summer day, my mother made a noodle kugel, with pasta and hoop cheese. It tasted delicious and we all complimented her on it, "This tastes so good! Thank you!"

But instead of accepting our appreciation, she became very angry. "Do you have any idea how much work that was and how hot it was in the kitchen? I'm never making it again!"

Of course, if we had ignored her efforts, she would've been mad also.

I remember that my grandmother used to send a care package of baked goods periodically and they were all delicious. Rugelach, hamantaschen (triangular-shaped pastries) with poppy seed or prune filling, sinfully buttery cinnamon coffee cake, halvah (sesame seed candy). My mother didn't know how to bake any of these things.

I saw matzoh balls for the first time in Arizona at my grandmother's house. I thought they were the weirdest things — huge round balls sticking out of a bowl of soup.

There was a whole other issue around food with my mother. When I was nine, she decided I was overweight and put me on a diet.

"You are eating too much and if you keep it up, you will get fat. You need to eat less. Use your willpower and don't eat desserts!" she told me.

When I ate less, "Good girl!" she said.

And when she thought I ate too much she pursed her lips, a favorite passive-aggressive expression.

As an adult, when I started dealing with my compulsive eating issues, I went looking for childhood photos to see how fat I had been. I looked through all the photos, from infancy to high school graduation, and to my surprise couldn't find any in which I looked fat. I wasn't as thin as my sister, but simply average-looking. I don't know what she feared or why she did that to me, but it made me feel fat, and was the beginning of my love/hate relationship with food and my using food as a drug.

My Father, Henry

I wasn't very close to my father for most of my childhood because he was away from us physically at work, and distant emotionally; partly because of his depression, and partly because my mother made all the decisions about our lives.

When I asked his permission for something, his standard answer was, "Ask your mother."

I do remember as a very young girl that my mother allowed me to walk down to the end of the block and meet his car when he came home from work. I thought that was exciting and special!

Henry was tall, and thin at this time because he had ulcers and stomach problems. His hair, what there was of it since he was half bald, was dark. He had a loud lovely laugh, which instantly made everyone around him want to laugh. Unfortunately, a lot of the time he was sad, not cheerful. He would wander around the house or sit glumly in a corner with a stricken look in his eyes, withdrawn from all of us to the realms of depression and self-hate.

But he was very good to me sometimes. I remember that he used to make up stories just for me about a character named Thumb-bum, who was his thumb, but was also alive. He had a home base underground and went on many adventures.

Henry also made up stories for my sister and me about the gophers in the backyard who had families, drank tea, and also had their own adventures. But when in the real world, my parents decided to call an exterminator to get rid of the gophers, my sister and I were devastated, because the gophers were people to us! I'm sure he regretted making up those stories.

From my father, I also gained some political and cultural awareness.

My father sang three kinds of songs when I was growing up. Although he would hardly talk about his experiences in World War II, when he was a non-flying cadet based in England, he did sing some songs from the military and Broadway musical war songs.

Henry also sang a few union songs and Yiddish songs he had learned from his parents. One was a poignant love song, *Her nor du schejn Maidele* about a young girl who works washing clothes and loves a poor young man. Just that one song later made Klezmer music and Yiddish theater music feel like a little piece of home.

My father's parents were atheist socialists, and he was what's called a "red diaper baby," i.e. a child of socialists or communists. He knew union and Marxist songs, including *The International:* *"Arise ye prisoners of starvation. Arise ye wretched of the earth"*; *Union Maid: "There once was a Union maid"* (a proto-feminist union song); *Joe Hill: "I dreamt I saw Joe Hill last night."* Joe Hill was a union organizer killed by the "bosses." Another song was half in Yiddish, half in Yiddish-accented English about The International Ladies' Garment Workers' Union, which his parents had belonged to: *"The Cloakmachers union is a no gutten union, it's a company union for the bosses. So, join the International Garment Workers Union, the only true workers' union . . .*" I have a photo I cherish from the early 1900s which shows my grandfather and other members of his union; and along with the union banner, there is a banner that says "Suffrage Vote!" I absorbed some awareness about injustice and political struggles early on.

My father worked for the L.A. Department of Water and Power. He went back to school, finished his BA and completed an MA in Political Science, but was never able to turn it into a career. I think he felt he couldn't take a chance when he had a family to support. Years later, he said he wished he'd gone to law school instead. He was a drafting engineer but didn't really like it. It was a job he put up with, not a source of satisfaction.

However, he did make some good friends at work, Lonnie, who was Black, and Gallegos who was Mexican-American. I met them and their families, but we didn't really socialize. I don't know if it was the pressure of Downey or perhaps my mother's discomfort with people who were "different."

Atheist Jew

My spiritual connection through books was not linked at all to religion. The whole concept of religion was very alien to me. Although I knew we were Jewish, that was about it. I knew hardly anything about Judaism, religious holidays, practices, prayers in Hebrew or Jewish spirituality, or even Jewish culture and food. We didn't celebrate most of the holidays; we didn't go to services. I had never eaten a bagel because they weren't available where we lived. I didn't even know what it meant to "look Jewish," nor did I understand that I, like my parents, talked with my hands more than the WASPs (white Anglo-Saxon Protestants) and Catholics who surrounded us.

I had a little friend on my block named MaryAnn. We had the kind of relationship where we would go and knock on each other's doors and ask, "Can Mary (or Lorry) come out to play?" I don't remember ever being in her house, but we were companions and made up games together.

After she started Catholic school with the nuns when she was five, she came over to my house and stood on the porch crying and sobbing in deep fear, repeating over and over, "I don't want to go to hell! I don't want to go to hell!"

Clearly the nuns had terrified her with what would happen to her if she made any mistakes or did something wrong or committed a sin. It made a deep impression on me. Her anguish was intense, and I didn't have a clue at age five how to help her. But I always remembered how religion could be used as a weapon to make people feel terrible about themselves.

My parents did send us for a while to Saturday school at a synagogue where we were supposed to learn about Judaism. But because they weren't part of the community, and didn't take us to Friday night services, we were outcasts and strangers there as well. I found out years later that my mother had actually grown up in a rather close-knit if dysfunctional Jewish family that celebrated all the rituals, but she gave it up because my father believed religion was the opiate of the masses. I don't remember learning anything even vaguely spiritual at the synagogue either.

My parents thought of themselves as free of prejudice. They were liberal Jews who talked and felt a lot about the need for justice and equity. But like most of us, they had a number of areas where unconscious bias crept in. One time when I was six or seven, I remember my parents, my sister, and I went to see fireworks for Fourth of July at a park in a neighboring community. My mother, so worried as always that we wouldn't be warm enough, had brought enough sweaters for a family of ten. I started talking to a little Latina girl about my age who had shiny dark hair and eyes, and warm cinnamon-brown skin. She was also there with her family. They hadn't realized how cool it would get when the sun started going down. My new little friend was shivering in short sleeves.

"Can we lend them some sweaters?" I asked my mother.

She wouldn't let me. In a whisper, she said, "We don't know them. They could be dirty."

They were dressed a lot like us, and I couldn't understand. It felt awful to me to have all those extra sweaters and to be forbidden to share them. I don't remember anything about the fireworks themselves, but that incident stuck in my mind.

The Making of a Writer's Block

One of the worst manifestations of my mother's control was about my writing. My mother insisted on correcting or editing or completely rewriting everything I wrote from the time I was nine until I left home at eighteen. I'm sure she genuinely wanted to help me be successful in school and achieve success in life, but the message I received was something quite different.

Since love in general felt conditional in my family — dependent on being good or achieving academic success -   I felt that love would be withheld if I didn't let her edit my work, so I could get the best grade possible. And I heard the message loud and clear that who I was and what I wrote and how I wrote it wasn't good enough without her.

"What are you working on writing for school? Let me see it," she would say. With sinking dread, I would reluctantly show it to her.

"Let's see," she said. Pencil in hand, she would correct my paper and tell me what I had done wrong, and change it without asking me.

I sat there time after time in sullen passive-aggressive resentment. I hated being there, hated her, and hated myself. I hated her treatment of me, and her manipulative martyrdom.

I didn't believe in God, but I begged God repeatedly, "Please, please don't let me be like her when I grow up!"

And I would silently say over and over, "I hate you!" I had a writing block for almost twenty years after these experiences.

Childhood Nightmares

I've never liked horror movies, maybe because I had nightmares a lot when I was young. I think they were a way for releasing all the fear and anxiety I felt on a daily basis. Being chased by animals was a recurring theme. Most frequently large dogs, sometimes wolves or tigers or lions and at least once a giant bear rearing on its hind legs with huge teeth and claws. They would all growl and bare their teeth at me. I would run away as fast as I could, but they would gain on me and I would desperately try to wake up, dimly aware it was a dream. Often, I would wake myself up, screaming, before they attacked; though once in the dream a dog bit my hand.

Other nightmares didn't have an animal chasing me, but contained an overwhelming sense of dread, of being stalked by some horrific invisible being. I remember one nightmare where I was in a dark house filled with small dogs, some up on the walls, maybe pugs or bulldogs with large eyes. They didn't move, except their eyes followed me everywhere. And I knew absolutely, with utter terror, that something far worse was after me and on the verge of finding me. I woke up in the nick of time!

The first movie I saw in a movie theater, when I was five, was *Darby O'Gill and the Little People*. There was a very scary (to me) banshee in it and I cried and put my hands over my eyes, terrified. We also went to Disneyland for the first time when I was five, and the wicked witch in the Snow White ride also terrified me. Even as an adult, a horror movie would scare me terribly and could trigger nightmares for days.

Aggressive Christianity

Downey was a very prejudiced environment. Most of the students were some brand of Christian — either Protestant, Evangelical, or Catholic. Jews and Armenians, being darker than the light-skinned, light-haired majority children, were suspect and were sometimes bullied or ostracized for how we looked.

I had dark hair and brows and olive skin that tanned easily in the Southern California sun, and it mattered. It marked me as the "other." There was a lot of prejudice and insulting language about Black people. And some children, especially as I approached sixth grade, expressed very prejudiced attitudes towards Jews, believing and saying that they killed Christ; even that they had horns and a tail, and that they were going to hell. I didn't take on all their beliefs, but I surely didn't fit in or feel like I belonged.

There were no Black or Latino children in Roger Casier Elementary School. Although redlining (refusing insurance or mortgages to Black or brown families) was no longer legal, racial covenants (racism written into property deed agreements), and steering (discouraging Black or brown families from looking in certain towns or neighborhoods), meant no Black or brown families bought homes or lived in my neighborhood. It was a clear manifestation of systemic racism. When I was in fifth grade, a little girl from Mexico came to the school. She was of African-Caribbean descent and some parents protested and didn't want her in school with their children. My fifth-grade teacher, Mr. Miller, gave an angry rant about people's prejudice and how wrong it was.

Finally, and only because the school officials affirmed that she was from Mexico, which was deemed marginally more acceptable than Black, did the protest die down and she was allowed to stay. She spoke almost no English. There were no special classes or services to help her learn. The Administration pulled me, the smart Jew, out of class to tutor her in English. I don't remember that I had any say in the matter: I was obliged to do it. I don't think they asked my parents' permission either.

Sixth Grade Outcast

Life wasn't much easier at school as I got older. Although I did very well academically, only athletic ability, of which I had none, gained respect and positive attention from other students. By sixth grade, I was a total outcast in school. I was pushed around and bullied and called names. My worst and most persistent tormentors were a pair of girls called Candace and Natasha. Candace was very Anglo-looking, light-skinned with blue eyes and soft curly blonde hair, a turned-up nose, and a sugary sweet voice. Natasha, who had bonded with her, was a dark-haired, Armenian with olive skin. I think now that Natasha hated and targeted me because she believed if I was the scapegoat, it would save her from the same abuse. I distinctly remember many times Natasha pushing me around, punching me in the arm, while Candace joined in taunting me.

One time, someone I never saw pushed me so hard from behind as I was walking past the boys' bathroom that I fell to my knees in the doorway and the swinging door closed on my fingers. It hurt! Since my fingers were small, they weren't broken but my knuckles were torn and bloody. No one noticed. No one took me to the nurse. No one saw my tears. My mother cleaned up my hands once I arrived home.

Another tormentor at school was Rowena. Maybe she felt competitive because I always did better in class than she did, but she was unmercifully mean to me.

I did tell my mother about the abuse at school. She was dismissive, and I felt all alone and unsafe. I concluded, again, that there must be something wrong with me and that is why I was bullied. That somehow, I wasn't okay, and the other kids knew it. The fussing by my mother had already set me up to believe this.

I tried talking about these experiences once to her years later when I finally realized that what had occurred was anti-Semitism, and she said, "Oh no, I don't think so."

Perhaps it was her own denial, even though she had experienced similar things as a young adult looking for a teaching job in Minnesota; and she had told me about them.

Another place I didn't really fit in and didn't understand why was Girl Scouts. I was a Brownie and later a Girl Scout with the same small group of girls in the local troop. I became friends with Cynthia, the daughter of the troop leader. One year, the Girl Scouts were doing a folkdance performance as part of a bigger, regional Girl Scout presentation. We were allowed to choose whatever partner we wanted, and Cindy and I really enjoyed dancing together. We were both good at it — learned the steps quickly, had a good sense of rhythm, and a bit of flair.

But Cynthia's mother didn't like it, perhaps because I was a Jew or possibly because my family didn't have as much money as hers. So, after telling all the girls they could pick whatever partner they wanted, she split Cynthia and me up, making an excuse that we were supposed to dance with different people. I was very upset and disappointed and so was Cynthia. Neither of us understood why we couldn't continue dancing together. She pestered her mother to explain, but she wouldn't explain or relent.

Looking Jewish

I found out later that I wasn't the only Jewish kid in my grade level. There were two boys, Barry, and Edward, and another girl, Barbara Rose. None of them were picked on and bullied the way I was. I'm not sure about why that was true for the boys, but Barbara Rose was tall, blonde, and good at sports, so she looked more like the other girls and had the athletic skills that were highly admired.

Some teachers were prejudiced against Jews as well. Miss Tremiere, my second-grade teacher, who was Catholic, favored a little Catholic girl named Maureen and convinced the rest of us that she was the best and most outstanding student. I couldn't have been more than six or seven when my mother came to an open house for the school.

Instead of wanting to show her my artwork on the walls, I tried to steer my mother to look at Maureen's artwork, "Come look at Maureen's drawing, Mommy. It's much better than mine."

My mother pursed her lips and smiled tightly. "No, I don't want to see her work. I want to see yours!"

Sad for a little girl to sincerely believe that her own sweet artwork was inferior!

None of my differentness was so bad when I was really little; kids didn't notice differences much, and they hadn't been brainwashed by their parents' prejudices. But with each year, the bullying became worse and worse. The nadir of it all was in junior high (middle school).

I was in a special program called Mentally Gifted Minors, (MGM), which those of us in it called Mentally Gifted Monkeys. In fifth, sixth, and seventh grades we did get some advanced course work and materials, which was fun, but the program also had a class bias — the well-off blonde students were included, it seemed, regardless of academic achievement, while the working-class kids were only included if they were exceptionally smart.

Anywhere but Here — Escaping into Books

One of the big gifts I was given in childhood was the gift of reading. Both parents read out loud to my sister and me. My father, Henry, worked in downtown Los Angeles and he would go to the huge children's department in the main L.A. library, and get the librarians to help him choose books for us. The librarians adored him; it was unusual then for a man to do this for his young daughters. He would bring the books home in his black metal lunch box, and I still remember the excitement and anticipation we felt to see what treasurers he had brought!

I read my first "chapter" book when I was very young, and I have been reading, mostly novels, with memoirs, self-help books, and other non-fiction thrown in, with delight and enthusiasm ever since. I once estimated the number of books I've read in my life and I'm sure, conservatively, it is well over 12,000. My Aunt Rose also sent beautifully illustrated hardback children's books each year for our birthdays, like *Little Women, Alice in Wonderland, A Little Princess, Black Beauty*. Some of them I still have.

In my challenging childhood, books were my friends, my comfort, my escape, feeding my sense of wonder, and offering a window on a bigger world. They were also my key to understanding other people and other cultures. I read an article a few years ago which said that people who read novels tend to be more empathetic, because they enter into the lives, perceptions, and feelings, of people very different from them. This is certainly true of me and explains why I can easily feel empathy for people who have had a very different life experience from my own. I probably spent time with someone like them inside a book.

I particularly loved historical novels and fantasy and science fiction, appreciating the bigger escape not only from my particular life, but my time, my world, and my American culture.

The public library in Downey was small and limited, but once I was old enough to go, I loved it. I read almost everything in the children's section by the time I was nine or ten, and moved on to the few shelves of young adult books.

The young adult section had a system of labeling that involved putting small pieces of sticky white tape with red symbols on the spine. There was a rocket ship for science fiction books, two hearts for the teen romances, and a magnifying glass for mysteries. I read everything.

The first science fiction book I read was by Robert Heinlein. It was either *Rocket Ship Galileo* or *Orphans of the Sky*. My imagination was captured by these outer space adventures that involved kids. I still have a soft spot for well-written science fiction and fantasy.

Then, by age eleven, I switched to the adult novel section. I would start at the As, and stop when I reached the maximum number of books I could take out. I read trashy novels and classics indiscriminately.

My parents, though nominally Jewish, were somewhere between agnostic and atheist. I was a spiritual seeker from a very young age, though I didn't realize it at the time. Nothing in my life let me know

Spirit could be part of my reality. As a very young child, I went crying to my mother, afraid of dying and wanting to know what happened after death.

"Am I going to die? Will I go to heaven?" I asked fearfully, craving reassurance.

The best my mother could do was say, "Some people believe that. And some people believe in angels."

I asked her repeatedly, desperately, "Do you believe that?"

But her only answer was, "No. Some people believe that, but I don't."

This response didn't soothe or comfort me at all.

Even when my mom belatedly started taking us to High Holy Days services, I don't believe I ever heard anything about how to be a good person or about anything spiritual. Like many Jews, I absorbed by osmosis even more passion for justice.

But, without realizing it, I longed for connection to Spirit, and I looked for signs of Divine love, a benevolent Universe, miracles and magic, in books, particularly fantasy books. I kept searching, and I found comfort and hope in Narnia, in Middle Earth, in *The Mists of Avalon*, in enchanted castles and ships that flew, in fairytales, in books about magic rings and crystals and unicorns and fairy dust, and mystical voyages and time travel, and heroic quests (particularly by girls); books about swords and sorcery, wise women healers and warriors and sorceresses, about courage that could move mountains, and about happy endings after endurance. I had a special fondness for young girls who seemed ordinary and turned out to have extraordinary powers that they could learn to use to save themselves and their people.

As a young adult, I thought I had to leave these magic realms behind in order to grow up. But then I discovered crystals and herbs and chakras and psychic healing and meditation and dowsing and intuition. I realized with great joy that magic *was* real after all. And Spirit did exist. That delight and longing has in some ways transformed my whole life. But first, I had to survive middle school and high school.

I went to North Junior High to start seventh grade. It was a challenging transition in some ways, even though I hadn't really been happy in grades four through six, but it did further my enjoyment of words and reading.

I more or less liked all my classes except PE (physical education), but the best parts of seventh and eighth grade were my English and Drama/Speech classes. My eighth-grade English teacher was Mr. Townsend. I think now he was gay, just from his style and body language. He was a dapper dresser who never talked about a family. He didn't help us learn to write, but he opened up the world of literature and the delight of learning new vocabulary. His class was a safe haven where I felt smart, engaged, and respected.

Drunk on Words

We were supposed to read as many books as possible. Mr. Townsend had his own paperback library in the classroom and he encouraged us to borrow. And we each had to keep a vocabulary notebook. When we came across a word we didn't know, in one of the books, or in a newspaper, or on the radio, we had to write the word down, look up the dictionary definition, and quote a sentence, which used the word in context. I found the process fascinating and this began my lifelong love affair with words.

To this day, I love words and synonyms. In my professional writing and speaking, I do my best to use direct, simple, effective words, but when I'm feeling giggly and free, I use lots of the words that I used to call "big," polysyllabic and complicated, because I get drunk on words! Post-Mr. Townsend, I don't think I formally studied words or meanings very much, at least in English, until graduate school. It was more of an organic process. Reading a novel, coming across a word I didn't know, puzzling out the meaning from context, later encountering the word again and getting more ideas about the meaning. I will say that I enjoyed TV's *Jeopardy* because I almost always knew some of the answers, partly because of my vocabulary, and partly because I have a huge grab bag of trivia about history and culture from reading so many novels.

I also really enjoyed the Speech and Drama classes I took. I found I could be a persuasive speaker. I could recite poetry with passion, clarity, and drama. And I was a lead in one of the eighth-grade short plays; and the MC at the Christmas show.

In middle school for the first time, when we were absent, we had to go to the office upon our return and get a small form with multiple carbon copies. We had to take it around to all our teachers and have them sign it. I began to have a new kind of dream, not exactly a nightmare, but filled with anxiety, that I forgot to get the signatures or couldn't find my teachers or classrooms, or somehow did it wrong and was in big trouble.

As I think of it, once I became a teacher, I had similar dreams. I couldn't find my classroom, or would have to go through mazes or tunnels or down slides or climb walls to get there, or I was naked and had to teach. Or I was teaching but didn't know what subject I was supposed to be teaching and didn't have a lesson plan.

Middle School Misery

Along with the classes I enjoyed, P.E. classes and being in the locker room continued with the bullying I'd experienced in elementary school.

The locker room was divided into sections, and I was put into a section with girls, all white, who I didn't know, and who had all attended the same elementary school. They didn't like me.

Again, I had no idea why, but when I walked into that section of the locker room, they would say, "What's that smell?" or directly, "You smell." Or hold their noses and pointedly move away from me.

I was tormented by their verbal taunts and insults every day, ceaselessly. One girl would poke and elbow me and at least once tried to slam my hand in a locker. I told my parents about this, and my mother said to fight back and I did.

The next time the ringleader taunted me, I punched her in the arm and burst into tears. With the current zero tolerance for physical fighting, these days I would've been called into the principal's office as a problem. But back then, I didn't get into trouble and it worked. She stopped tormenting me. I don't really know if it was the punch or the tears but they all ignored me after that.

One girl in seventh grade named Cecilia and I became friends of sorts. When she found out I was Jewish, she was very concerned that I was going to hell. Her church had taught her that's where people went if they weren't baptized. I tried to explain to her that that was what *her* religion taught, and I was fine according to *mine,* but she couldn't grasp that distinction. She had no concept of different beliefs for different cultural or religious traditions. I could make no headway against her narrow beliefs.

Tormented Monkeys

I remember seeing a film in middle school, which made a deep, hurtful impression on me. I have no idea why they showed it to us, but it was about an experiment that had been done with baby rhesus monkeys to test the bonds between mother and child and the effects of a lack of socialization. They divided these poor little rhesus monkeys into three groups. One group was with the mama monkeys, one had a bare metal "mother," and one group had a metal "mother" covered in terry cloth. The poor little monkeys separated from their real mothers cried and cried inconsolably. The ones whose metal "mother" was covered with terry cloth clung to her but were never comforted. And the ones without even the terry cloth just huddled and cried.

And I cried, witnessing this total cruelty. I empathized and identified with the tormented baby monkeys. The movie narrator said that the two groups of babies without mothers never learned to socialize properly with other monkeys and were always outcast. I thought that was totally wrong and that no scientific conclusions could justify it.

Chapter Two

Valley Girl

When I was fourteen, my mother started worrying that I, and soon my sister, would want to date Gentiles (non-Jews) and at that point decided to move to the San Fernando Valley. But so much damage has been done to all of us by that time. As Jews, my parents were misfits in Downey too, and didn't make friends with any couples. In ninth grade, moving to Van Nuys, California was a tremendous relief — to be at schools that were filled at that time about half with Jewish kids.

But the school I was assigned to, Van Nuys Junior High, was a year behind North Junior High in Downey. No one noticed and it didn't even occur to me that I could speak up about it, so I basically repeated a year of school even though I absolutely did not need to. And while I knew I was Jewish and I was supposed to date and eventually marry someone Jewish, the culture and religion were still pretty invisible to me.

Still a Misfit

Even in Van Nuys, surrounded by Jews, I was still a misfit. My mom made me wear ugly orthopedic shoes. Options for girls' sports shoes weren't widely available or acceptable for wearing off a court or field, so it was either flimsy, pretty, uncomfortable shoes or the ugliest beige old lady lace-up shoes you can imagine. I can't really even blame the other kids for making fun of me; they were that bad.

And a junior high with Jews was still junior high. Once my breast was grabbed by one stupid boy daring another. They didn't even look at me during their assault — it was all about them laughing and bonding — and it really felt awful.

When puberty hit, my hair which had been wavy, grew very frizzy, and I was teased and tormented about that and called Frizzball. The surfer look, with flat bone straight hair was in. Girls were ironing their hair to make it straight. But my mother wouldn't let me, and honestly, it would probably not have lasted long. My waves and curls were persistent. My beautiful wild hippie hair was ahead of its time, and I was being called names and hating myself.

A Dream of Prom

Among all the books I read as a young adult, was every teen romance novel I could find. A lot of them followed a consistent plot trajectory. A young girl was unhappy, didn't feel attractive or appreciated by family, didn't have a boyfriend or a life purpose. But, somehow, she would have experiences in high school that made her feel grown-up and valuable and she found True Love. I absolutely believed the stories and thought that they were guaranteed to happen to me too, in high school.

I remember getting ready to go to tenth grade, the first year of high school in my school system, with so much anticipation and hope. But the minute I walked onto the campus for the first time, I could see it was exactly like middle school. The kids were a bit bigger and a bit less mean, that was all. It was a devastating disappointment to me. I was a misfit in middle school and it really looked like I was going to be a misfit in high school.

Right away I thought, *"Oh my goodness, I guess I'm not going to prom,"* a dance which had featured prominently in these teen romance success stories.

It seemed extremely unlikely that I would meet an attractive, popular boy in the lunch room or one of my classes. I wasn't destined to be a cheerleader or the lead in the class play, and there didn't seem any opportunities to do something heroic that would bring me positive attention.

Nerd Haven — Grant High

Although I was never popular, and my prom queen fantasy was busted up, I did fit in a lot better at Grant. The teachers and students there valued education and academic achievement above all else. It was literally a school that always won the knowledge bowl and never the football games. And half the students were Jews, so they didn't think I was weird. In a startling contrast to Downey, Grant High virtually closed down on the Jewish High Holy Days; no explanations of our strange holidays needed. It was ok to be a smart Jew!

Finding a Nice Jewish Boy

I wanted to date boys. I'm not sure I was truly attracted to them, but dating was a major indicator of status and success, and an important aspect of the teen novels I'd read. So, I joined B'nai B'rith Girls, an organization of high school Jewish girls that did some service work, but whose main purpose was to help us meet AZA (Aleph Zadik Aleph) boys. I went to a bunch of socials, and it was always about notches, in this case phone numbers. How many boys were interested in you? How many asked for your phone number?

One time I was so disappointed that all the girls except me had been asked for phone numbers at a social. I felt like a total failure, even though in retrospect one of the boys was interested in me as he was driving us home.

Date Safety

Looking back, I am very grateful that when I did go on dates nothing bad ever happened to me or to the other B'nai B'rith girls I knew. I'm not sure now I would like a daughter of mine go out on a date alone with someone whom I knew so little about as I did with these boys. But the worst thing that happened to me is that they would forget I was there and walk too fast for me, or we wouldn't have much of anything to talk about. I met one boy who was very sweet and kind, but when I found out he was two years younger than me — I was sixteen and he was fourteen — it felt like an insurmountable obstacle and I wasn't interested.

When I was a senior in high school, I went to one Hillel dance, which was really for college-age Jewish girls and boys, and I met a very nice Jewish college student named Mike. He was tall and handsome and muscular, although in a beefy way that wasn't my ideal. He lifted weights, the first person I ever met who did that. He was interested in fast cars, and his goal in life was to be an industrial designer and design automobiles. He didn't read at all, and when we went to see a movie, he couldn't understand why I wanted to analyze and discuss it.

He said once, "It was a good movie, period." He felt no need to say more, which I found very frustrating.

I did find him attractive and enjoyed kissing him, and I was proud that I was dating a college boy. And I invited him to my prom and he said yes! I chose a prom dress, received a corsage, and went to the prom! I had a sense of pure satisfaction and joy.

Oh, Euphoria!

It wasn't about my prom date, and it wasn't about the dance. I had arrived! I entered into the fantasy that I had read about in so many books!

I wrote a haiku about it: *Oh Euphoria, what fun to float and gently bounce on the ceiling!*

I was disappointed that Mike didn't want to go with me to grad night at Disneyland, another milestone of success that I craved, but at least I had gone to prom!

Married People Touch Each Other Too

Mike's best friend was Bob, another student at the industrial design school. He was married, and Mike and I would double date with him and his wife, Gina. They were so affectionate to each other, holding hands and kissing, using endearments.

I remember thinking in surprise, "I didn't know people still did that after they got married!"

I knew boyfriends and girlfriends touched each other, of course, but because my parents almost never showed affection to each other, at least where I could see, I had unconsciously assumed that all married couples were distant. It was a sad realization about my parents and their relationship.

Nice Girls Don't

In high school, all I knew about having sex besides studying the reproductive system and understanding there was a connection between having sex and getting pregnant, was the stereotype I grasped from my mother and other girls I knew, that "nice" girls weren't sexually active, only "trashy" girls.

Propaganda in "Health" Class

I remember seeing pitifully outdated black and white movies from the 1950s in health class, designed to scare us about sex and drugs. In one movie, within fifteen minutes, a girl raided her parent's liquor cabinet, started smoking "reefers," a supposed gateway drug to hardcore drugs and addiction, and then became a prostitute with a swinging ponytail.

In another movie, some boys chased after some "bad" girls outside a movie theater, and one boy immediately caught a venereal disease and gave it to his girlfriend when they had sex once (off screen) in his car. She had a disgusted shamed look on her face after they had (presumably) had intercourse, and then she suffered a lifetime of regret. I knew these movies were false and silly, even when I didn't understand the specifics.

My only tiny indication that there were real girls who might be having sex in high school was once walking around the track during a P.E. class and passing two girls who I didn't really know, because they weren't in my academic track classes. They had hair teased up high (which only the "bad" girls did) and lots of dark makeup, wearing low-cut T-shirts, chewing gum and talking as they ever so slowly sauntered around the track. They seemed to be discussing their boyfriends, and maybe sex. As I passed them, one was saying to the other, "You know how messy it can get?" And the other one answered "Yeah."

The Mystery of 69

But this was the tail end of the '60s, so attitudes and acceptable behavior were starting to shift. I graduated from high school in June 1969. I was so ignorant and naive that when my fellow students joked about "69," I laughed because I knew it was supposed to be dirty/funny somehow, but I actually had no idea what they were talking about.

Early Admission

I earned very good grades in high school, and was invited to be part of an early admission program to UCLA. A select group of us high school seniors were allowed to take college classes, and get college credit while we were still in high school. We could only take classes in the early afternoon, after we were allowed to leave school early, which limited our selection, but I still managed to take some pretty fascinating classes such as archeology of ancient statues, many of which had an "archaic smile," a feature of the way they were carved; non-Shakespearean Elizabethan plays, mostly bloodbaths like *The Revenger's Tragedy* in which everyone died, comedy plays translated from Latin, and Restoration comedic novels. I would never have been exposed to these ideas without this program. It made my senior year a lot more interesting.

Not Applying to College

Then in the Spring when it came time to apply for college, I didn't do it. I knew I could go to UCLA because I'd already been admitted and I was so afraid of failure or not being good enough or being rejected and intimidated by the paperwork, that I just didn't bother to apply anywhere else.

Other students in the program with me applied to Berkeley or Stanford or even Harvard or Caltech, but I didn't feel good enough. So, I went to UCLA. My parents weren't rich, but they had saved their money and were willing for me to live on campus. I was very scared to go — partly I guess because I was young and had never been away from home, and partly because my upbringing had given me very little confidence that I could manage on my own. I had no vision of what I wanted to learn or any sense of a career path. I simply saw no alternative to college.

Chapter Three

Invitation to a Wider World

One of the great gifts of going to college was (finally) being exposed to a larger world with a wider range of people and getting to see for myself that my parents' attitudes, fears, and limited perspectives were not the only way to be. I began to believe I could survive without my parents' micromanaging guidance and start thinking for myself. It gave me more room to breathe and start discovering who I was. I still felt all alone in a hostile universe, and thought I had to accept the fact that I hated myself and felt insecure and somehow keep going, but it was a start.

The Myth of the Vaginal Orgasm

The first piece of feminist literature I read was a pamphlet one of my dormmates, Kate, handed me my first semester there. It was called *The Myth of the Vaginal Orgasm*. Since I was a virgin at the time and had never even masturbated, I really didn't understand the article or its relevance to feminism at all.

Learning to Listen — UCLA Helpline

My first year, I heard about a peer helpline at the college and was very drawn to it. My response to my mother's misery had sensitized me to the feelings of others, and I thought I'd be good at listening and peer counseling. I had been powerless to help my mother, but maybe I could help others.

In the training, we learned the basics of active listening skills, which I still use to this day, as well as information about local resources and how to talk people out of committing suicide. I was still miserable myself, but I think I and the other peer counselors helped some people, despite our youthful limits. People need to be listened to desperately, and we did that. I know we gave people valuable resource suggestions and intervened with some people who were despairing and suicidal.

I liked the other student counselors, mostly misfits like me, and began taking regular shifts and hanging out with some of them. That's where I met Tralee, who is still a friend of mine. It sparked my interest in psychology, which I pursued for a while.

Carl Rogers on Steroids

At this time, Carl Rogers, the psychologist, and his client-centered non-directive therapy were new and cutting edge. A lot of his observations and approach, including listening skills, were phenomenal and better than what had gone before, but when my peer counseling group embraced this, we carried it to extremes. We would never state an opinion, set a limit, or even make observations. We would continue asking questions to elicit thoughtful responses from the clients. It is a useful skill but only to a point! I saw how manipulative it could be, almost passive-aggressive, to try to "get" clients to reach some insight without being direct.

How Do You Feel About That?

The way we peer counselors used it with each other was safe and cowardly — we never had to say what we really thought in meetings or anywhere. Coaching as a field didn't exist back then, but some people now trained as life coaches follow the same teaching that *everything* has to come from the client. My own opinion, especially working with conflict and communication, is that if all the solutions and approaches could come from inside a client, they wouldn't need us. Of course, clients are the only ones who can decide what is right for them, and listening to them is crucial, but people find it hard to break out of patterns of thought, resentments, and patterns of behavior without some suggestions and tough love clarity as well as questions.

Dating Around in College

In my first year of college, I was still with Mike, the boyfriend I had in high school, but our relationship really didn't work very well anymore, and at the end of my freshman year we broke up. I began to meet and date other young men through the Balkan folk dance group and at my dorm. I went out once with a man named Jay. Looking back, I wonder if he was gay and closeted and just trying to date women as a cover, because there was truly no safety in coming out at that time. Whatever his reason for going on a date with me, he clearly wasn't interested in getting to know me or in getting close physically.

Another man I didn't exactly date, but hung out with was Jim, a rich kid from L.A. in the same dorm as I was. He was the one who introduced me to "pot," as we called cannabis, which I was curious to try. He also attempted to offer me tobacco cigarettes, which I recoiled from in horror, unlike my response to cannabis. He had a very messed up rich family and wasn't given much attention or love as a child.

I also met a man who was Jewish, and had converted to Hasidism, a rather extreme branch of ultra-orthodox Judaism. There was a resurgence of a Hasidic movement within Jewish communities, even on the campus in L.A. I came to understand that they adhered to a rigid code for worshipping, eating, dressing, and living.

As he told me with a smile, he didn't subscribe to the no touching rule between men and women, but he was starting to follow a lot of the other rules. I went out with him a couple of times. He was a good, kind person, but seemed to be committing more and more to this new/old way of practicing Judaism.

One time he took me to Friday night dinner at Chabad House, a center of Hasidic Judaism. I met the rabbi and his wife, who wore a wig. All the women covered their hair, and assumed very traditional and limited roles. It felt very alien and archaic to me and not at all in line with the empowerment and liberation of women that I was starting to experience in feminism.

I ran into him once after we'd stopped dating, and he had become even more traditional; wearing the side curls called "payos," a hat, and black garb.

"Nice" Girls Have Sex (For the First Time)

One of the subjects about which I changed my mind was sex. A lot of girls I knew were being sexual with their boyfriends. And they seemed like "nice" girls, who had career aspirations and were doing well in college. I started becoming more open to the possibility.

My junior year I met a Turkish graduate student named Müfit. He was very muscular and handsome with olive skin, prominent cheekbones, and an impressive mustache. He went to the Balkan folk dance class that Hillel offered solely to meet girls and seemed quite interested in me. I was very flattered and attracted, but I really didn't have a lot of skills to set boundaries, say no, or know what I wanted separate from him. He convinced me to have sex with him and I did. I wasn't at all sure that I liked it that first time. And he put a lot of pressure on me, assuming that of course once I had started, I had to continue to be sexual with him, and I did, although I'm really not sure that I wanted to; "nice" girls don't always know how to say no either.

We used condoms the first few times, and then I went to the UCLA health clinic to get a diaphragm. I remember looking around surreptitiously at the other young women in the waiting room and thinking well, they look like nice girls not prostitutes, so maybe it's ok. I still had a lot of shame and I knew that my parents would utterly disapprove.

In some ways, Müfit was interesting to me because he was from a different culture. It's funny now looking back, because of course when I later taught ESL (English as a Second Language) I had many students like Müfit and understood his homesickness, cultural differences, and culture shock much more than I had when I was twenty and in relationship with him.

I started to enjoy having sex with him, although I certainly wouldn't consider him a skilled or subtle lover. But problems with my parents began.

My mother started suspecting that I was involved in a sexual relationship. I didn't know until afterwards, but she started calling my dorm room at all kinds of odd hours to see if I was there. My roommate went home a lot on weekends to spend time with her (single) mother, so neither of us were there to pick up the phone.

From Nice Girl to Slut (In My Mother's Eyes)

One time, Fran caught me on the phone unexpectedly and started screaming hysterically at me. "Do you have a boyfriend? Are you having sex? Are you pregnant?"

In that moment, I just blurted out, "Yes, I have a boyfriend. Yes, we're having sex. No, I'm not pregnant."

My mother totally flipped out. "You slut! You whore! Don't expect us to give you money for college if this is how you are going to act!"

When I went home for the summer, she practically kept me a prisoner. I don't believe she ever had a very healthy attitude about sex, and the fact that Müfit was Turkish and Muslim and she wanted me to marry a nice Jewish boy completely pushed her over the edge.

I asked for family therapy, not because I felt I needed it, but because I was really worried that my mother was having a nervous breakdown. Fran told me much later that she had turned away from someone she was very attracted to and married my father instead. She liked Henry, and he felt like a safer choice somehow. I never heard the details, but I believe she was frightened of her own passion.

My father came to see me privately at school and told me that he had had sexual relationships with other women before he started dating my mother. But, out of respect for her, they hadn't had sex before they got married, even when they were sharing an apartment after moving to California together. And then he said I should also respect my mother by not having sex, which pretty much makes no sense. She was his partner, not mine.

This was a very hard time for me. I was moving away from my parents and their view of me. It was past time for me to become my own person, but it was hard to be attacked and unsupported. I still hadn't found a place I fit or could truly be myself.

Steps Toward Independence

I found a part-time job for the first time. I couldn't earn enough to completely support myself working part time, but I figured if they did stop supporting me, I would be able to somehow continue my education. It was a start at financial independence. I knew lots of students never had the privilege I had of being given money for college, but it was frightening to have a sudden threat of losing financial support.

Müfit, seeing me as a free-spirited American girl compared to his sister or other young women in Turkey, really didn't understand the difficulties I was having with my parents. He wanted me to choose him, to live with him, and probably get married and move back to Turkey with him eventually. Through him I met another couple, a Turkish man and an American woman, Mary, who were married, and I didn't really like what I heard from her about the challenges and difficulties that she had. It seemed like Mary was in constant battle with his expectations and what she wanted to do. It was before the fundamentalist wave hit the Middle East and Turkey, but the cultural differences were still very difficult.

Eventually, when I was a senior, the relationship with Müfit felt unsustainable. It wasn't that I believed what my parents were telling me, but it simply didn't feel right anymore. Even though I knew I needed to leave him, I had never been seriously involved with someone or had sex before, and I felt like my heart was breaking when I ran into him or saw him on campus afterwards. I didn't know then that I really wasn't capable of making a long-term commitment to any man because I was meant to be with women.

Heartbreak

Another Jewish man that I met folk dancing was named Layne. He was a tall, handsome, golden-haired, blue-eyed, secular Jew, who always had lots of women and girls around him and chasing him. He had spent part of his college years working and studying on a big ship called University at Sea. He never lacked for girlfriends or opportunities. I think he fell in love with me partly because I wasn't chasing him.

I liked him, but I was still hung up on Müfit. I remember one time after I'd broken up with Müfit, I was talking to Layne on the campus and caught a glimpse of Müfit. I abruptly ended our conversation, and ran to talk to my ex. Layne looked after me with a kind of hurt, rueful expression, perhaps recognizing the irony of all the women after him but the one he wanted loving someone else still.

Seeing Women Who Looked Like Me

Another delightful thing about the folk dancing, was that for the first time in my life I saw women who looked like me. Growing up in Downey, I looked very different from the people around me, but the Balkan folk dance attracted a lot of younger Jewish men and women. I saw women who had noses and faces shaped like mine, hazel green-gray eyes like mine, and golden skin tones. It was the oddest feeling to not feel unique, but instead part of a tribe.

A College Education

Although going to UCLA was more prestigious than going to a community college or a state college, I don't actually think I received a particularly good education there. A lot of the classes, especially when I was a freshman and sophomore, were in huge lecture halls and students really only interacted with the Teaching Assistants — graduate students who generally weren't as interesting or knowledgeable as the professors.

I started out as an English major because I'd always been so very good in English, but when I turned in my first essay for freshman composition the teacher gave me a C. I was absolutely shocked and unable to deal with the failure. I thought I was supposed to be perfect, especially in English; and never make mistakes. I'd always scored As without trying, and never had to work at improving my writing.

The TA who taught that freshman composition class didn't explain that writing well was a learnable skill. She didn't have training or access to any of the tools and processes that I learned later about how to teach writing and guide students to write better. She gave us no guidance or instruction; she only told us to write and then critiqued it severely. It's funny that I eventually did a full circle and came back to getting a Master's in English.

Switching Majors

Being completely unable to cope with even slight failure, I immediately, even before finishing that semester, switched to a psychology and political science major in which I thought I could achieve better. I don't regret having had a different major for undergraduate, but it seems like English could've been a much better experience.

A lot of the psychology classes were boring and useless, since, unfortunately, UCLA at that time was very behavioral psychology-oriented. I didn't find it interesting, to run rats through mazes and make conclusions about behavior from that. And some of their curriculum decisions didn't make any sense.

Freud Lite

For example, we had huge, thick psychology textbooks in various classes, and each one would have a little section on Freud. Instead, in the same amount of time, we could've read some of the books actually written by Freud. It was a poor model for education.

Nonetheless, a few classes I took were fascinating. I had one psychology class on learning theory which was full of mind-expanding information about how the brain works, how memories form, how we learn. It is a subject I still follow to this day.

I took another class through the psychology department that was really a mind-blowing feminist consciousness-raising class that Tralee and I took together. And we continued to explore feminism and progressive psychology movements in other classes and on our own.

I took a class on Middle Eastern history and politics taught by a professor who was somewhat pro-Palestinian. I hadn't even known there was a different point of view from that of the pro-Israel Jews I knew.

Mickey Mouse Classes

I took a History of Jazz class, one of the classes that had a reputation with the students for being a "Mickey Mouse" class or "mick" for short. Those were classes that didn't require much work and in which you could get an easy A. But the instructor had actually known and played with many of the jazz greats such as Billie Holiday. His stories about his experiences made it far more worthwhile than merely an easy grade.

And I do remember one of the psychology professors in a giant lecture hall who repeated over and over "correlation does not imply causation." I found that a very useful concept for understanding politics and life.

Lying with Statistics

I also took a class on statistics for the psychology part of my major. I wasn't very good at this kind of math, and since I took it in the summer, there wasn't a lot of time to learn. I studied very hard and ended up with a B-minus. But I learned from studying statistics that numbers could be manipulated by people intent on doing so. All a study had to do to be valid was prove a significant difference between the categories. But as I saw, a "significant" difference could be so small as to be meaningless outside of the statistical world.

I never felt the same about statistics and percentages again, knowing how carefully you had to look at them to understand what they were showing and if they really meant anything.

Milgram Torture

I saw a film about the Milgram Experiment. This was the one in which innocent test subjects were on one side of a wall and actors on another. A scientist in an impressive white coat told subjects to give electric shocks to the people on the other side.

Many people would persist in giving the shocks when the scientist told them to, even when the actors, who they thought were real people, seemed to be screaming in terrible pain at them to stop. Many of the people felt awful about continuing, but nonetheless obeyed an authority figure. It was an absolutely chilling demonstration of the effect of authoritarianism on ordinary people. Only a few of the people had the courage to say no, they would not do it. This was an important lesson in thinking for myself and not following an authority blindly!

Other studies I read about showed how people would defy the evidence of their own eyes if a group was affirming false information, even about something as simple as which line was longer. With my family background of genocidal pogroms and anti-Semitism, this obedience to authority and "group think" terrified me.

Blocked

During this time, I experienced the true horror of my writer's block. It is in some ways a miracle that I made it through college, since every time I started to write, horrible negative voices would come up and tell me that what I wrote was no good and would never be good enough. Although I was very smart and willing to study, I was almost completely blocked and self-hating about my writing, even after I left the English department.

I remember endless hours of suffering, sitting in the library, trying to write a paper. I would write one line on a piece of paper on my notepad, and inner negative voices would begin screaming at me. "This is no good! You will never be able to write this paper. Anything you write is shit. You are not good enough."

The voice of criticism was so loud and overwhelming and intense that I would crumple up the piece of paper and throw it down near my desk. This would happen over and over, and after two hours, my chair was completely surrounded by crumpled-up pieces of paper with only a sentence or two on them. I was exhausted and crumpled-up in misery myself, and I wouldn't have even made a start on the paper.

And because I felt inadequate and the inner voices that I still heard from my childhood experiences with my mother and writing were so hateful, I was paralyzed with procrastination. I could only write under the intense pressure of a last-minute deadline, desperate and hating every minute of it.

When I Wake Up in the Morning, My Heart Is Beating (Sometimes, Always, Never)

As a psychology major, I had to be a human guinea pig for the graduate students and professors working to test theories or conduct experiments in order to earn credit for a number of classes. The experiments were often tedious, sometimes interesting. I had to take the Minnesota Multiphase Personality Inventory, a test designed to measure psychopathology. The questions seemed odd and sometimes laughable. One of them has stuck in my head all this time. The statement read, "When I wake up in the morning my heart is beating a) sometimes, b) always, c) never." My fertile imagination started musing about who would answer that their heart wasn't beating every day when they woke up. Vampires were one possibility.

Other tests were very different. One was to measure psychic ability a la Duke University experiments. We were supposed to guess symbols and shapes on cards without seeing them. I wasn't any good at it. Another tested biofeedback and alpha waves. We were hooked up to machines and put on a set of headphones. When we produced alpha waves, the machine would beep in a certain way.

I could do it some, by breathing and consciously calming myself, which was pretty remarkable since I was a nervous anxious person with no training or practice in meditation. But as soon as I started having alpha waves and the beeping started, I would think, "*I'm doing it!*" which immediately made it stop.

I didn't learn to meditate at this time, but it did plant a seed that became important later.

The Hat Snatchers and Other Tales of Bullock's Department Store

The part-time jobs I started getting after my parents were threatening to cut off support for college were educational in a different way. The women I worked with didn't talk about feminism, but they were out in the world and supporting themselves or helping their families in a way that many of my fellow students weren't. My very first job was working in a children's clothing store. It paid minimum wage which at that time was $1.65 an hour. It doesn't sound like much, but probably could buy more than minimum wage can today.

Then I heard that they were hiring sales associates at Bullock's, which at that time was a fairly high-end department store with a branch so close to the UCLA campus that I could walk there. I began to work there part-time. For a while, I floated around different departments.

For a few weeks, I was a hostess in the elegant lunch room. We were given a meal ticket, but we didn't get to eat any of the delicious food that the patrons were eating, only greasy, miserably over-fried food and cheap hamburgers in the employee cafeteria. That hostess experience led to being a dresser for the models who would do fashion shows in the tea room with some of the new clothes. The models liked me because I moved fast to help them change.

Eventually, I settled into working at the fine jewelry department. They had complicated procedures, with multiple keys and sequences to open up and close, and they appreciated having a "college girl" because I caught on quickly to all the rules and processes.

Of course, not as many people bought expensive jewelry as visited other departments in the store, so I was bored a lot, sitting idly on my stool behind the glass-topped counter, waiting for people to come along.

A lot of the people who came by were rich, self-absorbed, and smug, believing their money let them ignore us sales associates or treat us like servants.

One even laughed delightedly, saying, "Oh, I was completely ignoring you!" as if that were charming.

Some people who stopped by still stick in my mind. One was a young woman who had gotten engaged. Her husband-to-be was in the service, and he had picked out a ring to give her without any consultation with her. She was looking at rings to guess what he might have chosen. I remember that all her fingernails were bitten down to the quick and I wondered if it was her relationship, his deployment, or something else causing her stress.

Another woman, pretty and blonde in a wispy young Mia Farrow kind of way, came and sat at one of the stools at the end of the counter. The fine jewelry department was located near the north entrance, so it was a convenient place for her to sit. She confided in me that she had been living with a man for a long time, but was waiting for another man, who was married, to pick her up because they were having an affair. When he arrived, he was every bit as blonde, wispy, blue-eyed and attractive as she was.

But I could tell from what she said and her manner that the real issue was that she was bored with her life. And I felt even at the time that it was too bad she didn't go back to school, or start some kind of brilliant business or career, instead of creating misery for both couples because she didn't know how else to get some interest and excitement in her life.

Another young woman came in with her fiancé and his mother, to look at rings. She was a young Latina woman, he was older, a red-haired Anglo, very reserved, and still living with his mother. For the first time, he was venturing out to get married and live with this woman. It was clear that his mother micromanaged every aspect of his life and planned to continue doing so. He seemed fearful about leaving his mother's house, and I didn't envy the young woman having to deal with a mother-in-law like that and a husband who most likely wouldn't stand up to his mother.

One other woman who visited the fine jewelry department stood out because of her nails. She was very rich, with perfectly manicured nails in a bright color. But there was something about her nails that made them curve like a parrot's beak with a distinct arch, more like talons than manicured nails. Nonetheless, she displayed them proudly. It gave me the creeps and reminded me of horror movie characters.

Fine Jewelry Feud

The man in charge of the fine jewelry department was an older white man, with a lined, craggy face and red cheeks and nose.

There were two women who worked there full-time, both older than me, both gorgeous, and both from Spanish-speaking countries. One of them, Suzette, had long naturally red-gold hair. She was from a very wealthy Argentine upper-class family, had attended private schools, and led a very privileged life. She told me she had come to the US to marry an American psychiatrist after her fiancé in her own country had cheated on her.

She had clearly, from what she told me, married him on the rebound, and was not in love. She gained about a hundred pounds from her unhappiness and she was always dieting. She also confided in me that she had had a nose job to give her a gently curved nose instead of the dignified aquiline nose that she had had and her mother still had, which I saw myself when her mother came to visit.

The other Latina woman, Ramona, had long dark hair, an expressionless face, and a voluptuous body. She said she was also from an upper-class background, but it seemed to be a lie for which Suzette scorned her. Per Suzette, Ramona gave herself away in a hundred ways that revealed her humble background. Suzette claimed Ramona had been extremely poor and had clawed and kicked her way up to respectability any way she could, mainly using sex to get what she wanted.

And I myself witnessed that Ramona let the manager "take liberties" with her in the back room. I saw them embracing with her leg wrapped around his buttocks and his hand under her skirt and up her thigh. I don't think it was a full-blown affair outside of the work situation, but he let her get away with a lot, coming late, leaving early, because of their physical relationship.

The two women hated each other. They each had total contempt for the other person because of their different lives and backgrounds. They wouldn't even speak Spanish with each other although it was their mutual native language; and barely communicated in English.

Love and Hats

The hat department was across the aisle from the fine jewelry department, and I became quite friendly with two young women who worked there. One was named Marcy, a young fresh-faced, newly married white woman, and Carmen, a single, young Mexican-American woman with broad cheekbones and big brown eyes who was very shy and sweet. While we were working there, she met a young Anglo man named Tim, who was also rather shy. They began, little by little, to chat, and then quickly fell in love and became engaged. It was beautiful to watch these two quiet people find each other and see this love story unfold before my eyes. Carmen's new happiness and serenity were splendid to behold. It gave me hope that we don't have to be glamorous or extroverted to find our soulmate.

They're Taking Your Hats!

One day, I was sitting on my stool behind the fine jewelry department, totally bored and staring straight ahead. Marcy had gone in the back room for a moment and no one was watching the hats. Two tall, muscular Black men came in with a bag, no guns fortunately, and began removing all the hats and putting them into their sack. They looked right at me and ignored me. I should've called security, but I was instantly angry that they acted like I wasn't there. With no thought at all, I jumped off my stool and around the counter.

I told them, "Stop taking the hats!" and grabbed one out of the man's hand.

I yelled to Marcy, "Marcy, they're taking your hats."

The men looked very startled, took the hats they already had, and ran out of the store. I followed them out the door and saw them get into a car. I went up close to the car and memorized the license plate, kept repeating it to myself until I came back in and wrote it down. Because of my actions, they caught one of the men, probably the one with the car, and I had to testify at his trial.

My supervisor was really angry at me. He said, "Don't you ever do something like that again! Don't you know how dangerous it was?"

In retrospect, I realized it was a very foolish thing to do. I could have been injured or even killed, but in that moment, I was so mad they had ignored me that I didn't think about the risk to myself. And, though it was misguided, the impulse was really the same burning determination for justice and rightness and not being invisible that later guided some of my social action work.

The prosecutor asked me to describe what happened, and what the men had looked like.

Then they showed me a picture of the car with the license plate and asked, "Is that the license plate and car you saw?"

Being completely honest, I said, "I don't remember. But, I am positive that the license plate I wrote down at the time and gave to the police is the correct one."

And that was enough to satisfy them.

The defense attorney, probably a public defender, only asked three questions.

"Do you wear glasses?"

"Yes, I do," I answered.

"Were you wearing them on the night in question?"

"No, I wasn't," I said.

"How far were you from the car when you saw the license plate?" he asked.

"One foot away," I answered, which shut down whatever argument he was trying to make about my vision and not seeing the license plate accurately.

Focus

All this was happening while I was in college and partly while I was seeing Müfit. Funnily enough, I earned the best grades of my entire college career after I started working there. I was afraid my grades would slip because of all the hours I was working, so I studied harder in a more concentrated and focused way than I ever had, and garnered straight As. Once I realized that I could work a part-time job without my grades slipping, I let go and went back to my procrastinating ways and my B-plus average. If I could've kept up the focus, I would probably have graduated summa com laude instead of magna!

I didn't go to my college graduation, feeling no connection with the other students, and not much sense of real accomplishment. I had no idea what I wanted to do with my life in any way, and with my procrastination and self-hate, I didn't believe I could accomplish much.

Chapter Four

The Personal is Political
in Berkeley

I still consider leaving L.A. in 1973 to be the single best decision of my life. I never fit in there. I never felt part of the beach culture, or the pretentious, narcissistic Beverly Hills beauty culture. I never liked the heat. I grew up there, but it was never my true home. A young folk musician I met, named Charlie, talked about leaving L.A. and moving somewhere else, and my imagination was captured.

I wasn't thinking of leaving with him, but I began to understand that I didn't have to be trapped or stuck in L.A. — that there was a whole world out there, and maybe I could find the courage to explore it; to ignore all the fearful messages that would hold me back. I'd never lived anywhere but Downey or Van Nuys, but I was desperate and ready!

Escape from L.A.

Carol, a college friend of mine, was getting married in Santa Barbara, and I decided to go up to see her and then continue on to Berkeley. I knew one person in Northern California, barely, a friend of a friend named Amy, but she was kind enough to let me stay with her and her family until I figured out my life a bit.

Amy lived in a typical Berkeley brown shingle house with her mother and father and younger sister. The whole family was kind, generous, and accepting. Her mother was a Bohemian artist and spiritual seeker who wore loose brightly embroidered clothes and lots of scarves. She had a vivid way of speaking and gestured dramatically. She kept the house going sort of minimally because of her creative work. The father had a regular white collar 8-to-5 job, which provided the finances. He looked weary when he came home from work, but he and his wife seemed to truly love and enjoy each other.

The Personal Is Political in Berserkeley

I stayed with them for a week or so and then started looking for a place to live. There were lots of notices for collective living situations or for roommates. I wasn't very good at that time at tuning in to what people were really like, so I made some spectacularly bad choices.

I'm grateful I didn't end up in the house with the month-old baby who cried all the time, or the one where they had divided one of the bedrooms in half with a piece of plywood, or where the lease holder wanted me to be her instant best friend. I did pick a house in a very nice neighborhood in the Rockridge area of Oakland because I loved the beautiful aesthetics of the dining room, with a colorful Indian Blue table cloth and a gently curved vase in the middle of the table that complemented it. One of the white men who lived there, Jonny, was a gentle person, although he had a hyper-critical girlfriend who spent too much time there. But the lease holder, Mark, was a truly awful man. I think now he might have been an alcoholic, but for sure his personality changed for the worse when he drank, which was often. I also found out that he was charging us a lot of extra rent so he could live there rent free, merely for holding the lease.

I was lucky nothing really bad happened while I was living there, but it wasn't a safe place. The final straw for me, two months later, was that one weekend my sister came to visit me from Stanford. Jonny and his girlfriend were going to be out of town, and when I asked, he was happy for my sister to stay in his room. In the middle of the night, drunk, Mark went into the room where my sister was, having offered the room, without checking with Jonny, to a friend of his. It really scared my sister and me. I yelled at him, but it seemed safer at that point to have her in my room with me rather than stand on principle. I moved right after that. I moved four times that first year.

I had some savings, but I needed to find work and purpose. My parents had acted like I'd dropped out of high school rather than taking some time off after graduating from college, so I was truly on my own.

People's Energy

I started volunteering with a small radical labor group. They had a little storefront in Oakland. Drew, who was white and Jewish, ran the organization called People's Energy that was supposed to transform the way people worked. Most of us were in our early twenties. People's Energy shared the space with a related publication, *Workforce Magazine*, run by Carey, one of the tallest, blondest men I've met. The 'zine had articles on unions, socialist approaches to work, calls to revolution.

Emily, who was very slender, short, feminist, and pretty with shiny dark hair, fair skin, and big blue eyes, became lovers with Carey. Drew had a long-term relationship with Andrea, his much more conventional girlfriend from his life in New York. She wasn't really into these radical ideas, including Drew's desire for open relationships and free love.

This was all very confusing to me. I found Drew quite handsome, and I flirted with him and with the idea of open relationships. But it didn't feel right, especially since Andrea was clearly unhappy about it. Warner was a librarian, stout, plump, balding, like a big teddy bear. He was much older than the rest of us and had left a marriage and run away to Berkeley. He knew how to set up indexes and catalogue, which came in handy. Many other people floated in and out.

I worked on magazine production and layout. This was before desktop publishing, so I learned to use a light table, ruler, instant-print letters, and other labor-intensive tools. It was fun actually. I also worked with Drew "counseling" people who wanted to drop out of regular 9-to-5 work and find their passion. I know I helped at least a couple of people, but I didn't really believe what I was saying. I had merely memorized what Drew told me, so I felt like a hypocrite.

After a while, Carey, Emily and some other folks and I moved in together in another Oakland house, this one closer to the Montclair neighborhood in the hills. It was a lovely house physically, but it wasn't easy to live there with all the strong personalities. I remember our trying to process everything collectively, but it didn't work very well. And Carey's and Emily's relationship fell apart as she realized she really was a lesbian. We all moved out.

I moved to Albany where I met Alan who became my boyfriend, although I called him my lover because boyfriend seemed too bourgeois a label.

Alan, who was white, Jewish, and gorgeous, with shiny, long, wavy hair and a handsome face, was sitting in a wheelchair the first time I saw him. I assumed he was disabled. I was totally startled when he got up out of the wheelchair to get something to drink! He was only sitting there because the living room didn't have enough chairs.

I liked him right away. The other two housemates were ok enough — a blonde male musician who spent all his time in his own room, and a dark-haired white woman named Gail who talked a lot, had a strong New York accent, and spent most of her time with her boyfriend Barry. I still remember his name because she used it every other sentence she spoke! "Barry says" was her constant refrain.

But Alan and I really bonded. It turned out that we had gone to the same high school, US Grant in Van Nuys at almost exactly the same time. His best friend Ernie went to prom with my best friend Karen, but we had never met. We were both Jewish but not religious.

At that time, he called himself an anarcho-syndicalist, a very obscure branch of progressive politics, which I found interesting. Most important, he was kind and attractive and listened, and we talked and talked.

Fairly quickly, we became romantically involved, and when it became harder and harder with the other roommates, we decided to move out and get a place of our own. We rented a place in a shabby but architecturally beautiful old apartment building in Oakland that had survived the 1906 earthquake. It had crown molding, high ceilings, hardwood floors, and old-fashioned, intricately designed, octagonal black and white tile in the bathroom.

After my sister graduated from college, she moved into another apartment in the building next door with her boyfriend, Steve. We were still close at that time and it was wonderful to have her there. My sister never told my parents about her boyfriends until she was out of the house on her own. She learned from my drama-trauma example that honesty was not the best path in this situation.

When she finally told my mother, Fran's response was to sigh and say, "I guess things are different now."

A far cry from her over-the-top response to me three years earlier!

Neither Alan nor I really knew how to cook, but we decided to learn together. We took turns choosing recipes and then would cook together, puzzling out the parts of the instructions we didn't understand. He was tidier than I was, and didn't watch sports, so he definitely busted some of the stereotypes that cause women to complain about men!

Alan had dropped out of college after being an anthropology and then a music major. He landed a secure but physically difficult job sorting mail in the post office at night. We weren't able to spend much time together, and we were struggling to live together. My sister broke up with her boyfriend and moved back to L.A. so there was less tying me to the apartment.

Eventually, although we didn't break up, Alan and I decided not to live together anymore. I found a little cottage in Oakland on 42nd Street near Market behind the house of a tiny, elderly but vigorous Italian widow, Flora Carlevaro. Alan moved into a collective house owned by a progressive Latino activist and radio personality who was a terrible landlord.

Alan had an evolving group of roommates, all white but very different in background and outlook. I became friendly with them when I spent time there. Rush and Mickey were a couple, both graduate students in biochemistry. Alan decided to go back to school in biochemistry too. Other roommates for a while included Ed, a long-haired, blue-eyed Vietnam vet who was a solar energy architect before it took off in the mainstream.

The Mutability of Walls

When Ed wanted to move in to the small downstairs room, he measured everything and realized his bed wouldn't quite fit in the room, unless he moved the doorway five inches. So, he moved it. I was amazed and impressed. (Aside: I met two of his architect friends, a couple who also had a very casual attitude about moving staircases and interior walls to suit their needs in their house.) I had always thought of walls and doors as immutable, but it was all a moveable canvas to them.

A Circle of Girlfriends

Ed almost always had a girlfriend staying overnight with him. He had at least five who took turns spending the night. They all knew about each other, and they all spoke of Ed fondly. I chatted with some of them, and they were attractive, intelligent women. I could never understand how he pulled it off, or why he wanted so many.

The awful landlord became too much, and Rush and Mickey and Ed decided to buy a house together. They found a house on Deakin Street, just around the corner from the Co-op grocery store, and fixed up the attic to have more bedrooms.

Some new roommates moved in. Allegra was an apprentice carpenter struggling with sexism in the trades, which were beginning to open up to women; and Tina, another young feminist. They were both rape survivors, still working on their healing, and they bonded around that experience. Another woman named Diana moved in as well.

Rush and Mickey broke up, and Rush became disillusioned with biochemistry after a colleague stole some of his dissertation research and published it as his own. Diana had a brother, Paul, who started spending time at the house, and he and Mickey started a relationship. Rush didn't seem to mind much, but Diana didn't really like Mickey and was dismayed, especially when Mickey got pregnant and she and Paul decided to raise the baby together.

Meanwhile, I had a friend named Kay who started seeing Rush. Kay and I had met through a women's anger group (lots of yelling and beating pillows and permission to be angry instead of sweet!).

More about Flora Carlevaro and 42nd Street

I ended up living in the little cottage behind Mrs. Carlevaro's house for fifteen years. It was a mixed situation in a lot of ways. I liked having my own place, but at times I was very lonely, especially after Alan and I broke up. And the cottage wasn't well built. I remember when I took a weaving class, I was trying to put together a frame loom, and realized there were no right angles in any of the doors or walls. The whole place looked like a distorted fun house to me for days! The cottage had wood strips on the walls and no insulation. It was very cold. And, there was black toxic mold that kept coming back on the walls. I didn't know then what a big health hazard it was, which I'm sure contributed to my later chronic fatigue and multiple chemical sensitivities.

Flora had a big garden, which she still kept up. I could pick the miniature carnations, and sometimes she gave me vegetables. That was the first time I saw and ate Italian flat green beans (Romanos), which I have loved ever since.

Lorry Vs. the Wasp

A recurring problem was wasps building nests in the eaves. Mrs. Carlevaro knocked one down from my porch, and I was quite impressed.

When the wasps came back and built another nest, I thought I should knock this one down, even though I was terrified of stinging insects. After all, if tiny Mrs. Carlevaro could knock one down, I reasoned, I should be able to as well.

Unfortunately, I picked the evening time to do it. I knocked down the nest with my broom, and wasps swarmed out! I didn't realize that during the day, when she knocked down the nest, the wasps were out finding food, while at night they returned to the nest to sleep.

When they swarmed angrily on the porch, I screamed and ran in the house, slamming the door shut! Fueled by survival adrenalin, I was so quick, that only one wasp slipped in! But I was terrified of insects, particularly stinging ones, and that one wasp was a catastrophe.

The little cottage was what is called a railroad flat. One room, which I used as a living room, had a door to outside, next to it was the bedroom, also with an outside door, then a kitchen and bathroom all in a row. The wasp appeared in the bedroom because I had gone out that door with my broom. I ran in the kitchen and slammed the inside door between the bedroom and the kitchen. But I couldn't go to bed until I banished the wasp!

I cautiously opened the door, broom in hand, and the wasp circled toward me. I screamed again and slammed the door shut. I repeated this sequence several times, but every time I tried to get the wasp, it came toward me and I screamed and slammed the door. Then in desperation, I began opening the door, throwing books at the wasp, a pot, and anything else I could find. It would evade the object and come towards me, I would scream and slam the door shut again. Between the thumps of thrown objects, the doors slamming, and my high-pitched screams of terror, I'm surprised no one called the cops.

Finally, I cautiously opened the door and didn't see the wasp. Broom in hand, I warily reentered the room. No wasp. I looked everywhere in the room, walls, behind furniture, under and behind the bed but saw no living wasp or wasp corpse. Finally, nervously I picked up all the books and pots and went to bed. I never found the wasp. And I never knocked down a wasp nest again either!

My House as Cultural Anthropology Site

My friend Kathy was taking a cultural anthropology class and asked if she could take pictures and use my house as a "site." I said sure, so she came over and took pictures, writing up a report. Her fellow students became very excited because I had an actual altar with candles, flowers, and a picture of La Virgen. I also had up some magic marker drawings that little Lorry, my inner child, and I had drawn in therapy. The students concluded that I was a Catholic Latina single mother!

Culture Mix on 42nd Street

972 42nd Street was in an old neighborhood with small, mostly shabby houses. There were three distinct groups that lived there. For many years, it had been an Italian neighborhood, and there were still a few elderly Italian immigrants, like Mrs. Carlevaro, who had lived there for decades. Then it had transitioned to a Black neighborhood, and there were a number of African Americans, mostly middle-aged with some adult children living there too. And the most recent group, a mix of renters and owners at that time, were young and white. When I was there, people were still pretty friendly, but by the time I left, drugs and gang violence were becoming issues, as they were in so many neighborhoods in Oakland.

One of my neighbors, Stacy, was young and white with a Black boyfriend, two large dogs, and an art studio in her garage. She made beautiful stained-glass art, especially portraits of famous Jazz singers and musicians like Billie Holiday, which she sold at jazz festivals. She didn't make a lot of money, and I found out later she supplemented her income by getting cannabis through the mail from a contact in Hawaii and selling it. She was caught after several years and was very lucky to avoid prison. But she had to turn informant on her contact/dealer.

A Neighborhood Thanksgiving

One of the older Black families was very kind, and invited me to Thanksgiving dinner at their house one year when I had nowhere to go. I accepted, but it was pretty uncomfortable because I didn't really know them at all and felt shy and very much an outsider. I couldn't seem to find a topic to start a conversation, and silence felt awkward too. Of course, I used to feel totally uncomfortable with silence. It was interesting that they had dishes that represented different Thanksgiving food traditions from what my family had — potato salad with sweet pickles and collard greens with bacon, neither of which I had had before.

Another year I had nowhere to go, I cooked an entire Thanksgiving dinner for myself — turkey, stuffing, yams, gravy, cranberry sauce, and pie. I wanted to prove I could take care of myself even when I was all alone, but it also gave me scope for my compulsive overeating.

Sisterhood Is Powerful!

At the same time, I was starting to get involved with the feminist movement. Emily introduced me to some people, and I became part of a year-long training program to be a feminist activist in the psychology realm. The women's group met at the Radical Psychiatry Center, which promoted the work of R.D. Laing, about the value of madness and going through it rather than medicating it. It was revolutionary and not at all spiritual.

Our particular group had a Maoist-feminist approach. For a brief shining time in the '70s, many progressives believed that Mao Zedong and the new People's Republic of China were leading the way to a true revolution. And Maoist slogans, such as "*Women hold up half the sky,*" and "*The personal is political,*" were exactly in line with our passionate, radical feminist beliefs that eliminating male supremacy as well as racism, homophobia, and economic disparities were essential to create a new, just, and equitable society. We read in Mao's little red book, "*Where do correct ideas come from? Do they fall from the sky — no! They come from social practice.*" And we read R.D. Laing with his radical anti-psychiatry ideas of allowing people to go through their madness, and to honor the genius and creativity that traditional psychiatry "treated" with mind-numbing medications and electric shock. Women were particularly victims of this harsh treatment. We applied these ideas to feminism and assertiveness training and unlearning sexism, and psychology. We were self-righteous and quick to condemn each other in the name of sisterhood. But what powerful, heady new ideas. And I learned the basics of facilitating meetings in the group, a skill I've been using ever since.

Red — an Old-Style Butch Lesbian

Most of the women in the Maoist-feminist group I was in at the Radical Psychiatry Center were white, and newly lesbian feminist, doing our best to act and dress in an androgynous style to show our freedom from traditional femininity and from old Butch/Fem roles among lesbians as well. There were also some people who didn't quite fit the paradigm. Some women who previously identified as heterosexual were trying out calling themselves lesbian and being romantic with women for the first time. One woman had an older Butch style, wearing men's clothes and shoes rather than the new androgynous look, because she had been around and out since the 1950s. Her name was Red Jordan Arobateau. Red was working-class and mixed race (white, Latina, Black) and had come from the bar culture, with a lot of the struggles written about in the lesbian pulp fiction books, such as *Woman in the Shadows*. She herself wrote autobiographical and explicitly erotic lesbian books about sex workers and other marginalized women. Everyone accepted her, but we didn't really understand what her life had been like or who she was. She was part of our history, but we didn't know our history well. Of course, years later the dichotomy of Butch (very masculine) and Fem (very feminine) looks absolutely came back as accepted lesbian styles. Butches wore suits or leather jackets; Fems wore heels, makeup, skirts and dresses. Both were much admired, and I'm sure Red fit in much more comfortably. I heard she later transitioned and became a trans man.

The Heavy Fist of Political Correctness

Alan, who is still a friend of mine, ended up being my boyfriend from 1973 – 1979. I didn't yet know that being with a woman rather than a man was right for me romantically, but I was definitely hanging out with hard-core feminists and lesbians. A lot of what we were discussing and taking action around was truly cutting-edge, about women's rights to our own bodies, to our lives, to our careers, and how we saw the world.

One of the popular slogans, expanded from the Maoist one, that exemplified this new feminist movement was, "The personal is political, and the political is personal." It was a way of saying women's lives and concerns and empowerment mattered. And we knew "Sisterhood is powerful." and we could be allies rather than rivals.

It is always a bit of a shock to me when I realize that some of these ideas are new and exciting now to more mainstream women exploring these issues for the first time, while to me they are foundational and almost traditional after forty years.

Along with all the beautiful progress and freedom these new ideas represented in the '70s, there were some negative aspects as well. One of the worst was the concept of political correctness, which came from a socialist or Maoist sensibility but was carried to absurd and constrictive reaches of radical conformity. There was a right way to talk, to think, to act, to dress. There were absolute judgments about who you could be sexual with. If you dressed too femininely, you were an instrument of the patriarchy, and you would be scorned and ostracized. One lesbian accused another of not being a "real" lesbian because she "caught her" wearing (gasp) earrings. It is ironic to look back and reflect on how radical and free we thought we were, but the pressure to conform was as great as in the most traditional sorority.

There was a clear hierarchy and rules. Lesbians were higher on this ladder of status than straight feminists and bisexual women were reviled. Living on the margins of society ranked higher than having a regular job (i.e. working for the Man). The more Karl Marx and Betty Friedan you could quote, and the faster you could fling accusations at those less pure, the higher your status. Any styling to your hair, a trace of makeup, accessories, or any clothes other than jeans or work pants and flannel shirts, were anathema.

If you used the wrong language to describe oppression, or minorities, or feminist thought, you were interrupted, admonished, corrected and sometimes ostracized. And what made it very tense and difficult was that the correct terms changed frequently, with the latest feminist/socialist guru or publication or book. So it was a constant challenge to keep up.

And at times, there were epic battles of political correctness between different women or schools of thought. The judgments were definitely a PC (politically correct) version of what we would now call "mean girls."

Some feminist women said they were lesbians and had same-sex relationships only because the pressure was intense; although their true romantic attraction was toward men. At the same time, for lesbians in these progressive circles there was an increased level of acceptance. But Ms. Magazine and the mainstream feminist movement still feared lesbians would give them a bad name and it kept them from being allies for a long time. There was a lot of tension and strife.

I was ashamed to admit I still had a boyfriend because then I was automatically a lesser being. I was very careful to wear the right kind of flannel shirt and pants and not wear makeup, which I didn't know how to apply anyway, so I would fit in at first glance. I scrambled to learn the right language, feeling ashamed if I said something in a wrong way. My friend Laurie Ann told me recently, "While you were feeling disrespected for having a boyfriend, I was totally hiding the fact that I was bi." Bisexual women were at the time thought to be straight women who were "experimenting," toying with the feelings of real lesbians, and guaranteed to dump them after satisfying their curiosity.

I wanted to fit in so much. I wanted to belong to this beautiful sisterhood and this burgeoning movement. But I didn't understand the perils of this intense judgmentalism or the destructiveness of having to toe the fanatical party line. It was a very different set of standards from those of my childhood, but my feeling less than and straining hard to be good enough and fit in, were all too familiar. It deeply undercut the central feminist ideal of breaking barriers, being free to explore all of ourselves, only valued as wives and mothers or young ones in training, but as full, powerful, creative human beings.

Don't Call Me Sweetheart!

Sometimes my own anger and fanatic adherence to these ideas came out in exaggerated ways. My sister had a sweet, handsome boyfriend named Rob. One time, I was looking for her in Moffitt Library on the UC Berkeley campus and ran into Rob instead.

"Hi, sweetheart!" he greeted me.

"Don't ever call me sweetheart!" I responding angrily. "It is demeaning and disrespectful!"

Now, if someone said that to me in a friendly way, I would simply say, "Hi, sweetheart!" back.

Marriage as Patriarchal Slavery

Another area in which I was completely in harmony with the politically correct stance at the time was about marriage. From having a close view of my parents' unhappy marriage and with all I was learning about the ignominious history of marriage, of women as property transferred from their fathers to their husbands with no rights or freedom, I was completely opposed to the whole institution. With great relish, I even wrote an exaggerated, macabre poem about this, the first line of which was, *"A coffin of the mind, institutionalized."* Creepy and dark!

The Wonderland of Berkeley

In so many ways, my real education began when I moved to Berkeley. Feminism was a big part of it, but far from all. At that time, Berkeley was a cutting-edge caldron of new ideas and revived ancient ones. During the time I lived in and near Berkeley, I learned about herbal medicine, homeopathy, psychic and spiritual healing, acupuncture, the power of massage, shamanism, an economic analysis of capitalism, and following the money in politics. And all kinds of history that had been left out of textbooks — people's history, history of women and healing, union history, queer history, plus more styles of music than I had ever known existed, including women's music.

Some of these topics I learned about in groups and classes, but many topics I learned about first through KPFA, a remarkable progressive radio presence bringing so many different voices and perspectives to the airways. And Berkeley was full of artists and musicians and healers and community leaders, so vibrant and alive. I took many workshops to learn about all this, and taught some too. My brain was constantly full of new ideas, and after the narrow fearfulness of my childhood, I was hungry for them all.

The Sicky-Sweet Crystal Peace Center

I truly loved what I was learning, but there was also a lot of spiritual competition and phoniness. I knew women who changed their names to "Rainbow" and "Crystal Vision" and there was definitely a battle, similar to the feminist one, about which spiritual or healing path was true and who was most enlightened.

One time, I took a workshop on crystals which met on a Friday night and all-day Saturday. I was responding to a flyer and hadn't met the woman leading the group. I showed up for the Friday evening, and as soon as she opened her mouth, I knew I would never make it through Saturday. She had a soft, ultra-sweet breathy voice, and listening to it was like eating too much cotton candy. It set my teeth on edge and made me feel a bit sick. I knew I couldn't stand to listen to her for a full day, no matter how useful the information might be. I let her know I wouldn't be able to come back Saturday.

But this experience inspired me to create an imaginary spiritual healing center, which I called the Sicky-Sweet Crystal Peace Center. She was the first presenter who I "signed up" for the Center. And since then, whenever I run across pretentious spiritual speakers or workshops, I include them too!

Lesbian Home Fries

One of my favorite places to eat at this time was a small restaurant called The Brick Hut Cafe, owned and run by lesbians. Alan and I used to go there, and I also went there with my women friends. They had good food and a radical sensibility. It was a hub for new information and events. Alan used to talk in his sleep and one time he said, "lesbian home fries." I thought this food item fit the Brick Hut perfectly! I really missed it when it closed.

Ladies Against Women

There was a lot of serious passion in Berkeley and San Francisco, but other awesomely talented people wanted to change the world through comedy. My favorite of them all was Ladies Against Women. This group of women comics was an offshoot of The Plutonium Players, who started as an anti-nuclear activist group.

I will always remember a flyer of theirs, which I picked up off the ground on the UC Berkeley campus in the mid-'70s. It had a drawing of a group of protestors marching with a banner proclaiming "Unleash the Fury of the Ruling Class!" Participating groups included "Voices of the Unborn," "Billionaires for (HW) Bush," and "Ladies Against Women." It looked serious, but I knew it had to be a joke, and I very much wanted to find out more about them. Any group, a leftie improv troupe, as I learned later, who could poke fun at the left and the mainstream establishment at the same time were my kind of people!

Ladies Against Women offered an evening of "consciousness lowering." I attended one at the Julia Morgan Center. Their slogan was, "One step forward and two steps back." I bought a button from them, which I kept for years until it totally rusted. It said, "Tupperware preserves the family."

They also taught us an "aerobics" workout, which involved standing up, waving our hands and saying, "Excuse me. Could you pick that up? It is too heavy for me."

Feminist View of My Mother

During this time, I visited a feminist counselor who helped people understand their mothers in light of feminist history. It was the start of my having more compassion for my mother, Fran; how she had been influenced by the sexism and pressures on women to conform, especially in the 1950s after World War II. For her to get a college education, thanks to her mother's insistence, and have a career was a bit unusual still. And I know she felt totally coerced by shame, guilt, and expectations to stay home with my sister and me when it was like torture and ongoing frustration to someone like her, who was only happy out in the world practicing her profession as a psychologist and teacher.

Fat is a Feminist Issue

Another beautiful and freeing new concept I learned about through the women's movement was about fat as a feminist issue. Although the condemnation of makeup and feminine clothes was taken to extremes, the idea that society had contempt for fat as a way to make women conform, feel small, or be ashamed, was very powerful. The idea that our bodies were beautiful at all different sizes, and that we didn't need to diet to be attractive and healthy was radical in the most liberating way!

Pinup Girls throughout the Ages

Once in a bookstore, I saw a big coffee table book called *Pinup Girls throughout the Ages*. The farther back in time the pictures went, the bigger and more voluptuous the women were, except for the 1920s. Women who have been considered fat for the last fifty years were at one time the ideal of feminine beauty. These historical photos helped me understand what the women's liberation movement was saying, that fat and fashion and beauty were shifting constructs that kept women hating themselves and putting all their energy into looking and being a certain way, instead of claiming their power and using it to transform and run the world.

Of course, issues around health and healthy food, about using food as a drug, are complex and real, but with my "sisters," I set a goal of loving myself and my body exactly as I am. I still find old narrow judgments against myself coming up, especially as I am getting older, but I keep working on it! Recently, there have been a lot more women claiming their beauty at any size, and more models and actors who are not thin, but we still have a long way to go.

Our Bodies, Ourselves

Another empowering aspect of the feminist movement was the way feminists began to change our relationship with our bodies and to stop believing what society told us. Fat as a feminist issue was part of this, but there was much more. A visionary yet practical book by the Boston Women's Health Collective called *Our Bodies, Ourselves,* was published at this time. It was designed to teach women all about our bodies, to help us love our bodies and cherish them and listen to them and understand them and have control over our own health and healthcare.

I remember a cartoon showing Wonder Woman holding a speculum. The caption read, "With my speculum I am powerful!" Women, including me, were learning how to use speculums and examining our own vaginas. Artists were drawing beautiful pictures of labia. I bought a labia coloring book that showed different beautiful shapes of women's genitalia.

The goal was to see how beautiful we were, to not accept society and men's contempt and belittling and seeing us as "dirty." Some of us also began to reclaim witchcraft and witches as wise women who had been later demonized. We promoted the idea that we didn't need men to define us.

Being independent, having our own identities, our own careers, our own paths apart from men, was another liberating idea!

Lesbian Barfly (ing)

I wasn't a big drinker, but I did go to a lot of lesbian bars for the dancing and camaraderie. Bars were older venues for lesbians to meet and experience their own culture, and the bar scene continued alongside newer women's centers, bookstores, and coffee houses.

There was a lesbian bar on Solano Avenue in Albany, a couple of blocks north of Berkeley, called the Bacchanal; a gay and lesbian bar on Telegraph Avenue called the White Horse; a women's bar and nightclub further down Telegraph called Ollie's, which had a big room called Radcliff Hall, a wordplay on the name of the lesbian writer who wrote the classic lesbian novel, *The Well of Loneliness*. There was also a country-western lesbian bar called Jubilee in East Oakland. Then, in San Francisco, were Maude's and Amelia's.

I never really liked the crowded chaotic energy of bars, but I did have a lot of fun sometimes dancing and mildly flirting. One time when I was still single, I went to a Halloween dance at a bar. I was dressed as a harem girl, and I met a woman dressed as a pirate. We had a very steamy flirtation on the dance floor and met for a drink once after that, but we didn't really have much in common.

I remember meeting two other women there, who were dressed as a bride and groom, but both wearing Groucho Marx glasses, with the dark eyebrows, mustaches, and big noses.

I commented at the time, "Isn't it strange how married couples start looking like each other?" And we all laughed.

But it was a perfect example of the ironic and funny social commentary with which people subverted costumes and roles.

And at the Unitarian Fellowship in Berkeley, there was an extraordinary series of women's dances, some with live music and beautiful musicians, where we would get together and dance with no alcohol — my favorite of all.

I Swing Both Ways (On the Dance Floor)

I went to a lot of parties for lesbians, particularly dance parties. Because I knew how to lead a little, I was very popular on the dance floor and had fun, even though I wasn't the butch some of these women hoped I was. I used to joke that I could swing both ways. That expression was (condescendingly) used to describe bisexuals, but for me, it was only true on the dance floor.

I remember at one party, I decided to dress a bit Butch. Although I definitely tend to be more feminine, sometimes I like to experiment with other looks. I wore a tailored green-on-green long sleeve shirt with pants and buttoned it all the way up to the collar, and went to the dance. There was a woman there I knew from one of my meetings, who strongly identified as Butch. She had short dark hair and a very masculine way of acting and dressing. She'd always been nice to me, but when I was dressed more butch, she clearly felt very uncomfortable around me. My dressing differently somehow affronted or challenged her expectations. She didn't want to dance with me because I guess it felt like a role violation to her.

Politically Incorrect but Happy

After Laurie Ann and I met in the Maoist/feminist/radical psychiatry group, we discovered that we shared a common interest in ballroom and social dancing, which was dreadfully politically incorrect at that time.

My boyfriend Alan had bought an old book at a garage sale called, *Foxtrot Made Easy*, complete with diagrams with black silhouette footprints and arrows that taught people how to do the Foxtrot. Laurie Ann and I learned the steps and practiced dancing together, using that book and her old vinyl recordings, doing our best to follow the footprints and recall ballroom dance lessons we both had had when we were young teenagers. We were secretly self-taught, but rather good at it. I always led because I was six inches taller. We went to a few regular lesbian dances and tried out our moves, and people seemed to feel all right about our style, but it wasn't the right music or situation.

Jorene Jackson's Big Band

Then, along came Jorene Jackson's Big Band, an all-women swing band. They first played at Ashkenaz, a dance venue that had originally started with folk dancing, but branched out. Laurie Ann had hung out with drag queens a whole bunch, (her drag name was Hothouse Rhubarb) and she had found or made great vintage clothes to wear for swing dancing.

She inspired me to buy a gorgeous vintage '40s-style black dress with a square neckline, shoulder pads, rhinestone buttons, and side drape panniers, which I wore with seamed retro stockings, rhinestone diamond earrings, and a flower in my hair. Laurie Ann didn't have stockings with seams, so I painted lines on her legs with an eyeliner pencil. We primped and dressed up, and went to the dance.

Picketed!

As we approached the entrance, we saw angry white lesbian separatists picketing outside. They thought this dance was a demonstration of women's subjugation and, somehow, of capitalism at work. I remember one woman in particular with very short hair and very angry blue eyes really getting in our faces and screaming at us. These protestors were filled with rage. It was an intimidating gauntlet, but we made our way through the angry shouting picketers and to the entrance of the dance.

As we walked through the door, Laurie Ann tossed her hair over her shoulder and said defiantly to me, "We may be politically incorrect, but we're happy."

In essence, we were choosing joy instead of doing what we thought we "should." And we did have a wonderful time doing our Foxtrot to the big band. We were much admired by some of the butch lesbians inside who liked Fems, including one tall gorgeous motorcycle Butch named Glenn. It was a big lesson for me in charting my own course and not being intimidated or controlled by other people's ideas, even when I respected them.

Butch for an Evening

I enjoyed getting all dressed up, but it was a lot of work. It so happened that Jorene Jackson's band was playing again at the Women's Building in San Francisco a few days later.

I was complaining to Alan, my still boyfriend, that I didn't really want to do the whole dress thing again. He said, "Why don't you go Butch?"

My hair happened to be very short, and in my closet, I had a tailored black pants suit and a plain white-on-white rather mannish shirt.

I'm more of a Fem, but I thought again, "Why not try something different?"

I slicked my hair back and wore the John Travolta-ish outfit (think *Saturday Night Fever*) with my shirt open to show a gold chain. I still wore my own women's sandals.

Laurie Ann was very startled when I picked her up, because my look was so different without the flower and the dress, but she liked it. And I felt different. I opened doors for Laurie Ann, and offered her my arm, feeling rather powerful and protective. We had a lot of fun dancing again. But my dressing Butch had an unforeseen consequence.

The Terror of Cross Dressing
at Ali Baba's Ballroom

In Oakland at that time, there was still a big old-fashioned ballroom called Ali Baba's that had been there for decades. They put on well-attended dances with live bands and all kinds of dances — Foxtrot, Swing, Rhumba, Tango, Waltz. But same sex couples were not allowed, and Laurie Ann knew a lesbian couple who had been thrown out for dancing together, even in their beautiful evening gowns.

Laurie Ann was consumed with the idea that I should try to pass as a man and take her there. Now there is a huge distance between dressing a bit Butch and actually passing as a man.

I had no interest in doing that, and told her so emphatically, "I can't pass as a man! No way!"

But oh, that girl could push. "Why not? Come on! Do it for me!"

And "You already have the clothes. I know you can do it."

"But what if they figure it out?" I asked fearfully. "I don't know how to act like a man."

"They won't." she insisted. "I really, really want to dance there."

"I don't want to be busted! It would be totally humiliating."

"You won't get busted. Where's your sense of adventure!"

She persisted and persisted, asking me, begging me, cajoling me, answering my objections until she finally wore me down, and with great trepidation I reluctantly agreed to do it. "Alright. I guess I'll do it. But for three dances only!"

My voice would never pass as a man's, so I couldn't talk, and I wouldn't be able to use either bathroom, so three dances was the limit.

Laurie Ann agreed to my stipulations, "Ok, that's fine."

And we set a date. I don't think I have ever been as apprehensive about going anywhere as I was going to Ali Baba's as a man.

We went up to the ticket counter, and the woman there said, "I'm sorry, sir, but you can't come in without a tie."

Then she looked at me more closely, and added uncertainly, "Or are you a woman?"

I looked at her with as much macho scorn as I could muster, silently of course, and she quickly apologized. "Sorry, sir."

So, we left. Laurie Ann wanted to go find a tie for me and come back, but I was done. I've never tried to pass as a man again.

Flowers in Our Hair

Years later, Laurie Ann and I reconnected and went dancing together several times. One dance at the Women's Building was called a "Butch-Femme Soiree." We dressed up in our same retro dance dresses (I had an even bigger hibiscus flower in my hair.) and went to San Francisco. I was driving and parking was hard to find.

I finally found a smallish spot around the corner from the Women's Building, and began to pull in. It was tight and I slightly touched the car behind me. The car was full of dressed up Latino men. I jumped out of the car and apologized very sincerely. They were utterly charmed by me, my dress, and the flower, and graciously accepted my apology, especially since there was no damage to their car. But if they had known we were going to a lesbian dance instead of being traditional models of femininity, they might not have been so nice!

We walked into the dance and one of the first women we saw was decked out in a shiny green satin full-length evening dress with bare shoulders, a plunging neckline, and a high slit on one side. She was even wearing high heels. Ironically enough, it was the very same blue-eyed woman who had picketed us and screamed at us outside of Ashkenaz. From one extreme to the other, but she still had short hair!

Return to Ali Baba's

Around this same time, Laurie Ann and I finally realized our ambition to dance at Ali Baba's. My beloved gay friend, Rich, had become my companion and dance partner. He was totally into going to Ali Baba's and bringing a friend for Laurie Ann. So, we made a date and went!

We were all dressed up, and although it turned out it was a "casual" dress day, we received so many compliments.

"Oh, you look so nice."

"It is great to see young people so interested in ballroom."

"You can really dance."

We smiled sweetly and thanked them. Although we were dancing with opposite sex partners, me with Rich and Laurie Ann with Howard, it still felt like a seditious victory to dance inside notorious Ali Baba's!

I gradually lost interest and opportunities for ballroom dancing, but Laurie Ann began seriously studying ballroom dance, eventually teaching social dance professionally here and internationally.

The Last Gasp of My Atheism — a Rant against the Goddess

One time when Laurie Ann and I were having breakfast at the Brick Hut, she told me that she had begun praying to the Goddess. At this time, I was a feminist and an atheist, and I thought Laurie Ann was misguided to be doing that.

I launched into a passionate and extensive rant that went something like this:

"If you pray to something outside yourself, you are lessening your own power as a woman. We have to learn to access our own strength, make our own decisions. Giving up your power to some external deity undercuts feminism and diminishes you. We are powerful by ourselves, and claiming that is how we change the world!"

Laurie Ann just smiled at me and didn't say anything, but it was obvious I hadn't convinced her. It seems funny now because my relationship with the Divine (Goddess) is the bedrock of my life. This rant was perhaps the last big expression of my atheism before I realized how deeply I longed for the support and love of a benevolent Divine presence.

God Is a Woman

I also connected with the work of pioneering anthropologist Marija Gimbutas and the beautiful archaeological goddess artifacts that showed the female divine. We were the source of life; we were beautiful and powerful.

Remembering the Divine Female

And all this had been forgotten as men, envious, tried to steal our power and push us down. I still hated my menstrual period, I must confess, but I did understand that there was a very different way of looking at it and embracing it as part of the sacred female. (We bleed yet have no wound).

And the idea that we were all Goddesses, that we were made in Her image, giving birth to new life, was magical and mystical. It was a healing antidote to the overwhelming misogyny in society. I read a number of books including Merlin Stone's *When God Was a Woman*, and later Barbara Walker's *The Woman's Encyclopedia of Myths and Secrets,* and Starhawk's *The Spiral Dance.*

I hadn't yet connected this ancient wisdom to my own spirituality, but it was the beginning of envisioning the Divine in a way that worked for me. I began to set up altars and to love Goddesses of all sizes from different cultures, especially Kuan Yin and the Great Mother of Willendorf.

The Women's Refuge

After leaving *Workforce Magazine*, I was hired for a (not well-paid) job as coordinator for Berkeley's Women's Refuge, one of the first shelters for battered women in California. Although I was definitely a feminist, I knew nothing about the issues facing battered women. Domestic violence and battered woman's syndrome was barely starting to be more generally understood. I think I read the first pamphlet ever written about it. But I couldn't understand then why some of these women stayed with their abusers or went back to them. Sometimes the women showed up beaten up, in terror, clutching their kids and a few possessions. I know now how much courage it took to leave, especially if they were economically dependent on their abusers.

The Trial of Inez Garcia

I attended the 1974 trial of Inez Garcia with some of my coworkers at the Refuge. She had killed her abuser/rapist and was on trial for her life. It was perhaps the first case in which a woman cited self-defense as a reason to kill the rapist/domestic abuser. And the judge still seemed to believe that someone who was raped or beaten was always "asking for it." At a rally outside the courthouse, the women were angry and vocal. I felt intimidated. I wasn't comfortable then with women expressing their rage so openly. But working with battered women at the shelter, I began to see how common domestic abuse was (and is) and how little recourse women had to protect ourselves.

Give Me Shelter

The shelter was a program of the YWCA. We had an office, living room, and big dorm room at the center. We meant well and having a place to go did help some of the women. And we were pretty good at listening, and connecting them to resources for housing, and financial assistance.

But we were a group of young judgmental feminists, mostly lesbian, and we missed many opportunities to be of deeper service. None of us had ever heard of PTSD. And we lacked the skills to create community and support groups. We individually supported the women, but did nothing to help them support each other. The shelter closed down during the day, and none of us, sadly, understood how hard that was on the women staying there, so we didn't fight to change it. In general, we staff were as much focused on proving how politically correct we were to each other as we were to really being of service to these women.

I had a hard time also dealing with the uncertainty and violence and the limits of our grant. The Refuge's mandate was that women and their children could only stay for a month, which most often wasn't enough time for them to regroup and start a new life, so we were always looking for other emergency shelters and services for them on a crisis basis. This wasn't our fault, but didn't offer a good model for solid, effective help. It was hard to witness their horrible situations and feel powerless.

Fashion vs. Lesbianism

One of the women who worked at the Refuge when I was there was Reyna, who I first met as a Latina lesbian. She broke up with her girlfriend and found a boyfriend instead. I saw her after she had left the Refuge and stopped identifying as a lesbian, and she was an exquisite fashion plate — makeup, jewelry, a pretty dress, high heels, even a hat. She looked a lot more comfortable in her skin, and radiant too. I think the restrictions we all felt about how lesbians were supposed to dress had cramped her preferred style. Now, no one would question her being a lesbian looking stylish and feminine, but then, with feminist lesbians and all the judgments, I'm sure it felt impossible.

Member of the Mob (To My Shame)

One of the white women who worked as a counselor at the Refuge, Wendy, was different from the rest of us. She wasn't a feminist; she was very pretty, a feminine and conventional young woman who wore makeup and nail polish and high heels. She didn't share our perspective on life, women's rights, or the oppression of makeup.

She related very well to the women who stayed at the Refuge, and I believe it was easier for them to talk to her because she wasn't as weird and alien as we radical feminists.

But, we judged her and didn't accept her. We complained about her to our supportive supervisor, Barbara, and framed it in a way that she felt justified in firing Wendy. At the time, we all were completely self-righteous, and it wasn't until many years later when I was being mobbed at a college and researching the topic, that I realized we had mobbed her.

It was a humbling realization for me that I had been part of a group that treated her unfairly and was responsible for her firing for the crime of being different. When I realized this thirty-plus years later, I tried to find her to apologize. But I couldn't remember her last name, and the Women's Refuge didn't exist anymore. I did remember Barbara's last name and tried very hard to find her, but none of the several women I found online with her name ever responded to me. I also contacted the Y, but they didn't have records of that time anymore except in a whole warehouse full of mixed-up file boxes.

I decided I could make living amends by talking about what I had done whenever I teach a class on bullying. Most of my life I have been the victim/survivor of bullying or mobbing — in grade school, junior high, at work. But, in this case, I was one of the perpetrators. The good thing is that my sharing this helps people understand we need to address the *bullying behaviors,* not label and dismiss people as bullies and enemies.

Chapter Five

Europe (with Backpack)

The Women's Refuge actually fell apart not long after — maybe Karmic payback? — and we all lost our jobs. I was burned out from trying so hard to help these homeless women when I lacked sufficient inner resources, or outer resources for that matter.

And working towards a revolution was all very well, but in some ways Berkeley was a self-contained universe, and I was curious to see more of the world. Alan was at loose ends too, and we decided to take advantage of the time off by going to Europe for an extended trip, which ended up being about three months.

We took backpacks and bought Eurail passes. Since it was kind of last minute, we found a cheap flight there but had no return tickets. I went with $2000 and after three months, still came back with money! We stayed in the cheapest pensiones and hostels, and ate a lot of yogurt and muesli for breakfast and bread, cheese, and apples for lunch. We generally only ate dinner in restaurants.

We wandered around Europe without a plan, visiting England, France, Italy, Spain, Belgium, Switzerland. We were superficial tourists, but it was still enthralling.

The Old-World Beauty of Europe

Growing up in Southern California, in a tract house that had been built right before my family moved in, and which looked exactly like everyone else's tract home, I was blown away by the age and variety of buildings and places in Europe where people had been living and working for hundreds of years.

And oh, the art! I'm not sure I had ever been to an art museum before I went to Europe, or if I had, it hadn't made much impression on me. I drank it all in and had an insatiable appetite for more beauty, more art. I knew nothing about the artists or art history, but I will always remember some of what I saw. I could see how beauty was an expression of Spirit.

In Florence, I saw Botticelli's paintings of gorgeous, soulful women. Michelangelo's David was breath-takingly grand, while Caravaggio's Medusa shield in the Uffizi Gallery had all the power of a terrifying horror movie. And in the same museum, I saw a rather amusing version of *The Annunciation*, by Simone Martini, with an angel telling Mary via banner that she was going to bear God's child. She looked utterly sick and unhappy about it all! And a painting of the Resurrection in which Jesus looked like a stoned, long-haired hippie dude rather than the Messiah.

In Paris, I saw the ethereal *Lady and the Unicorn* tapestries in the Musee de Cluny, crafted hundreds of years ago by unknown women artists. The original *Mona Lisa* in the Louvre was far more powerful than the many images and copies I had seen. And in Père Lachaise Cemetery, I also saw where Oscar Wilde was buried, surrounded by flowers and other tributes from gay men. On one part of the wall was a powerful bas-relief sculpture of the murder by firing squad of the Communards, who were members and supporters of the Paris Commune, a far-left revolutionary government that briefly controlled Paris for two months in 1871.

We also visited Carcassonne, a medieval walled city. It is still intact, not a ruin; and I was amazed to actually walk inside such a city and have a glimpse of what it might have been like hundreds of years ago. In Rome, I was most impressed when we wandered piazzas and side streets at random, seeing architectural elements from different time periods all mixed together. And, with a shudder, visiting catacombs where monks had piled human skulls and bones into artistic patterns.

I had a sense of the fullness and richness of history that I had never known before.

Alan and I also visited feminist and political bookstores. I missed my women friends so much! I met some feminists who were also part of the Catalan independence movement and had stickers about women's empowerment written in Catalan. It was hard being completely disconnected from women and from a stable life routine. Without an itinerary, many times we skipped meals or didn't have a place to stay. One time, we were planning on spending the night in Marseille, and there must have been a lot of events going on, because we couldn't find any place to stay, so we climbed back on the train. Alan and I had money, so it was only temporarily uncomfortable, nothing like the experiences of women I knew who were really homeless.

Soldiers on a Train

Alan and I used our Eurail passes a lot. Unlike the U.S., Europe always kept and expanded its train system, and it was a good way to get around. In Spain, we happened to be on a train with a lot of Spanish soldiers. I left our compartment to go to the bathroom in the middle of the night, and then got turned around and couldn't find my way back to Alan. My Spanish at this time was minimal. One of the soldiers befriended me, but somehow thought that I was fleeing an abusive relationship. He did help me find Alan, but was very suspicious of him and my Spanish was insufficient to really explain or reassure him that I was ok. Fortunately, it didn't get physical and he left, still casting dubious glances back at us. I was thoroughly relieved to be back with Alan and my backpack!

Paella and the Competitiveness of "Mellow" Hippies

One of the places we went without a plan was Valencia, a port town in the center of the east coast of Spain. It had beautiful coastal vistas. We stayed at a cheap hotel, and met another guest, a white redheaded woman in her late thirties, who was on her first trip ever outside of Australia. The proprietor of the hotel was immediately attracted and began courting her. She was flattered and liked the attention. I don't know what transpired, but it certainly seemed like she might end up living in Spain with him.

We wanted to try Paella a la Valencia, the signature dish of the region, and arranged to have dinner at a nearby restaurant. We wanted to eat at six, and the restaurant owner said that was fine, but at 6 P.M. the food wasn't done. Nor at 7 or 8 or 9. We didn't know then that the typical time to eat this meal was at 10 P.M., and the owner had no intention of feeding us earlier. It was awfully frustrating, but when we finally ate, my first time having paella, it was scrumptious.

We ran into an American hippie couple twice on a train. The first time, they told us all these stories of sensational, serendipitous experiences on their travels, far more dramatic and interesting than anything we had experienced. The second time we saw them was just after our visit to Valencia. When we told them about visiting the beach there and eating paella, their attitude of acceptance and mellowness fell away. They questioned us sharply and looked sick with envy, crestfallen that they had missed this opportunity. I must confess I enjoyed very much being the mellow one with marvelous adventures to tell!

The World Diversity of Earl's Court

One of the places we stayed in London was in Earl's Court. At that time, it was the area of London where all the new immigrants came. We met and saw people from Australia, from the Middle East, from Africa. This was before the resurgence of Muslim fundamentalism, but we saw many women wearing various kinds of veils and face coverings, depending on where they were from.

One day, Alan and I were doing laundry. We didn't have many clothes with us, so I wanted to wash as many as I could. I put on my tennis shoes and a skirt,which stuck out awkwardly below my rain jacket. In the lobby of the hotel, a group of women from somewhere in the Middle East were sitting, wearing leather masks.

The masks surrounded their eyes and had a piece that ran down their noses and connected with a second part of the mask which covered the bottom half of their faces. I now know they were Bedouin women from Oman, but at the time it was the most surreal face covering I had ever seen. They looked to me more like masks for an S&M dominatrix than conservative face coverings. I stared at them, and they stared at me in my bizarre (only clean clothes) outfit, and I don't know which of us was more amazed, bemused, startled.

Jane Austen Hated Bath

One of the places I definitely wanted to visit when we were in England was Bath because Jane Austen had lived there, and had set one of her books, *Persuasion*, partially in Bath. I had read enough about Jane Austen to know that she hated living in Bath, and her main character in *Persuasion*, Anne Elliot, hated it also.

Nonetheless, I adored Jane Austen and she *had* lived there, so I wanted to experience a place where she had been. The baths, where people came to take therapeutic waters, were still there. And there was a museum showing furnishings and clothes of the time. I was able to wander around some of the streets that Jane Austen might have walked on. It felt like a pilgrimage to go there and think fondly of all her books that I had enjoyed so much.

I don't really know when I first read *Pride and Prejudice*, my first and favorite of all her books, but I do know that I requested *Pride and Prejudice* as the special present my parents wanted to buy me when I had my tonsils out at age twelve. So, I must have really cherished the book before then. I still have that copy of the book plus more editions.

The Vulgar Opulence of Brighton Pavilion

Another place I wanted to visit was Brighton Pavilion. I had read all about the Prince Regent and about the pavilion he created in Brighton, a sea resort in England. This knowledge came from some of the books of Georgette Heyer, who wrote Regency romance novels.

My sister and I read about fifteen of them; and a vivid description Georgette Heyer had written about the Brighton Pavilion stuck with me. Alan and I were able to go, and it was indeed spectacularly and impressively vulgar and overwhelming, with brash and clashing colors and designs in the most expensive fabrics possible, precisely as she described it. There was no order or harmony or attempt at serenity.

Although the Prince Regent was royalty, the Pavilion had more of a Nouveau riche sensibility than the restrained snobbery of old money. The only thing I ever saw in the United States that was even remotely comparable was Hearst Castle, which had a similar aesthetic of vulgar pomp and opulence.

And of course, I knew enough about the Prince Regent to know what a decadent and debauched womanizer and gambler he was. He laughed cruelly at his mad father, the King, and chased women very inappropriately. He had many mistresses and squandered the money of his realm on gambling and lavish parties, and spent one big chunk of money on the Brighton Pavilion.

Chapter Six

The Personal Is Also Spiritual

After I left the Women's Refuge and came back from Europe, I took a job at the food Co-op as an education officer. I didn't really understand the politics or purpose, but I falsely pretended enthusiasm. I felt like a total hypocrite and didn't enjoy working there. At that time, I would say anything to please potential employers and be the person they wanted to hire, even if it wasn't my truth.

The Co-op had started as a small Berkeley all-volunteer food co-op, with a radical approach to food, favoring organics and bulk food, in which every shopper was a member/owner. It had become much more mainstream and bigger, but they still had special positions like education officer, and a number of members who were actively involved in governance.

My Friend Erna, Pioneering Peace Activist and Black Journalist

One of them was Erna. At the time I met her, she was about seventy, and the stories she could tell! She had grown up in Kansas at a time and place when there was a lot of segregation and severely limited opportunities for women, for African-Americans, and especially for African-American women. But her parents were strict, loving, and passionately pro-education.

Erna became one of the first African-American women journalists in Kansas. She worked for newspapers in Kansas, and then L.A. She became a peace activist and was very involved with the Women's International League for Peace and Freedom and the Esperanto movement, which believed that a universal language would promote peace.

When I met her, she had retired from having her own print shop, but was still very active in local progressive politics. She was also kind, incredibly funny, and a wonderful storyteller with a unique, eloquent way with words. She and I became very close.

She often gave me sage advice, and confided in me stories that weren't generally known. She had a beloved friend and roommate during World War II who was German and under curfew as an enemy alien, even though she had never done anything even vaguely against the U.S. This roommate married a man who, according to Erna, had had only gay relationships up to that point, but vowed that if the friend married him, she would be his one and only, a promise he kept.

Perhaps her biggest secret, which she shared with me, was that she was a lesbian. She hadn't had many opportunities for relationships, but it was women whom she loved romantically. I was the only person in her life who knew she was in love and courting a woman she'd met at a peace conference. She also had a bit of a crush on me.

She described me by saying, "She is bright and beautiful and shines like fine old polished gold."

I was deeply flattered, but though I loved her, I wasn't interested romantically, partly because of the forty-five-year age difference.

I Run Away

Our relationship didn't end well, due to my co-dependence. Because I was the only person who knew she was gay, I took on a self-imposed burdensome sense of responsibility and felt like I had to constantly be there as her confidante; which wore me out. I ultimately ran away. I moved north and completely lost touch.

By the time I had some awareness of my own issues around caretaking and people pleasing, and started working on this in a 12 Step program, she had died. I wanted to apologize, and I did by writing a letter to her, reading it aloud, and burning it. But it wasn't the same as seeing her. I looked her up when I started writing this memoir, and found out an affordable housing complex in Berkeley is named after her. She would have loved that!

I have to forgive myself.

She was a remarkable woman, who let nothing stop her and I feel lucky that I became friends with her. But it is one of the regrets of my life that I didn't find my own healing in time to reconnect.

My other regret was that I wasn't able to support her very well after the death of her younger sister, Gaynelle. She loved her sister deeply and tenderly. Erna was enough older than her sister that she helped raise her. She had actually chosen the name Gaynelle from a novel she wasn't supposed to be reading. Her sister didn't have much money, and all I saw was how much money Erna was sending her that she really couldn't afford. I had never lost someone I truly loved at that time and I didn't get it at all. I wrote about this too in the letter.

While You're Munching your Organic Raisins, Don't Forget to Smash the State!

Even beyond the Co-op, food was another area where Berkeley people were strikingly progressive and forward-thinking but also had very rigid political correctness and judgment. There used to be a small organic food store run by the workers, a collective of course, called *Ma Revolution Natural Foods* store. They had bins for bulk food, which was new and radical at that time, organic produce, and a political agenda, as you might guess from their name.

I remember a big poster that they had up on the wall, perhaps by the great cartoonist R. Crumb, which showed a big burly muscular man with tied-back long hair standing in front of a bulk bin and looking back over his shoulder at us. The caption read, "*While you're munching your organic raisins, don't forget to smash the state.*"

There was a cafeteria-style restaurant on Telegraph Avenue called *One World People.* I wandered in there one day and a (seemingly) blissed-out long blonde-haired hippie guy behind the counter proudly showed me the meal of the day. It was comprised entirely of beige colored beans and white rice. I was completely bewildered and couldn't imagine why anyone would want to eat that.

Similar to early feminism, the new food movements expressed a lot of opinions about what was correct and incorrect to eat, and a lot of radical ideas that became much more mainstream and very important later. The idea of people having control over our own food and food sources, the idea that pesticides were destroying the earth and that we needed to stop using them, the idea that we could eat whole, beautiful, organic vegetables and less processed food, were all new then but have been embraced more and more in the mainstream.

I remember reading Frances Moore Lappé and other writers to understand the importance of food and health, how food shortages were caused by political decisions and inaction, and that starvation was completely unnecessary if food resources were given to the people who need them; and if people were given the space to grow their own healthyfood.

The Gifts of Ahbi

While I never turned away from feminism or progressive politics, I began to feel that external political agendas, no matter how valid or important, were not going to be enough for me to fix the wounds and misinformation of my childhood and have a happy life. I was still filled with self-hate, shame, resentment. I felt stuck and helpless, unable to find love, to figure out what I wanted to do for a career, or even thoroughly enjoy a day without worry or frustration.

I was lucky enough to find the perfect therapist, Ahbi, to help me heal and become a more whole, self-loving person. This was an important part of my spiritual journey as well.

Ahbi and I were almost exactly the same age, though she looked even younger, short with lush curves, creamy white skin, big brown eyes, and shiny dark hair. She was still an intern when we started, but she gave me so many gifts that were the foundation of healing and a better life. I worked with her a total of eight years, and I will always be grateful.

When I described my childhood to her and my experiences of being bullied at school, she immediately told me, "You are describing anti-Semitism."

I was shocked. "Really??" I said. "I thought it was all me."

"No. Not at all. Everything you've told me about what happened indicates anti-Semitism," she said. "I'm Jewish too, and I grew up in the South. I experienced a lot of the same things you're describing."

Her personal experience and calm assurance convinced me she recognized anti-Semitism when she heard it!

It was a tremendous relief. I had had no idea, although it made so much sense as I explored it more with her, that what I had experienced was at least partly caused by prejudice. I thought it was something deeply wrong and bad about me as an individual. This new information planted a seed of healing.

My Beautiful Inner Friend, Little Lorry

Of course, learning for the first time that I had experienced anti-Semitism didn't change my shame and negative feelings about myself all at once. But we also started working on my inner child, whom I call Little Lorry. One of the most important gifts from my work with Ahbi, was to get to know little Lorry and heal my relationship with her.

First, I had to meet her in dialogues and guided visualizations and then convince her to talk to me and to believe that I would listen. When I first met her in a session, she was sullen, angry, and so very unhappy. I dialogued with her, I listened to her, I apologized for having ignored her and her needs. I started showering her with love. I created hand-made cards for her, let her pick some activities and have a say in what we did. Over time, she blossomed into a sweet, loving, playful little girl with oodles of joy and creativity.

I discovered that it didn't take big expensive gifts or extravagant events to make her happy. Getting to draw, seeing a flower garden, dancing, spending some time in a Redwood grove, or sitting (virtually) in my lap filled her with delight.

I have continued to cultivate the relationship with her that started at this time, and today, she is my creative partner in teaching, designing graphics and slide presentations, writing, and having fun! And she has a lot of compassion for other people's inner children. She loves them, invites them to feel safe, express their feelings, and play too; which adds a wonderful dimension to my coaching and teaching. Ahbi guided me and supported me in this initial process.

I began to recognize all the negative, unhelpful messages I had absorbed from my well-intentioned but fearful parents. In a visualization, I had a vivid experience of feeling psychically smothered by my mother. I couldn't breathe, feel, think, from the pressure of her feelings, her expectations, her desperate needs.

At the same time, I also began to find compassion for my parents, who I realized, also had inner children who hadn't felt loved or cared for. Over the years, I saw more and more clearly those little inner children inside my parents, and it helped me forgive them for not being able to give me what I longed for — unconditional love and acceptance. I understood that they couldn't give me what they didn't have.

My Mother's Apology

One time, when I went down to visit my parents as an adult, my mother apologized to me.

Her tone was self-pitying (it was still all about her), but I think she was sincere. She said, "I'm so sorry for all the mistakes I made when you were growing up. I feel really bad about all the things I did wrong."

And fortunately, I had enough perspective that I could respond to her gently and truthfully. "Mom, there was a lot I wish had been different in my childhood. But I know you did the best you could. And now, I'm an adult. It's up to me to create a good life for myself; it is not your responsibility anymore."

That was a healing moment for both of us.

Little Lorry Sticks Her Tongue Out

Little Lorry has enriched my life immensely with her warm heart, unbounded creativity, and honest emotion. Once I was sitting in a meeting and someone walked in who I was still very angry at because of a difficult encounter we had had. Little Lorry was upset. I visualized tucking her in my heart where she would be safe and loved, and told her to let me, the grown-up, handle this. She agreed, but then, in my mind's eye, she put her little hands on the opening in my heart, popped her head up and stuck her tongue out at the person! She ducked back down, but popped up again three more times and stuck her tongue out each time. I could hardly keep from laughing out loudat this image, but it was very satisfying, and I wasn't as angry after that.

Learning to Channel the Goddess

With Ahbi, I also found the Goddess, who has been part of my life and approach to spirituality ever since. The books I had read were helpful, but the heart of my wonderful new connection with the Goddess was the guided visualizations I did with her. The first one was imagining myself sitting on the lap of a divine woman, the Goddess, and feeling Her loving arms around me. The Goddess became the unconditionally accepting mother I had always longed for.

Channeling the Divine

I also took a workshop on channeling the Divine with a group called *Windsong* and began dialoguing with Her. In the workshop, we were introduced to the idea of doing automatic writing and allowing the Divine to speak/write through us. In some ways, it was a difficult experience. The class met multiple times and I found myself being very fearful of how I looked and whether my clothes were clean. I never wore dirty clothes, so I had to ask myself what was going on.

I realize that almost all of the people in the class were white and blonde, and it had triggered some feelings left over from Downey of being called dirty because I was Jewish and different. But after I recognized the source of my discomfort, I decided to continue in the workshop, and I'm very glad I did, because that is where I first learned how to channel the Goddess. And, I have been doing it ever since.

I still find my very first channeling I wrote beautiful and affirming.

I asked Her — *Do you, can you truly love me?*

Here is Her answer in part:

> *Beloved, does a dove have wings? As a dove wings its way to the heart of its beloved, so do I love you. My love is infinite, all encompassing. You have but touched your lips to the rim of a cup which is filled to the brim with love everlasting. You can drink and drink from now to Eternity and not lower the level by so much as an inch. Is this not the magic of true joy?*

This channeling in particular changed my life forever. The love, power, and tender beauty in these lines was palpable, and it was clearly not my style of writing. It reminds me of poems and prayers like the *Desiderata*, but it came from my letting the Goddess guide my pen. I couldn't be an atheist or agnostic after that. I believed! And although I didn't feel it every minute, the experience of unconditional, unlimited love began to change me.

My Honeymoon with the Goddess (Born Again)

After the initial channeling and the loving visualizations I did with Ahbi, I had a six-month "honeymoon" of bliss. I felt that I had been reborn in the Goddess. I felt Her loving presence with me constantly. I was filled with peaceful joy and love for myself and the world. I truly believed that from then on, all my lessons would be learned in love and not from hardship.

But like any honeymoon, that blissed-out period ended.

I still had and have a daily relationship with Her, sometimes filled with love, but also with arguments and resentments. I still had many difficult experiences, as you will see, and they've taught me a lot that I couldn't have learned if I had stayed "high" on the Goddess. Nevertheless, I knew and know that I am not alone in a hostile universe. I have a loving Being with me at all times — I just have to remember.

Eight Important Years

I saw Ahbi for almost eight years, and I am grateful for every one of them. I remember one session in particular, when an issue that I had brought to her years before, came up. I felt ashamed, like a failure, to have to deal with it again.

And she said, "No, you are not in the same place. This is a spiral not a circle. You are looking at the same material but you have grown and your perspective is not the same."

I still find that helpful and comforting when my character defects come up or I make the same mistake again!

Talking to My Body

One of many themes I worked on with Ahbi was how to love my body. Believing the Goddess loved me unreservedly as I was and as I am now helped, as did the messages of feminism and images of Goddesses who weren't model thin. Ahbi also taught me how to dialogue directly with my body. I had a lot of frustrating problems with my knees, particularly my right one, which would swell up, hurt, and prevent me from dancing. I called my right knee my "bad" knee.

With Ahbi's guidance, I did a dialogue with my knee.

Immediately, my knee said to me, with sorrow and certainty, "Don't call me 'bad'! I'm doing the very best I can!"

I understood, and knew she was right! I began to call her instead my "special needs knee." It seemed to help.

Angels and Earthworms

Towards the end of our time together, I remember another extremely valuable session. I was looking at yet another mistake I'd made, where I revealed my imperfect, human self.

"But Ahbi, I don't want to keep making all these mistakes. I want to be an angel of light!" I lamented.

She looked me right in the eye and responded, "Then what would you do down here with all the rest of us earthworms?"

We both laughed and I have remembered ever since that I am in good company with the wonderful human earthworms!

Writing a Journal

I kept a journal the whole time I was seeing Ahbi. I poured out my fears, shame, self-hate, frustrations. I wrote about my hopes of finding a sweetheart, I wrote about insights I had in therapy, and I wrote down channelings and conversation with the Divine and dialogues with parts of my inner self. It was healing.

Looking back over years and years of my journal, I am in awe of this record of my courage and determination to heal, to grow; my persistence in working through the negativity of my early years. And, I realized later, with great gratitude, that all that journaling was key to breaking through my writer's block and being able to eventually write with a lot more ease.

Walking with the Goddess

As part of my search to connect more deeply with the Goddess, I signed up for a nine-month *Women's Mystery School*, which met one weekend a month at a big house near the beach in Point Reyes, California. It was led by Vickie Noble, author of the Motherpeace Round Tarot Deck, and Hallie Iglehart Austen, an author and spiritual leader.

It wasn't well-organized, but I had some powerful spiritual experiences and guided visualizations. One powerful experience was doing Tarot Theater. We would each pick a card, dress up in costumes, and act out the message of the card. The cards were always exactly right for some issue each of us needed to heal.

We did deep, guided visualizations to connect with the Goddess. We learned and sang beautiful songs by Lisa Thiel and others about various Goddesses and their stories.

Pushing the Car to Point Reyes and Other Stories of Recovery

While I was attending the *Women's Mystery School*, I was beginning to learn about letting go of control; especially of other people's choices or addictions. This dovetailed very well with what I was learning about the Goddess.

I didn't have a car at this time, so was dependent on other workshop participants for rides. One time, four of us were riding from Oakland to Point Reyes together. We met at Lisa's house, but she wasn't ready. Then, she had to stop for gas. When we finally started driving to the workshop, it was clear that we were going to arrive at least an hour late. I hated that!

As we were driving, I noticed that my stomach muscles were very tense. In fact, I realized I was trying to push the car faster with my stomach!

A sane little voice inside me spoke up. It said, "Honey, no matter how much you push, you can't make the car go even a quarter of a mile per hour faster. All you can do is give yourself a stomach ache."

I laughed out loud, and let go! Maybe a stomach ache would have been worth it if it could have made us go faster, but my stomach has no such power!

I Want to Live!

Around this time, I remember walking down Solano Avenue in Albany one evening. Solano Avenue was filled with restaurants, wine bars, coffeehouses, ice-cream parlors, and boutiques. As I passed by a restaurant, I saw an uprooted flower, a periwinkle, on the sidewalk. Someone, in an act of vandalism, had pulled out the flower and its root, and thrown it wantonly on the sidewalk.

I picked it up gently and looked around. I saw a restaurant with a window box that had brightly colored periwinkle flowers, and a gap in the row. The restaurant wasn't open, but I went into the wine bar next door and asked if they could give me some water. I was very emotional, and the bartender probably thought I was nuts, but he kindly rinsed out a wine bottle and filled it with some water.

I took the water and the flower back to the window box, gently put the flower and the root in the hole, patted the earth down around it, and gave it some water.

As I did, I whispered to it, "I want you to live. I want you to grow and flourish and have a lovely flower life."

I started sobbing, and realized that I was really talking about myself. I didn't want to die, not physically or in my spirit. I wanted to truly grow and change and live and flourish. It was an important moment in my choosing life, love, and healing. And 12 Step programs were becoming an important part of this process for me.

All 12 Step programs began with Alcoholics Anonymous. The founders came up with 12 Spiritual Steps, in part based on the Oxford Group, a Christian community, and in part from the experiences of doctors and others grappling with patients suffering from addictions. The 12 Steps were designed to help people recognize that they were powerless over their addiction, but by turning to a Divine loving presence, often called a Higher Power, taking responsibility for their mistakes, and forgiving themselves and others, they could ultimately transform their lives and have a daily reprieve from acting out their addiction.

Miracles of Fellowship and Spirit

My own first 12 Step program experience was motivated by relationships, how to take care of and value myself and not be codependent — i.e., pleasing or manipulating others. It was a revelation to me. First though, I only went to a few meetings, realizing "Ok, I'm codependent. That's good to know." I thought that particular insight was all I needed. I came back for a few weeks because there were lots of cute lesbians there, but I didn't really get the purpose or the journey.

But I recognized that I was unhappy in relationship or out, and neither therapy nor feminism nor political awareness were enough either. I began to understand I would never be happy unless I could heal my inner wounds and false beliefs about myself and others. The idea that things could be different for me personally, that I could be different and more peaceful, took hold.

In 1987, I started going to meetings regularly for spiritual and practical help and hope. The 12 Step program began to show me a different path, of letting go of control and forgiving myself.

In the 1980s in Berkeley and Oakland, there was a robust lesbian and gay recovery community. I went to two sequential lesbian meetings at the Temescal Library in Oakland on Monday nights, a beginners meeting followed by a regular meeting; as well as a lesbian and gay recovery meeting at the Congregational Church in Berkeley, which generally had sixty or more people on Wednesday nights; and a beautiful lesbian/gay meditation meeting that, in good weather, met under oak trees in Live Oak Park — a special place to meditate.

Two months after I started going to meetings, I broke up with my girlfriend of that time because I realized that if I wasn't trying to save her, fix her, or control her, we actually had nothing in common.

One big benefit of going to meetings was that we each had the opportunity to share what was on our hearts and minds. People would listen deeply and not interrupt. At the Wednesday night meeting particularly, I shared my whole journey, week after week, including the illness and death of my dear friend Rich. People there were very kind and supportive and they helped me get through it. And working the 12 Steps by writing about each one, looking at the ways I needed to change my behavior and thinking, accepting the mistakes I had made and sharing this with my sponsor and other program members, helped me connect more with the Divine.

I became much more willing to see that I was not and had never been in charge of my life. I felt hopeful about charting a new path forward with love and spiritual support. I didn't feel, as I had in college, that I would always hate myself and feel insecure. My fellows inspired me with the changes they were making.

Pretty Doesn't Mean Sane

One of the things I started seeing right away in recovery, was that looks had nothing to do with good or bad relationships. I had always thought that if I were thinner, prettier, better dressed, had more toned muscles, wore high heels or more makeup, or was somehow different, then I would find true love and have a happily-ever-after relationship. But as I attended meetings and started hearing people's stories, I quickly realized this was wrong.

In particular, I remember two different women at two recovery meetings sharing remarkably similar stories about their relationships. One white Jewish-American lesbian was quite overweight, and came to the meeting each week in a pair of grimy overalls and with messy, greasy hair. She talked about her problems with her girlfriend and how she tried to control her and please her.

Another woman, Chinese-American, at a different meeting was lithe and slender, with long shiny brown hair, and exquisite clothes. She looked quite different, but her story about her relationship with her attractive boyfriend was almost identical to that of the overalled lesbian.

I started understanding that if you were very attractive, you could find someone who was also very attractive, but that didn't mean the relationship was any more nourishing or functional; it could still be a total nightmare.

This was a revelation to me and really busted my belief about what I needed to do to have a good relationship. It wasn't about changing how I looked or how I presented myself; it was really about how much I could love myself and be centered, and let other people be who they are, with discernment but not judgment. This strengthened my commitment to healing my beliefs and my spirit instead of "looking good."

My Frenemy, Food

My first 12 Step program helped me with self-love and sanity in relationships as well as my addiction to worry and attempts to control others. But, I began to realize my favorite way to self-medicate, my truest drug of choice, was food and the act of compulsive eating. My childhood had set me up for an unhealthy relationship with food as well as with people. Since food was tightly controlled when I was a child, I couldn't really use it as a drug until I moved out of my parents' house. And my weight didn't actually go up until much later, because I was a pretty active person. But as soon as I was on my own, I definitely started using food to manage and soothe my feelings rather than as the nourishment we all need to live.

When I was alone in my little cottage in Oakland, if I didn't have a date or event to go to on Saturday night, I would go to the grocery store and stock up on sweet things like cheesecake, candy bars, chocolate cream pie, and ice cream; and on salty things like chips and dip. I would alternate eating sweet and salty items in a full-blown binge that lasted all evening.

It was my secret entertainment and punishment, my comfort and torment. I didn't tell anyone what I did. I lived alone for many years, even though I was lonely, because I was ashamed and didn't want anyone to see what or how I was eating or how hooked I was on sweets and excess food.

Years later, I saw *Brown Bag Readers Theater*, whose members wrote humorous skits and monologues about alcoholism. One of their pieces applied so much to me.

Translated to food, they said, "Bored? Have something to eat! Excited and can't sleep? Have something to eat! Oh, you lost your job — eat something; you'll feel better. Oh, you got a new job! Let's celebrate — with food! You fell in love — hooray! Let's eat! You broke up with your girlfriend — some food will make you feel better! Someone hurt your feelings — food will help. You don't know what else to do — there's always extra food!"

Tranquilized by Food

I didn't realize until I found recovery, how all my feelings and experiences were muffled and mediated by food. When I first found some abstinence and stopped using extra food for everything, my feelings were overwhelming. I would think, "Why is this such a big deal? I've done this before." Then I would realize I'd never done it "sober" without excess food.

I had to learn to live life in a completely different way, with more joy and more sorrow and more reality. And with gentleness, because I realized what a sensitive person I had always been since I was a very little girl. I didn't know how to manage those feelings and how to feel ok, so I had turned to food. And food did help me get through the misery of my childhood and young adulthood.

As I said earlier, my weight wasn't bad for a long time, but when I moved up to Carquenas for what turned out to be my horrific and dysfunctional job, and left much of my support system behind, all I had was my "frenemy" food; and I ate my way up to 215 pounds. When that happened, my drug of choice created consequences that were visible to everyone. I felt deeply ashamed of my weight, self-hating, and helpless to stop.

Doctor Who and the Adipose People

I started watching old *Doctor Who* episodes from the 1960s with my dear friend Rich; and when they rebooted the series in the 2000s. One of my favorite doctors was David Tennant and there was one episode called *Partners in Crime*, which I loved and really connected with because of my compulsive eating.

In the episode, there was a new miraculous weight-loss pill on the market. And it really worked, and people lost a lot of weight. But the people who took the pill also heard mysterious noises in their houses; the dog door would flap open and closed, or windows were opened. Dr. Who and his sidekick begin to investigate, and it turned out to be a deep alien conspiracy. When people took the pill, it would create baby aliens for the Adipose people out of their fat. The idea in the episode was that if this secret conspiracy were revealed, everyone would be horrified and the aliens couldn't keep doing it.

The episode itself was very amusing, with a final scene of all the baby aliens, looking like Pillsbury doughboys, giving the royal wave as they were drawn up to the Mothership, leaving behind their human nursemaid.

But I was even more amused because from everything I know about people who are food addicts or compulsive overeaters, most of us wouldn't care at all if our fat was making alien babies, as long as we ejected it and lost weight! The episode clearly contained some social commentary, but I don't think the writers understood the depth and lengths that addicted people would go to in order to be thin!

When I started the 12 Step program around food, I, too, only wanted to lose weight and keep eating compulsively. But gradually, as I received support, connected more with the Divine around my eating and feelings, and worked the Steps, I realized that the clarity, inner strength, and self-love I found when I took responsibility for my behavior, forgave myself and others, and didn't eat compulsively, were more precious and more satisfying than any food item could possibly be. From being my god, food has become a friend, who needs love and boundaries.

Now, I haven't had sugar or chocolate for over twenty-four years and have kept off fifty-five pounds for twenty-two years. But, like an alcoholic, I am never cured. I need to stay close to my food program, the 12 Steps, and the Divine, so I can "have a daily reprieve if I stay in fit Spiritual condition," as Bill W., the founder of AA said.

The courage and strength that abstinence has given me, helps me deal with any difficulty or challenge in my life, and I will be forever grateful. I eat delicious food that nourishes and doesn't trigger me, and stay close to Program because I never want to go back into shame and addict behavior or be without Divine love and support.

The Ethereal Realms in Berkeley and San Francisco

In my ongoing quest for healing, I also found my way to a white woman named Christina. She was the most unconditionally loving person I had ever met to that point. She was gorgeous too, tall with long golden-brown hair and big blue eyes. She actually looked like one of the beautiful women in Botticelli's paintings, but a bit more voluptuous.

She had had a healing power practice in San Francisco earlier and then had gone off traveling. Now she had come back, and was living in an ashram across from the Golden Gate Park panhandle. She had the true all-loving healer's energy, and people found their way to her, even though she didn't have an office set up. She saw people in her bedroom, curled up at the head of the bed while people sat at the foot of the bed. She knew how to dowse, using a pendulum with a crystal on a cord to obtain answers to questions.

Christina would talk about and dowse flower essences, crystals, and herbs for people. The flower essences she gave me seemed to help.

But I knew then and know now that the main draw was her ability to simply channel love, unconditional and complete. She was a priestess of the Goddess. She had her own personal limits and problems, but they didn't come across in how she worked with people.

Flowers in the Water

I became very interested in flower essences after this. Each flower had a different psychic or emotional property. You could make an essence with a bowl of water and the flower blossoms. Once they "steeped," you could preserve them with brandy or glycerin. I still don't understand why or how they work, but I experienced the evidence myself. They are a form of magic.

Rescue Remedy, a combination of several essences, was really good for shock and trauma; and other flower essences helped me with my healing.

Learning how to dowse, first using a crystal and then using my pointer and middle fingers, helped me access my intuition in a way I never had before. I had to let go of my thoughts and opinions so that I could sit still and be a pure channel for whatever divine wisdom wanted to come through. I gradually honed my skill, although if my busy brain was too active, it would short-circuit the information. This stillness later helped me with prayer, surrender, and meditation.

I bought a kit of flower essences in the Bach style, the original flower essences from Great Britain, and took trainings. Then later I went up to Nevada City for an intensive week and studied American flower essences with the Flower Essence Society.

For a while, during the time I was teaching at various colleges as an adjunct, I had a small flower essence practice and would see clients. I would interview them about their issues and listen closely.

Then, I would hold their hands and run a pendulum over the box of essences to find the flower essences it seemed they needed. I would double check it with the information I'd received from the interview and also by asking them again.

The Miracles of Flower Essences

Sometimes the results were very dramatic. I worked with one woman who was a new psychotherapist, but had absolutely no confidence in herself or her abilities. I gave her a combination of flower essences, for self-love, healing, and confidence. And the next time I saw her she was brimming with self-confidence and had been promoted at work.

I also saw a young man who had a severe phobia of crowds and was afraid to leave his house. He came with his girlfriend, clinging to her for dear life and shivering in terror on my couch. I gave him a combination of flower essences for fear and terror and past trauma, and it cured him. I knew that it wasn't me that had picked those essences, so being a channel in this way also strengthened my connection with the Divine.

In a workshop I taught, one woman was having trouble dowsing for herself. I held her hand and passed a crystal over the essences. Sunflower essence jumped out as right, and I asked her if she had a difficult relationship with her father. She almost fell off her chair because it was true, but I had no logical way of knowing it. Again, I knew I was simply a channel.

You Will Meet a Tall Dark Stranger

One of the things I did to try and have more flower essence clients, was to set up a booth at psychic healing fairs. I only did it a few times, because it wasn't a good fit for what I was offering. People would be drawn to my energy, but they were really looking for direct answers, someone to tell them what to do. Instead, I was offering a tool for healing. Of course, understanding what they needed was a psychic gift, but I wasn't offering the kind of advice that people wanted.

But I did have some interesting experiences at the fairs. At one, I took a break from my own table and went to thought-provoking workshop on past lives. The workshop leader explained how her process worked, and asked us to pick two topics. We came up with money and love. We explored money first.

A Prophet Unheard in His Own Land

The person leading the workshop had us envision a moment of time in the present and then visualize a time ten years in the past. Then we began to slide our consciousness back and forth between the two times. Then suddenly, instead of ten years, she told us to go back a thousand years. I had an actual vision. I was a man, with a deeply lined face and matted long hair and a beard; a prophet in the desert wearing a dusty robe whose bare feet in sandals were caked with sand. I both was this person and could see him from an observer's perspective.

I stood a few steps outside the closed gates of an ancient walled city.

The guards didn't want to let me in, because I didn't have any money. And I was pleading with them, "But I have something important to tell you. You need to hear this!"

I was totally sincere. I don't know what I wanted to tell people in the city, but I had a desperate urgency that they needed the information. I couldn't convince them to listen or to let me in.

I Won't Marry Him!

Then we explored the topic of love. The leader had us do a similar sliding back-and-forth of consciousness. I had a different and very clear image. I was a young brown-skinned woman wearing a white dress. I saw my hands holding a wooden bucket filled with water.

In the vision, I slammed down the bucket, saying "I won't!" My parents were telling me I had to marry someone, but I didn't want to.

I have no idea if these images were actual glimpses of past lives or metaphorical, but it was truly fascinating.

Life After Life

After this experience, I began to read books about reincarnation. In one book called *Life After Life*, the author, Raymond Moody, interviewed people who had near-death experiences and came back.

There were definitely common themes repeated over and over, of people hovering outside their bodies, of people going through a tunnel or a dark place towards the light and being asked (by an angel, by Jesus, by God, by a column of light), "What do you have to show me about your life?" or, "Are you ready to die?" which was in essence the same question.

They saw their whole lives laid out, and also felt unconditional love from this presence or being. They were all told to go back, that it wasn't their time yet. Many didn't want to return because they felt such joy.

Another researcher, Helen Wambach, who wrote a book called *Reliving Past Lives*, did guided visualizations for groups of people to lead them to experience a past life, and then had them fill out a survey form. Most of the people reported being poor peasants, living in a hut and eating mush of some kind. This ordinariness gave it a great deal more credence in my eyes. No one was Cleopatra or Napoleon or anyone rich and famous.

After my fearful childhood, the ideas that we have multiple lives and that a loving Divine presence will meet us when we die were comforting.

Your Handwriting Reveals Your True Self

At one of the psychic fairs, I also met a very kind and interesting man named Marcel Matley who did handwriting analysis. He claimed that he wasn't psychic, that he was using his expertise in interpreting handwriting, but his analysis seemed miraculously insightful to me.

I took a workshop with him to learn how to change my own handwriting, heal the past, and improve my attitude and life. It was after this workshop that I found a full-time job in my field, so it seemed to work. I also learned a bit about how to read other people's handwriting and understand what some of their issues might be. Above the line was conscious thought, below the line was unconscious, and the way your handwriting slanted determined whether you were optimistic or pessimistic. He could tell things about your childhood as well.

More recently, he worked more with the court system assessing whether documents were authentic or forged, but his ability to see who people were from their handwriting was astonishing.

The World is Filled with Magic and Healing

Exploring these topics in San Francisco and Berkeley, I came to understand how rich and mysterious the world was and how many paths there are to healing and being of service in the world. I continued taking different classes about healing modalities. I did more intensive studies about Chinese herbs and Chinese medical diagnosis at this time.

At one point when I was tired of being an underpaid adjunct faculty, I considered going to acupuncture school or naturopathic medical school. I actually took two of the prerequisites for the acupuncture school in San Francisco — Medical Terminology and History of Medicine.

A Biased History of Medicine

We had an assignment in the History of Medicine class, to write a timeline of healing. The class completely left out healing that wasn't from a Greek or European background, such as all the wisdom from the Middle East or Egypt or other parts of Africa. Instead of doing a timeline, I felt compelled to put together what I called a biased history of medicine, with cut-out photos, drawings, and a timeline that talked about the turning away from the Goddess, women's herbal wisdom, and natural healing.

During the time I was writing it, I couldn't stop, even though I knew I was doing far more work than the class required. I never did anything with the little book I created, but it was one of my first examples of being completely taken over by a creative project and being political at the same time. It was definitely working me, not me doing it. But neither acupuncture or naturopathic medical school stood out clearly as my path.

Sistah Boom!

In 1982, I joined *Sistah Boom*, a women's percussion Samba marching and dance band. The group fueled my creativity, my sense of community, and my awareness around racism. We all played drums: snare drum (Caixa de guerra), bass (Surdo), tenor drum (Repinique) or hand percussion instruments: a small Brazilian hand frame drum hit with a stick (Tamborim), and a double or single cowbell (Agogó). My friend Kay Sato invited me to attend a rehearsal. Kay was a wonderful singer and musician, a beautiful and gentle being. She and her parents had been in one of the Japanese relocation (concentration) camps in World War II.

Sistah Boom was quite something! I initially misunderstood what instruments they used and brought my Egyptian tambourine (Riq), but saw I needed a very different Brazilian tamborim. I was hooked immediately on the beautiful percussion and joined on the spot.

Sistah Boom was led by Carolyn Brandy, a professional drummer, composer, performer, and educator who had been with the Jazz group *Alive!*. And there were a number of other women in the ensemble who were also professional musicians such as Judy Grayboyes (*Blazing Redheads*), Michaelle Goerlitz (*Azucar*), Susu Pampanin (a well-known Middle-Eastern drummer) Gail Kissin, a percussionist and Yiddish music singer, Bonnie Lockhart (*Red Star Singers* and *The Berkeley Women's Music Collective*). My dear friend mica (she doesn't capitalize her nickname) had played in a women's band, *Witch 1*, in Vermont. Members included a number of other women who had studied percussion and played semi-professionally or in garage bands, and those of us who were inexperienced but had tons of enthusiasm and, hopefully, some sense of rhythm.

It was exciting to be in an all-women's group. Back then and even still a bit today, drumming was thought to be the province of men. To have women in the band, playing all the instruments, the big drums as well as the small stuff, was empowering and inspiring. And oh, did we have fun and make a joyful noise!

Although we didn't talk about it, it was a profoundly spiritual experience as well. I remember one rehearsal in particular where we were practicing a rhythm standing in a circle. We drummed our way into a blissful trance state. I saw and felt all our spirits soar, joining together as one above the circle.

We played Samba and other Afro-Caribbean rhythms and incorporated anti-imperialist and feminist chants in English and Spanish such as:

"The People, United, will never be defeated!/ El Pueblo, Unido, jamas sera vencido!"

Hey Hey Ho Ho _____________ (racism, sexism, war, etc.) has got to go!

Stand up! (boom BOOM) Fight back! (boom BOOM)

1, 2, 3, 4, We won't take it anymore! 5, 6, 7, 8, Stop the violence, stop the hate!

And more traditional lyrics:

Adios Mama, Adios Papa, Ya Me Voy, a La Comparsa (Goodbye Mama, Goodbye Papa, off I go, to the Comparsa) from a socially conscious music group.

The group started with the goal of marching in the San Francisco Gay Pride Parade, and although we expanded to many different events, such as pro-choice rallies, art events, the Dyke March, and Juneteenth celebrations, gay pride (which gradually became LGBTQIA Pride) was our biggest focus.

At our height, we had over a hundred musicians and fifty danc-ers, and as we marched in the Pride Parade, bystanders screamed for us as if we were rock stars. Hundreds of people along the parade route fell in behind us to dance along to our compelling rhythms. It was intoxicating! I have never had so much fun on a march or in a parade as I did during those years. It was worth all the rehearsals every Saturday at Aquatic Park in Berkeley, and the internal political correctness battles.

The March on Washington (1987)

Perhaps *Sistah Boom's* most exciting gig of all was marching and per-forming at the *March on Washington for Lesbian and Gay Rights* in 1987. We raised money for our airfare and hotels by playing on the streets and in the bars of the Castro, and by designing and selling buttons and T-shirts so that all the women, no matter their personal financial resources, could attend. My dear friend Angelica, a *Sistah Boom* dancer, generously financed the cost of producing these items, and our fans bought them all up. It took months, but we were dedicated and determined, and we hustled hard to transport forty members to D.C.

Washington was filled with gay activists who had come from all over to participate. It was a vibrant, energetic scene and we were an enthusiastic part of it. We played percussion as we marched as part of thousands. And, we even played on the main stage at the rally which followed the March, backing up Jesse Jackson as he spoke. The entire National Mall from the stage to the Washington Monument was filled with people, shouting and clapping. We were so proud to be there, to be doing our small part to fight for equal rights for lesbian, gay, and other queer people.

After the March, we met up with the *Batucada Belles*, a Boston-based women's percussion group. Picture two lines of women, all holding drums, or tamborims, or agogo bells, waving our drum sticks and hollering and coming closer together until we met and hugged our counterparts. We didn't know them, but they were our percussion sisters, for sure.

The next day, the National Mall was filled instead with one of the first major public displays of the *NAMES Project AIDS Memorial Quilt*. The project started in San Francisco; people made large quilt panels for their loved ones who had died of AIDS, showing with colorful fabric and embroidery their names, sometimes what they looked like or what they cared about in their lives. A group of us from *Sistah Boom* went to look. We all knew gay men who were sick or had died. We held hands for comfort and silently walked from one panel to another, overwhelmed with grief at the loss of all these young men. Already there were so many, many dead and no good treatment yet for this terrible illness.

Unlearning Racism

Sistah Boom was very culturally diverse, with white women, many Jewish and some not, African-American, Latina, including women from Cuba, Puerto Rico, and Brazil, Arab-Americans, Asian-American including Filipino, Chinese, Japanese, Malaysian. We were lesbians, straight, bisexual. We had a lot of love and passion for each other and the music and our mission, but, like most Americans, a lot of mistrust, assumptions, and stereotypes about other groups. And we were supposed to be sisters together, but some white women were fearful that if we communicated openly we might unintentionally say something racist. And the women of color had a lot of suspicion and fatigue about the well-intentioned but clueless white women. We never resolved these differences completely, but we did some courageous work.

We had workshops with Ricky Sherover Marcuse, who had a groundbreaking program series on unlearning racism, unlearning homophobia, and unlearning anti-Semitism. I took more workshops with her outside of *Sistah Boom* as well. The details are different but the underlying ideas for all these oppressions are the same. Some of our workshops were led or co-led by Gloria Rodriguez.

And I was part of these groups from both aspects — wanting to be an ally to people of color, and being a target as a Jew and a lesbian who had internalized homophobia, anti-Semitism, and sexism. I began to understand how much easier and more comfortable it was to see the ways I was oppressed and treated unfairly than to see the ways I had privilege as a middle-class white woman.

I remember one workshop *Sistah Boom* had with a riveting exercise called a fishbowl. All the willing women of color in the group sat in an inner circle and shared with each other some of their experiences of racism and prejudice, while white women sat silently in an outer circle and listened. Because of these courageous, risk-taking women, we witnessed some of their feelings and challenges around daily experiences of racism that are generally invisible to white women. It was revelatory! And it definitely deepened my understanding of the deep wounds of racism.

Sistah Boom — the Movie

Years later, director/producer Gus Van Sant, who remembered *Sistah Boom* fondly, was making a movie about Harvey Milk. The movie, called *Milk*, which came out in 2008, went on to win many awards, including Oscars for actor Sean Penn, Gus Van Sant, and writer Dustin Lance Black.

Cleve Jones, a prominent San Francisco gay activist who conceived the AIDS Quilt, cofounded the San Francisco AIDS Foundation, and worked closely with Harvey Milk, reached out to mica about *Sistah Boom* participating in the Milk film. He and the director were inviting us as a group to be extras in the film. What a fun day we had! We had to bring our own clothes but chose accessories, had a costume check, hung out in one of the "green" rooms, were invited to eat from the beautiful buffets, and then, after hanging around the whole day, we marched and played our Samba down a hilly San Francisco street, lined with vintage cars from the early '70s.

We heard "lights, action," but Gus couldn't get the timing right for the musicians. So finally he said, "Lights, Sistah Boom!" And we took it from there. We were so proud! Ultimately, our scene was cut from the movie, but we were included in special "thanks to" during the credits. Maybe the footage will be included in an extras video sometime!

Legal Power to the People

Still looking for a career path, I volunteered at Pro Per Collective, a self-help legal clinic, which I found out about while I was working at the Women's Refuge. The legal field was opening up more to women, and I thought I might want to go to law school. I didn't end up becoming an attorney, but I enjoyed learning some of the basics of defending people who didn't have access to legal resources.

I also met a Black woman who volunteered there. She was willing to take the time to educate those of us who were white about the legal discrimination against Black people and how unfairly they were and are treated in the legal system. I am grateful for her kindness and how she treated us as potential allies.

One of the important things she told me was, "Honey, we are all racist. You can't grow up in this country and this culture without absorbing the attitudes and having the shadow spots that institutional racism creates."

"This isn't about you personally. If you can accept this, and not be defensive, you can be a good ally."

I knew that what she was telling me was true. If I could be open and accept the gaps in my understanding of prejudice, then I could shift my attitudes. I could learn about what racism actually is, how it manifests, and what I can do to help without feeling attacked personally. This reinforced what I was learning in workshops with *Sistah Boom* and built my empathy and understanding of struggles different from my own.

Trying to Make Ends Meet

After working at the Co-op and Women's Refuge, but before I went back to school, I had a bunch of different odd jobs to pay the rent.

I had a series of temporary jobs as a research interviewer. Researchers would get funding to interview people about their pet subject. They trained us how to ask questions and write down the answers, and what they were looking for. One of my fellow interviewers had the most beautiful speaking voice I have ever heard, better than most movie stars. She was very successful because people would say yes to anything as long as they could keep listening to her.

When I started, I thought it was a cool job, but the meager pay was only based on how many people you convinced to let you interview them, with no money for travel or gas. I was stopped for a traffic ticket one time on my way home, which meant I paid out every bit of the money I received for that interview. It grew tiresome quickly, and I stopped taking extensive notes on people's answers.

I interviewed one fourteen-year-old girl from a Roma family. (At that time, I called them gypsies, not knowing this is actually a racial slur). In Rome, Alan and I had seen Romani begging on the streets, and some kids tried to pick-pocket our backpacks, but I had never before had a conversation with someone from that culture.

Although I was supposed to interview the girl alone, some of the time her mother insisted on being present. I had a romantic idea of the Roma people, but women's lives seemed hard and limited.

At least according to this mother and daughter, the culture didn't approve of education for girls. They should know how to read and know how to add and subtract numbers, but that was about all. These people were poor, but they had a huge bed with plush red velvet curtains and quilt, reflecting the importance of family unity, as they all slept together.

The mother accepted how things were, but was also angry, and some of it came out in controlling her daughter. The daughter, only fourteen, wanted to run away and marry, the only escape that seemed possible. She didn't seem to realize that her mother was just as trapped as she was.

At the end of my interview, the mother insisted on giving me a folded paper with dust to sprinkle on my doorway to bring me good luck.

I interviewed another young married woman and her mother. They were poor white working-class and didn't have much, but the love between them was sweet and deep. They supported and helped each other in many ways. It was very different from how I felt about my mother.

Temporary Growling and Biting

I also worked for a while through a temp agency, but I didn't have very good office skills, so I did the most boring, mind-numbing work. At one insurance company, my responsibilities consisted of taking a pile of physical files, checking each one against a ledger, and then refiling it; over and over and over all day long. The file cabinets were those long sideways files, three rows of them, from the floor up. The easiest way to replace the files in the bottom row was to sit on the floor.

As I worked my way up and down the file cabinet rows, I noticed that I felt happier when I was sitting on the floor. Since I was using very little of my brain on my task, I began to muse about why that was. After a while, I realized that when I was on the floor, I wanted to growl at the people who walked by and bite their calves, which were at my eye level! As soon as I received the visual image, I laughed out loud, and kept chuckling the rest of the day. It truly cheered me up because it captured how I felt. This experience fueled my desire to find a better way to earn a living!

I Have Bigger Balls than You

One of Alan's friends was Morris, who was also a musician. He joined the Jewish Renewal movement and changed his name to Moishe. For a little while, he also thought he might be gay, and experimented with jewelry, bright colors, and maybe relationships with men. I used to wear gold earrings in the shape of globes. Moishe had some too, and he came over to the house where Alan and I were living wearing them. He looked at my earrings and said, "Oh, your balls are bigger than mine." I couldn't resist, and responded in my deepest voice, "That's right, Moishe. My balls are bigger." He realized what he had said, and we both laughed a lot.

Chapter Seven

Women, Healing, and Social Change in Mexico

While I was going through the mail at the self-help legal clinic, a flyer came across the desk about a program called *Women, Healing, and Social Change*. It was for women to go to Mexico to study Spanish, herbs, feminism, and liberation theology in Mexico. I had always wanted to learn Spanish in some kind of immersion program, and this sounded a lot more intriguing than the standard kind. I also knew it would be a far deeper experience than my three months in Europe as a tourist with Alan. I was still interested in herbs, feminism, and different cultures. So, I signed up and went.

And I certainly learned a lot, though not exactly what I was expecting.

The program itself was kind of a bust because it was too ambitious and promised far more training of various kinds than the two leaders, well-meaning visionary Christians, could deliver. They created expectations that they couldn't possibly meet.

But the group of women I was with were fascinating. Some were Chicana healthcare activists, some were spiritual practitioners, some were Christian progressives, and there was even one Latina nun from a teaching order. They were from all over the country and spending time with them was an education in itself.

I was living with a few of the women at the home of a Mexican family; a mother Lucy, and her adult children, Connie and Angél.

This family and others I encountered helped me understand about traditional families and the beauty and restrictions of belonging.

My own immediate family was very modern and very alienated from their extended families. My parents moved across the country to California from the Northside of Minneapolis, and I barely knew my grandparents, aunts and uncles or cousins. I felt little connection to them. But, being a temporary part of Lucy's family, I witnessed the good aspects and the difficult aspects of a more traditional family.

They didn't seem to feel all alone the way I did, but part of a loving unit. And, at the same time, they were restricted and limited by the expectations their families put on them, and by their strong sense that family came first. They were supposed to sacrifice their individual desires and longings for the good of the family.

I knew that being who I was, I could never have survived successfully in that situation — I was American to the core, too individualistic, too selfish, too set in my belief that what I wanted as an individual was most important. And yet, I envied their closeness and sense of belonging because I completely lacked that.

What I began to learn about intercultural communication was also fascinating. I hadn't known before this — that although some universal concepts are the same, no language simply substitutes a different word to translate the same identical meaning; instead, each language has many words to express different ideas and alternative ways of thinking, which impact how people feel and act as well. In other words, you can say things in English or Spanish or Hopi or Yiddish, that you can't express as well in another language. My brain began to expand!

I loved beginning to really be able to communicate in Spanish, and I felt a freedom in speaking the new language that I had never known. It was as if in a different language, I was free to reinvent myself. And speaking directly to people from a different culture satisfied curiosity I hadn't even known I had. Finding ways to convey ideas and information with all the gaps in my vocabulary was a fun challenge.

However, it was hard and humbling when people didn't understand what I was trying to say. Sometimes they laughed at my mistakes or said the way I communicated was "cute." I wasn't trying to be cute! I was trying to communicate as best I could, but my vocabulary, accent, and cultural understanding were all inadequate. I struggled to understand what people said to me as well, especially if they spoke quickly or used a lot of slang.

Most people in Mexico were kind about my language deficiencies, but they were also sometimes condescending. This experience sparked my deep sympathy for people learning English for the first time.

You Say Hello, I Say Adios

One beautiful example of intercultural differences came when our group took a day trip to a tiny pueblo (village) called Tlayacapan. While I was walking down a dusty back street, a slender local housewife, wearing a faded housedress and apron, hair in a bun, approached me from the far end. As we moved closer, we both smiled, and as she passed me she suddenly said, "Adios."

Her remark disconcerted me. But I realized, after some thought, that our connection only lasted for a few seconds. So, saying "goodbye" certainly made as much sense as "hello." And "adios" could also mean "go with God," blessing me on my way. It had simply never occurred to me before that someone would address the end rather than the beginning of these extremely short interactions. And truthfully, if someone I walked past like this in the U.S. had said "goodbye" to me, I would have thought they were crazy. Being the "crazy gringa" in Mexico, who despite my best efforts, made frequent amusing or offensive mistakes in communication because of gaps in my cultural or linguistic knowledge, changed forever how I view these situations. I knew that different styles didn't mean either of us was wrong!

And there was so much abundance in Mexico. I had been to farmer's markets briefly in Europe, but the one giant mercado (market) at which Lucy did most of her food shopping, was so full of color and life and artistic displays of food! You couldn't imagine a place more different from the typical sterile American grocery store of that time.

Whole rows were devoted to fruit, some piled into pyramids, with huge papayas which the artistic vendors opened and cut into the shape of flames. Fresh mangos, mamey, which tasted like fresh roasted orange sweet potatoes, and so many sizes and colors of plantains. Platanos, our yellow bananas, dedos (literally fingers) which looked like miniature (finger-sized) yellow bananas, rojo (red) bananas, and platanos machos (we call them plantains). All delicious, although the plantains needed to be fried or roasted.

Some aisles had mountains of mole (pronounced moe lay), rich dark brown, or red, or green paste, and huge coarsely woven sacks filled with beans or dried fish. There were stalls devoted to herbs, hanging in bunches, with small good luck charms included. Other rows (which didn't smell as good) had raw chicken, beef, pork, fish. Everyone brought their own woven plastic bags for the groceries. They weren't thinking about the environment particularly; it was undisputedly the good way things were done.

And oh, the food in the restaurants. Even little hole-in-the-wall restaurants had incredible food. I had only previously experienced

Mexican food in California, which I now understood was merely Mexican fast food, a small subset of the richness of Mexican cuisine. I had the most delicious chicken vegetable soup I've ever had in Mexico City. Papas fritas (fried potatoes) fresher and better than I'd ever had in the U.S. in Puerto Escondido; a simple breakfast of black refried beans, scrambled eggs, green salsa, and fresh tortillas, delicious and flavorful in Cuernavaca.

One of my favorite restaurants in Cuernavaca only served posole, a soup with chicken, hominy, and vegetables, and many kinds of tamales. Tamales wrapped in corn husks with red sauce, tamales wrapped in banana leaves with mole and chicken filling, and dessert tamales, sweetened masa (corn meal) flavored with strawberries, pineapple or squash and spices. All scrumptious.

In Oaxaca, I had chile rellenos, but stuffed with chicken, pine nuts and pimentos instead of cheese. They were a gourmet delight! I was blown away by the quality and variety of culinary traditions from different regions of Mexico.

Mysterious Zanahoria

Once I was outside a vegetarian restaurant off the central square in Mexico City looking at the menu, though the restaurant was closed that day. One dish featured zanahoria, which I had never heard of. I thought it was a mysterious vegetable native to Mexico, but later I found out zanahoria means carrot! I had to laugh.

Alien with Blue Eyeshadow

Part of the time I was in Mexico, I was mostly around people who were Mexican, not Anglo. Once, I was on a bus and saw a blonde Anglo woman waiting at a bus stop. She had on bright blue eye shadow, and along with everyone else on the bus, I stared at her; she looked odd, like someone from a different planet! I knew I was a gringa, sans eye shadow, but I hadn't seen anyone who looked like her for weeks.

Chickens on a Bus

I took buses quite a bit in Mexico, to go from Cuernavaca to Mexico City (La Ciudad de Mexico), to Oaxaca, to Acapulco. Mexico at that time had a number of different bus companies. I enjoyed interacting with many different kinds of people but when it came to buses and distance travel, I confess my goal was always to find the best, most direct, fastest, most comfortable buses to my destination.

There was no central place to catch the buses; you had no choice but to go around to the different companies' bus stations and ask how long it took, how many stops, etc. Almost every bus company claimed they were the best and most direct, and most of them lied. Sometimes I was on fast, air-conditioned, direct trips, but other times, I ended up on locals that made many stops. I shared space uncomfortably with goats and other animals. One man climbed on the bus with a bunch of chickens with their legs tied together, flung upside down over his shit-spattered shoulder.

When I went to Oaxaca from Cuernavaca, I was unfortunately on a slower, older bus, the only "gringa," and it took forever to get there. The bus broke down in the dark in the mountains and the driver and his assistant didn't have a flashlight. I had a small one with me, so they borrowed it and jury-rigged repairs on the bus. Then we resumed the trip. They gave me back my flashlight, covered in greasy black fingerprints from the oil that I could never clean off. But if I hadn't had the light, I think we would have all had to spend the whole night on the bus. It would have been the worst for the animals and the people with small children.

The Queen of Mexico

One of the beautiful examples of art and spirituality in Cuernavaca and other parts of Mexico was all the portraits (retratos) of La Virgen de Guadalupe, (The Virgin of Guadalupe), a Latin-American version of the Virgin Mary with her own miracle story. This spiritual vision was casually incorporated everywhere, in murals and on the walls of paleta (popsicle) stores as well as in churches. Even though La Virgen was part of Catholicism, I knew she was also a symbol of the power and love of the Divine Mother, a manifestation of the Goddess.

La Virgen was always shown with a radiant aura all around her, wearing a blue cloak containing the starry night sky. Often, she stood on a curved crescent moon, one of the other symbols of the Goddess.

She was often surrounded by roses, and sometimes by smaller pictures telling her miracle story — how she revealed herself to a poor peasant, telling him the church needed to build a cathedral on that spot. She gave him a tilma (shawl) wrapped in roses, and when the peasant brought it to a bishop and they unwrapped it, a complete portrait of her was on the inside, with no brush strokes showing — a miracle.

I went to the Basilica in Mexico City where the tilma still is. I bought a souvenir card with her picture which said on it, "La Reyna de Mexico y la Emperatrix de Sur America" (The Queen of Mexico and the Empress of South America) — not heaven, but Mexico! I loved this certainty of who was really in charge. She became an important part of my pantheon of Goddesses.

I remember one exquisite little church I went to, beautifully maintained with a carved ceiling, whitewashed walls, and blue accents. Instead of statues, which I suspect they couldn't afford, they used department store manikins with wigs and biblical costumes to depict Mary, Joseph, and the rest.

Diego Rivera's and Frieda Kahlo's House

Cuernavaca had some of Diego Rivera's murals about the history of the Aztecs and other aspects of Mexican history and culture; and I loved his style and vibrant colors. I saw his exhibit at the big art museum in Mexico City as well.

One of my fellow students in the *Women, Healing, and Social Change* program, Irma, told me about Frieda Kahlo and her house in Mexico City and insisted I had to go. I had never heard of her (this was in 1978), but I went and was enthralled with her art and her style. It felt like a little bit of her energy lingered in the house. As well as beautiful examples of her art, there were photos of her in indigenous colorful outfits, photos of her and her husband Diego, and a whole wall of *Milagros* (miracles), little metal icons shaped like crowns, hearts, or other symbols to bring luck or healing that she had collected.

Love Affair with Mexico

I really fell in love with Mexico, and became infatuated as well with Lucy's adult son, Angél. He was a sweet man and we shared some passion and fun, but I didn't realize at the time how much my infatuation with Mexico was the actual fuel for my affair with him. He had velvety smooth reddish-brown skin and was very kind to me, but we didn't have a whole lot in common.

Interestingly, he learned enough about me and my mangled Spanish to be able to interpret for me, even though he didn't speak English. He could explain to me what other people were saying in Spanish so I could understand; and could explain my Spanish to people when they didn't understand me.

Spanglish Creeps In

Once I was trying to explain "sleeping bag" to Angél.

I went on and on, in Spanish of course, saying, "it is for sleeping in the country when you're outside and don't have a bed . . ."

He listened closely and then said, "Ah! Esleeping bâg."

I wished I'd tried Spanglish first! But false cognates also created a lot of trouble for me. I told another man I was looking for "adventuras," meaning exploration and adventures, not knowing that in Spanish "adventuras" meant sexual adventures.

The Wonder of Watermelon

Watermelon was another of the many fruits in Mexico. I had never liked it much when I had it in the U.S. Basically, I didn't like eating anything with seeds (or bones) in it. But one day I was running around Oaxaca by myself and I met these two lovely sisters who worked as seamstresses in Oaxaca because they couldn't find work in their small village. It was very hot that day, and I didn't have any bottled water. They took me to their house and offered slices of deep red watermelon. It was cool and delicious and satisfied my thirst. I have had a deeper appreciation of watermelon and what it offers ever since!

El Dialecto in San Juan

The sisters invited me to come spend a day with them in their true home, a small village a couple of hours outside of Oaxaca. A cousin gave us a ride in his pickup truck. I sat on a small low stool in the back of the truck. In a way, it was quite uncomfortable, but it was also glorious. I had nowhere else to be, and nothing I needed to worry about. The sky was an intense blue, the countryside we were traveling through was green and tranquil, with maguey and other crops growing on both sides of the road. I felt a peaceful joy and connection with the beauty all around me. It was another early experience of being completely present in the moment, instead of being divided between the past and future.

The village, when we arrived, was humble but sweet. The biggest surprise — most of the people there were speaking a strange language I had never heard, and they didn't speak Spanish at all. I asked my friends about it and they said it was "El Dialecto" (the dialect). This did not satisfy my curiosity, so I kept asking about what the language was and where it came from until I found out it was called Zapotec, the language of the indigenous inhabitants of this part of Mexico.

I knew nothing about the many languages that had been spoken in Mexico — not only Zapotec, but Nahuatl and Yucatan Maya among others. I was amazed and fascinated. I surely wished I could speak their language so I could talk to them about their lives, how they managed without Spanish, and how they had kept their language in the face of Spanish conquest and assimilation.

Some of the relatives invited me to stay in the village and spend time with them. I wish now I had done it, but at the time it felt overwhelming and scary to stay by myself where I didn't speak even a word of the language. The sisters had to go back to Oaxaca for work, so I would have had no translator at all.

Forever Monogamous

While I was down in Mexico, infatuated with Angél, my boyfriend Alan unexpectedly came down to visit. At that time, he and I were experimenting with an open relationship, so I wasn't "cheating on him" with Angél. But I absolutely couldn't be sexual with Alan while I was having a sexual relationship with someone else. My brain and body simply wouldn't work that way. Alan wasn't very happy about it, and as a result sought more involvement with his other girlfriend at the time, Patricia, who he has been with ever since and now has been married to for many years.

It was the beginning of the end for Alan and me. And it was all very uncomfortable and miserable feeling, especially since I hadn't figured out I was really a lesbian. However, whether with men or women, I never tried again to have more than one lover at once because I am truly monogamous.

Beach + Cannabis = Enlightenment

I went back to Mexico again for a visit, arranging to spend time again with Angél, but it turned out he didn't have the time off when he had told me he did, and also had a pregnant girlfriend. I was devastated, and purposeless, but managed to go off on some adventures.

I'm really lucky I didn't end up in a Mexican jail, because I took up with another man, Jorge, whose friend sold "mota" (cannabis). He had a whole airline bag full of cannabis and gave us some to smoke on the beach. I had never felt so relaxed and spiritually connected. But even at the time, I knew that what I wanted was more spiritual connection, and that drugs were not the best way to acquire it. Still, I'm grateful that the cannabis offered a sign post and glimpse of what could be. And Zipolite was an almost completely undeveloped beach community that we stayed in for a while. Sleeping on the beach in a hammock under a palapa, an open hut with a palm frond roof, was chilly but interesting.

Extra Large Virgin

After I returned from Mexico, I still loved Mexican art and Latin music. I remember going to the Mexican Art Museum in San Francisco soon after I returned to see some exhibits and visit the museum store as well. Among many beautiful items, they had T-shirts printed with a graphic of La Virgen de Guadalupe, and I really wanted one. At that time, because of my weight, I needed an XL-sized T-shirt and there weren't any on the rack.

So, I asked the woman working at the cashier station, "Do you have this T-shirt in any larger sizes?"

She nodded and shouted out, "We need an extra-large virgin up here." I burst out laughing, and after a moment of puzzlement, she did too!

Vamos a Bailar! (Let's Dance)

As another way to stay connected to Latin culture, I began to take Salsa dance lessons. Salsa is primarily from Cuba and Puerto Rico, but it overlaps with Cumbia, a popular dance in Mexico, and "Música Tropical" (Tropical music). I loved it and, after I finally learned to shimmy and bend my knees right, I was pretty good at it.

Dancing Like a Cubana

At one dance party I went to after my trip, they played some salsa music and I danced with a lesbian from Cuba. She paid me one of my best dance compliments ever.

She said, "You dance like a Cubana (Cuban woman)!"

As a *gringa* (Anglo) from L.A., I felt very flattered that my years of lessons and working on my shimmying skills had paid off!

The First Jewish Feminist Conference in San Francisco

After I returned from Mexico, I attended the first Jewish feminist conference, held in San Francisco at a middle school in the Mission District, across the street from Dolores Park. I walked into the conference, and the big room was filled with progressive Jewish women all talking at the top of their lungs, all gesturing with their hands, and almost all with impressive noses instead of tiny turned-up ones. It was absolutely transformative. I cried.

I had never ever been in a large group of women like me. And I realize that one reason why I had enjoyed being in Mexico so much was because people there also spoke loudly and talked with their hands. I felt more comfortable in a foreign country than I did many times with people from Northern European backgrounds in the U.S.

I went to workshops about the history of Jewish feminism, Goddess imagery in the Bible, and workshops about transforming Judaism to include feminism and nature. I knew many women who reclaimed their Judaism in a different way, incorporating these feminist principles.

One touchstone was putting an orange on the Seder plate. A very conservative rabbi had said that putting feminism into the Haggadah (religious script for Passover), and having Jewish women as rabbis, was like "putting an orange on a Seder plate," meaning impossible and wrong. Traditionally, the Seder plate which related to Passover and the Hebrews leaving Egypt, had items representing tears and the brick walls they built, bitter herbs, etc. But after this statement, many women, including me, and some supportive men, started putting oranges on their Seder plates to symbolize the new inclusiveness that we were embracing.

Although I attended other Jewish women's gatherings, this new Judaism never stuck with me the way it did for some women. I still didn't feel connected to the religion or most of the rituals. The stories in the Torah seemed far too cruel and patriarchal to attract me. I know many sincere men and women who reclaimed their Judaism in this way, combining it with feminism and progressive politics, but it never worked for me.

Later on, I did play hand percussion in the house band for Congregation Shomrei Torah, a synagogue in Sonoma County. It was a thoroughly enjoyable way to connect to a Jewish community. And a bit later, I started my own band *Salaam, Shalom,* to form a musical bridge between Arab and Jewish culture and support peace in the Middle East. We played Arabic music and music of the Jewish diaspora, singing in Hebrew, Arabic, Judeo-Arabic, Yiddish, and Ladino. Mary Harmon and Patricia Wilburn of the Community Media Center in Santa Rosa made a short documentary about us. Find it on YouTube: https://www.youtube.com /watch?v=MtVNh0Ut-eY.

Chapter Eight

ESL Lessons

When I came back from Mexico, I was no longer interested in pursuing a career in law but something related to cultural differences and understanding. My friend Kathleen told me about a program at San Francisco State University to study intercultural communication and become an English as a Second Language (ESL) teacher; and I jumped on it.

Returning to school to become an ESL teacher, my life became deeper, richer, and more complicated. I was learning a new professional skill and at the same time I was committing to my recovery around relationships, healing my childhood, finding two best friends, coming out, dealing with death and the AIDS epidemic, and connecting more closely to the Goddess.

The Living Beauty of English

My first class was History of the English Language. I have always loved words, and was fascinated to learn about the languages, geography, and the conquests and cultural/linguistic merging that led to the English language we have today. Understanding that language is a living entity, always growing and transforming, continues to intrigue me.

A River of Words

I was still very afraid of writing at this time, so I took the option of creating a project instead of writing a paper for the History of English class. I used a technique I had learned in my tenth grade World of Art class involving colored tissue paper, starch, and pen and ink. I created what I called A River of Words. I researched word origins using the OED (Oxford Unabridged English Dictionary) and, using different colored tissue paper "streams," showed when and where a word entered the English language and how it changed spelling and meaning along the way. I didn't realize at the time how creative the project was, because my motivation was simply to avoid writing!

Hooking Up with Phonics

I also had to take an introductory class in Phonics and the International Phonetic Alphabet. I struggled to learn all the unfamiliar symbols and the sounds they went with, and scored a D on the first quiz. I went to see the professor in distress, my worry and lack of confidence making me instantly sure I would fail the class and wash out of the whole program.

He only asked me one question, "Have you ever studied this before?" I said, "No."

He shrugged and said, "You'll get it after a while."

He was right and I passed the class with a B.

Grammar, Linguistics, and the Perils of Chalk

As in any academic program, there were classes I had to take that were frustrating and not very interesting. We studied Noam Chomsky's transformational generative grammar for an entire semester. It never made much sense to me and was utterly useless for actually teaching English grammar to anyone. I spent hours on my own studying English grammar and how to explain it to a second language learner because we didn't have a class for that.

Mixed Bag of Classes

Other classes were interesting and useful — Psycholinguistics about how people learn languages and what happens in our brains, Methodology, and Materials preparation. Methodology was a mixed experience — lots of wild theories and approaches that didn't work well in the real world. I remember one approach that used little polished wooden sticks of different colors and lengths — I can't remember now how or why they were supposed to work.

There was also enlightening information about learning styles — how to teach in a way that reaches people in all the different ways they learn.

Backwards Build-Up Extravaganza!

I found some of the terminology amusing. One technique to teach pronunciation was called "backwards build-up." You started from how to pronounce the end of the word and worked back. For an assignment, I created what I called a "Backwards Build-Up Extravaganza." Another pronunciation term I loved was "successive approximations," meaning you kept practicing and bit by bit approach the correct way to say something. I thought it applied to a lot of learning way beyond ESL.

Saudi Wives and Engineers

I still had some prejudice against people from the Middle East at this time (before my peace band *Salaam, Shalom*), because of the narrow pro-Israel attitudes I had grown up with. The class I took in college on the Middle East had helped me understand that there was more than one perspective on the deep-seated problems of the area, but I was still afraid my students from that part of the world would hate me for being Jewish.

When I became acquainted with students who were Saudi engineers at SF State and St. Mary's College, I saw they were people, smart and eager like all my students, who wanted to learn English and to be successful.

And their wives, who were allowed to take classes as well at SF State, taught me a lot. They loved being in the U.S. because they could leave the house freely, without needing a man to go with them. I realized how lucky I was to be a woman in the United States, even with the sexism that still existed.

I also realized that progress doesn't happen evenly in different places. I truly believed that the feminist movement had helped women everywhere in the world, but these women were back in the dark ages in many ways, with severe restrictions on their lives and freedom.

When I was at SF State, I also tutored a free-spirited Iranian girl from a wealthy family. She was tall and beautiful, with a long dark shiny ponytail, and wore jeans and tight shirts. This was before fundamentalism started constricting women's lives in Iran. She was definitely planning to return to Iran, and I don't know if she was able to have the career she wanted or was forced to become a house-wife. I'm sure she had to wear a Hijab (headscarf), and don't know if it was something she embraced or had forced on her.

Most of the foreign students I taught went back to their home countries after a few years of college. I generally lost touch with my students after our class or sessions together ended. But I've never forgotten the many lovely people, from so many different cultures, who touched and enriched my life and taught me a lot about their experiences in the wider world. And as I followed world events, and read about violence, fundamentalism, dictatorships, natural disasters, and revolutions, I prayed that they were all somehow okay, including my student from Iran; and found a way to lead safe, fulfilling lives despite the upheavals in their countries.

Gay Girls Just Want to Have Fun

It was while I was in graduate school that I realized I was a lesbian. Emily, one of my comrades from workforce magazine kept asking our mutual friends if I had come out yet. I think now that because of my repressive childhood, my sexuality was dialed way down and it took me quite a while to figure out who I was really attracted to. As part of my quest for fun and true love, I went to many lesbian-themed cultural events — concerts, documentaries, whatever I could find.

Aerobosex Girls

The Castro Theater had an LGB film festival every year; much bigger and with more letters added now (LGBTQIA). I remember going to one documentary about the history of lesbian pornography, which turned out to be fascinating. I was never much interested in porn, but the filmmaker used it as a lens to explore attitudes towards lesbians by "conventional" pornographers and lesbians making their own pornography, as well as internal and external Images of what lesbians (should) look like.

For example, as I experienced myself, lesbians in the '70s were "supposed" to look kind of androgynous, with flannel shirts and fuzzy hair. In that clip from a porno film, the images were soft and out of focus and the women looked like twins. Later, the Butch/Fem dichotomy (dykeotomy?) came back into fashion, and in one film clip, one of the women looked very handsome and butch, with very short hair, strong features and developed muscles, while the other lover looked very feminine with long hair, dressed in a sexy dress.

But my very favorite film clip, mostly because of the title, was called *Aerobosex Girls*. This mainstream film featured very feminine women with long hair, lots of makeup, and porn star looks enthusiastically sliding around on big slick sheets of plastic and grappling with each other. I could hardly look at what they were doing to each other, because they had very long nails and it looked like it hurt. But the title was priceless.

Lesbian Pulp Fiction

I always read a lot, and I began to read a sub-genre of literature called lesbian pulp fiction, which pretty much started in the 1950s. I went to a slide show with a local lesbian historian who had lurid original 1950s covers of many of the books and lectured about her research into the writers and the historical context in which they'd been written.

My friend Laurie Ann was the one who lent me my first book and ongoing favorite, called *The Girls in 3B* by Valerie Taylor. She had an original tattered paperback she had bought at a garage sale, about three young women who come to the big city to work and find love and careers. Only one of them turned out to be a lesbian, but her storyline had the happiest ending, in my opinion. I went on to read many more, some shared with Laurie Ann, like *Women in the Shadows* and the *Beebo Brinker Chronicles: Odd Girl Out* by Ann Bannon.

In order to be published, the writers usually had to include some tragic moral consequences, but many of the stories were subversive in the best way, lovingly describing hidden lesbian culture, and featuring lesbian characters finding their way to love and joy even if they weren't supposed to. And I learned that these dime store books were a lifeline to closeted lesbians everywhere who felt like they were the only ones.

A couple of small feminist presses, Naiad Press among them, began to reprint the books and also publish new ones. None of them were in the library, so I bought as many as I could afford from the local feminist bookstores, first from *A Woman's Place* bookstore, and later *Mama Bears* books, both in Oakland. Most of the newer ones weren't very well written — the plots were predictable and the characters did not feel developed, but I enjoyed them and they helped me stay hopeful that I could find true love with another woman too.

My First Woman Love

When I met Stephanie, a beautiful tall butch lesbian with broad shoulders, a kind smile, and a quiet charisma, I was instantly attracted. She had a committed girlfriend, Judy, and was co-parenting the girlfriend's children from a (heterosexual) marriage, so nothing happened right away. But Stephanie, it turned out, was quite the womanizer, with lots of affairs and many "friends with benefits." I'm a naturally monogamous person; I couldn't even pull off having an open relationship with Alan.

But I was so deeply attracted to Stephanie, that when she made overtures to me months later, I didn't even try to say no. She came over to my little cottage for breakfast and I kept dropping everything — the spatula, the eggs, the silverware. She told me later she was laughing inside, and any doubts about seducing me vanished as she could see how nervous and attracted I was.

We ended up in bed together, and it was a revelation to me. It felt strange, so odd to be touching a woman's body, to be kissing and caressing a woman instead of a man. And at the same time, I had a deep sense of rightness and belonging, of coming home, and a flooding intensity of passion, not merely of the moment, which I had never felt with men. Being for the first time a woman loving another woman, I knew I had uncovered an important piece of my identity.

Being a Lesbian Is Not *the* Answer

I was still very much trying to find myself and figure out who I was. For a while, I thought being a lesbian was *the* answer and revealed everything I needed for my life. But I quickly realized that, while knowing I was attracted to women was important, and would point me in the right direction for romantic fulfillment, it didn't help with my self-hate. It didn't help me with a career, it didn't answer all the questions about who I was and what my life path was, and it didn't of itself strengthen my connection to the Divine.

It turned out Stephanie didn't even want a non-exclusive relationship with me — her love life was so complicated and full. I heard much later that she had transitioned to being a man, so that might have been the missing piece for her to find a right relationship.

But, I remember joyously driving down to Palo Alto to visit her from Oakland, and being in bed with her when another woman she was involved with called her. Lying there, hearing the smiling intimacy in her voice toward this woman while she ignored me, hurt. I realized that she could never give me what I wanted, a true partnership. And yet, I have no regrets, because being with her was a precious gift and a tender milestone for me.

So, it was as a lesbian that I continued my graduate studies.

Adventures on BART (Bay Area Rapid Transit)

While I was attending San Francisco State to earn my M.A., and after I finished and found a job at City College of San Francisco, among other places, I commuted across the Bay on BART, the rapid transit subway. I saw many small dramas and traumas. A few times, I felt in danger, but luckily, nothing bad ever happened to me and I met interesting people and witnessed odd interactions.

One time, I saw two business people, an attractive, slender but hard-faced business woman in high heels and a suit, and a pudgy, slightly inebriated business man, also in a suit, having a sexually charged encounter in the doorway between the BART train car and the station. She was standing on the platform, he was on the train, and they looked at each other with both hate and desire. I couldn't hear what they said, but the energy was clear. Finally, she beckoned to him, crooking her finger in a come here gesture, and swaying slightly, still with an expression of contempt on his face, he got off the train to be with her again.

Another time I saw an adorably attractive young woman with sparkling eyes, who looked part-Black and part-white, being hit on by a much older, paunchy unattractive white man with messy stubble. He asked her to go out with him. She told him she had a boyfriend and he said, "Too bad," like he really believed someone like him had a shot with her. It was all about his desire, as if that was enough to "make" her want him.

Drunken Sailors and a Switchblade Knife

One time when I was coming home on BART in the evening, I kept hearing a repeating clicking sound, like someone using a nail clipper to trim their nails. But it went on and on, so I finally looked across the aisle to see what was happening.

A thick-set man was sitting there with a grim look on his face. The clicking noise — he was flicking open a switchblade knife, closing it, and flicking it open again, over and over. He looked like he was preparing for a violent encounter. At the next stop, I stood up and unobtrusively moved to another car. He wasn't threatening me, but it was awful.

The scariest thing that ever happened was on a different night. I was in a very quiet BART car, when suddenly at least twenty raucous drunken sailors in uniforms and sailor hats entered the car. I think it was Fleet Week in San Francisco. I was terrified, stories of gang rape running through my head. I didn't dare get up and move because I didn't want to draw any attention to myself. I sat there, perfectly still, willing myself to invisibility. It was the hardest few BART stops of my life. At the last downtown SF stop, they all exited, leaving me and another white woman on the train. We looked at each other, laughing and crying in relief that nothing bad had happened to us, that the sailors had been so engaged with each other that they seemingly hadn't noticed us at all.

Manspreading

A far more common phenomenon I had to deal with was manspreading, the practice of men spreading their legs wide and taking up more than their share of the space on public transportation. I experienced this long before the term was invented, but immediately recognized the concept when I heard the word. It was really uncomfortable and challenging to deal with. Sitting with my legs to one side to avoid contact was painful and awkward, but if I claimed my space, that would involve touching his leg, which could be seen as a sexual invitation. Finally, I hit upon the idea of using my always full backpack. I would put it on the seat between me and the man, limiting his ability to "spread" without it being seen as provocative. It worked! And I kept using that technique the rest of the years I rode on BART.

ESL Names and Customs

I always wanted to know about the languages my students spoke so I could compare them to English, and understand how to pronounce their own names correctly. This was sometimes quite a challenge, because there were names and languages I had never heard of, some of which sounded strange or awful to my ears.

I remember one student from Thailand whose first name was Cittiporn, which sounded like City Porn(ography) to me. I always said her name respectfully, but I secretly hoped she picked an American name so she wouldn't be teased. Later, I had a student from the Philippines, but her native language was Pangasinan, not Tagalog. I worked so hard to remember that odd (to me) language name, that I will probably remember it for the rest of my life!

Esperanto, Anyone?

The very first time I taught in front of people was with my fellow students in the materials preparation class. We were given a list of phrases. (The first one was "This is a pen.") We were to present these phrases in a short introductory language lesson. We weren't allowed to use Spanish, because too many of us knew at least some Spanish.

I asked my dear friend Erna for help. She had learned Esperanto, an invented mixture of a number of different languages, through the Women's International League for Peace and Freedom. The theory was that if everyone could speak the same language, it would promote peace and understanding. I asked her to help me translate the assigned phrases into Esperanto, and also asked how to say "good morning," "very good," "please repeat," and "thank you."

When I "taught" my fellow students the Esperanto phrases they were fascinated, having never heard of Esperanto before, and my extra phrases, like those a teacher would use, impressed my instructor, Steve Thewlis. He said, "You are a born teacher, Lorraine." I liked hearing that!

The Novice Teacher

I had the opportunity, after a couple of semesters of instruction under my belt, to have actual teaching experience at the American Language Institute (ALI), an intensive language program for foreign students improving their English skills for later university studies. The ALI hired graduate students in the TESOL (Teaching English to Speakers of Other Languages) Master's program.

I will always remember my first five minutes of teaching in front of a real class. The teacher asked me to prepare a short lesson on adjective clauses. It took me hours to study adjective clauses, and prepare a short script (which I wrote out word for word) with an explanation, examples to write on the board, and a short exercise. I had only been up at the board for five seconds when a student asked a question I couldn't answer. I had no idea what to do. I wanted the floor to open up and swallow me.

All these years later, I know that if someone asks a question I can't answer, I calmly say "Hmm. Good question. I'll have to check on that and get back to you." But at the time, I thought my teaching career had ended before it started.

Teaching at ALI, I also learned about the art of writing on the blackboard. You weren't supposed to fully turn your back on the class, so there was a precise and twisted angle to your body; so you could keep an eye on the class AND write on the board AND keep talking at the same time.

Chalk Triumphant

I was also fascinated with chalk and how to use it correctly on the blackboard. This was before white boards or smart boards. I remember an adjective clause exercise I created that was all about chalk, and ended with one of my characters creating a sculpture called "Chalk Triumphant."

This obsession was reinforced by Steve Thewlis when he observed my teaching. He was taking notes the entire time he was observing me, and I couldn't imagine what he was writing at such great length. At the end of the class, he gave me his notes and he hadn't written anything! Instead, he had made a detailed drawing, complete with arrows and arcs, of the correct angle at which to hold the chalk so it wouldn't squeak!

Although I didn't like every single class, I enjoyed the process of learning, and my fellow students were an interesting group. Many of them had roamed the world and had extensive experiences with different cultures from travel or the Peace Corps. Some of them had grown up abroad or had themselves learned English as a second language. They all had an understanding of cultural differences, which made them easy to be around. However, in one class, I did have an incident in which I felt at odds with my fellows.

Commie Dyke for a Day

In the materials preparation class I mentioned earlier, the teacher assigned each of us a chapter from a different ESL textbook and asked us to critique it.

What did we like about it? What could be better? Would we want to use it?

I was given a chapter about a rich white woman playing tennis. I hated it and thought it was culturally insensitive and inappropriate.

In class, when it was my turn to critique my chapter, I had a bit of a rant.

"This book is classist and racist because all the characters are white and rich! And it's sexist, too! This woman spends all her time playing tennis and shopping. She doesn't work. How could our students possibly relate to her life! All our students are either hard-working immigrants or hard-studying foreign students." I said this loudly and vehemently in the class.

A dead silence filled the room for a full minute before anyone responded.

Then one of the white men in the class said slowly, in a rather heavy and bewildered tone, "Well, not every textbook has to be a call to revolution."

I didn't say anything, but my heart sank. My immediate internal response was: "Oh my God! I'm the commie dyke for the rest of the semester!" I felt exposed and scared and vulnerable.

I went home and told Erna about it, and her comment was helpful in putting things in perspective. She said, "You think they all went home and talked about you, but they all went home and ate their dinner."

She was absolutely right. I never heard another thing about it in the class.

Graduating (with Breasts)

One funny thing happened around my own inner sexism when I was close to graduating. I was walking around campus and musing about how I was going to look for a teaching job.

I thought to myself, "I need to get an interview suit," and then I thought, "Oh, but I won't look really professional, because I have breasts." This thought streaked across my mind and I managed to mentally grab it and look at it as if it were a wriggling little creature.

I was shocked. "Where did that thought come from?"

As an ardent feminist, I didn't realize I harbored any thoughts like that. But there it was, my internal belief that men looked more professional than women.

Freeway Flying

Well, I went ahead and bought an interview suit anyway and started looking for jobs, full-time and adjunct. Of course, there were a lot more adjunct jobs available. We adjuncts were also called Freeway Flyers. We were the under-earning underbelly of academia. We were paid an amount per hour which would've sounded generous if it weren't that we were expected to put many extra hours in for free. We were only paid for the hours in the classroom, not for preparation, correcting tests or papers, or generally meeting with students. I once figured out the actual hourly wage came out to $5 or $10 an hour. Nonetheless, getting more experience as an adjunct was the only path to the Golden prize, a full-time tenured job at a community college or four-year college.

The first place I was hired after graduate school was Golden Gate University, a private business college in San Francisco, which had some ESL classes for its international business students. It was in downtown San Francisco, about forty-five minutes away from my house in Oakland on BART. It was an awful situation. The person in charge didn't understand anything about effective teaching or ESL. She wanted us to share books and classes with other teachers instead of being assigned our own.

This was unheard of and very confusing as well as being a lot of extra unnecessary work. I didn't last there very long. But Carol, a fellow teacher, told me they were hiring adjunct ESL faculty at City College of San Francisco, so I applied and scheduled an interview. It was in South San Francisco, so over an hour commute for me on BART, but they paid better.

When I showed up for the interview, the division chair never came. She must have had some crisis or other that she had to deal with. So, I sat and talked with her secretary/assistant. We had a pleasant chat and I guess she must've taken a liking to me, because she told the division chair to hire me and she did.

I began teaching a class or two, never more than three, each semester at City College. I was there for seven years. In some ways, it was a tremendous place to teach. The students were from all over the world, primarily China and Vietnam but many other countries as well. I learned a great deal from my students, including how to actually teach grammar and writing. I tried out some innovative teaching techniques, like using journals and writing journal entries myself to model them for the students. It was an effective way to help the students connect to writing, but way too much work, so I only did it once. It was a steep learning curve: learning how to teach, how to manage my time, how to support students but have boundaries.

Sometimes I was self-righteous and full of ego (it was all about me) and took my student successes or failures personally. It was years before I learned how to manage that more gracefully.

Teaching and Divine Love

Learning to love and accept my students also helped me understand Divine love better. Once, I was giving a grammar test to my students. I was at the front of the class, and they were all intently focused at their desks, each one's busy brain working through the questions on the test.

I felt an overwhelming sense of love for them. Each one unique, each one precious, in all their differences and shared concentration. Some struggled more than others; they had different strengths and challenges. They were all human and imperfect and I loved them all equally. The thought immediately came to me — this is how the Divine feels about all of us.

Some of my students were affected by the prejudice against people with darker skin. I remember one beautiful student from the Philippines with perfect skin of a rich deep brown color. She really believed that she wasn't as attractive as her lighter-skinned sisters and friends back in the Philippines or here.

She didn't see her own beauty. I told her that her skin was a gorgeous color, but hearing that once, no matter how sincerely, isn't enough to counter that horrible prejudice that pervaded beauty magazines and the culture in general that White and lighter are better.

Another of my students, a young man from Vietnam, had completely fallen for a young woman, also from Vietnam.

To me, she was pleasant looking, not out of the ordinary, but he said to me with awe and deep appreciation in his voice, "She is so beautiful; her face looks like a flower."

When I looked at her a little bit through his eyes, I could see that her face looked like a chrysanthemum, that all the round curves did form a harmonious whole.

I Need Hazard Pay

One semester, I had a student who was out of control and inappropriate — meaning she interrupted loudly, and made comments that didn't make sense. She acted out in my class, and I found out from talking to other adjunct instructors that she had slapped a fellow student in another class. At that time, instructors still could ask that a student be removed from their class, so I put in a request.

The division chair didn't understand that I thought the situation was dangerous, so she wanted *me* to tell the student I was throwing her out of the class. I was very scared and worried about it. And then I realized I could step up in a different way.

So, I went to the division chair again and said calmly, "My intuition and experience tell me there is a potential for violence in this situation. I'm willing to ask her to leave, but I would like campus police to be there to prevent anything bad from happening. It might not anyway, but I am not getting paid to risk my life or safety, so I am asking that they be there in case I need help."

Her face turned white. And to her credit, she took it very seriously and not only campus police, but she as well, was close at hand when I had to tell the student to leave. The student said she felt humiliated, but I certainly felt a lot better not risking my or my students' safety in that situation.

You've Described an Orange Very Well

Graduate school gave me a start learning what I needed to know as an ESL instructor, but there were so many issues my classes had never addressed. One of them was how to make appropriate comments on student writing.

There was a lot more to say about the writing of the more advanced students, but when giving a very simple assignment to lower-level students, such as *"What does an orange look like? Explain using details and adjectives,"* it could be very challenging to figure out what to say, to encourage the students and yet point out the mistakes they had made.

One of my fellow instructors who I liked a great deal, a gay man named Gaetano Bandaera, once wrote on the student's paragraph "You've described an orange very well."

For whatever reason, this seemed to me to get to the heart of the existential dilemma about what to say. It was kind and supportive, but also a funny thing to say about a student's paper!

The Cookie That Ate San Francisco

Among the many gifts I received from my students was a greater appreciation of the English language and a more detached perspective on its many quirks.

In a grammar class, I was explaining passive voice to a class of intermediate students. I used as examples, "Yuan ate the cookie" vs. "The cookie was eaten by Yuan."

One very bewildered student asked, "What's the difference between 'The cookie was eaten by Yuan,' and 'The cookie ate Yuan?'"

I laughed out loud and acted out a giant cookie, terrorizing the city and eating Yuan. We all found this very amusing, and I'm sure she always remembered that lesson!

ESL "Poetry"

Idioms, because they are not logical, are particularly hard on ESL learners. My students created their own very creative versions of "on the other hand," including "in the other eye," "on the other foot," and "in the other sock." They actually make as much or as little sense as ours, but sound so funny!

Another student wrote a paragraph about the beach, including the sentence, "*The sun has been bathing me all the day,*" which I found charming and poetic.

Holding Hands and Hugging

Many of the countries my students came from were still very accepting of same sex affection. Don't get me wrong: there was deep prejudice against "homosexuality" but they didn't link that with girls and women walking arm-in-arm or men walking with their arms draped over each other's shoulders. I remember one party for the ESL foreign students where at least eight of the girls piled on a couch together, thinking nothing of it.

One young woman told me how she had held hands with another in San Francisco, and awful people yelled insults at them. It deeply scarred her and made her afraid to be affectionate any more, which I thought was so sad.

I've read a lot of novels from a hundred years ago or more, by authors like Jane Austen or Louisa May Alcott, and most of the young women were affectionate with others in the same way, while touching young men was absolutely forbidden. It is sad that prejudice and fear around people being gay has lessened this simple human contact.

Poignant ESL Stories

In writing classes, I frequently asked students to share something about different aspects of their lives. The idea was that if you are an "expert" on the topic, it is easier to write about, even in English, a foreign language.

I read raw, unvarnished accounts of taking a small boat from Vietnam and barely escaping with their lives. Or almost being killed in El Salvador, or the dangerous illegal crossing from Mexico, or how they had to abandon their professions in their home country and start over with much humbler jobs.

Some of the stories were about the distance and miscommunication in their own families. One common sad theme was about immigrant parents who have to work two or three low wage jobs to keep food on the table and a roof over the family's head. They were gone so much that the younger children didn't learn Chinese or Vietnamese or Spanish. The parents didn't have time to learn much English, so these children and their parents literally didn't share a common language.

Gay and Didn't Know It

I had a few students over the years, particularly in San Francisco, who were openly gay and talked to me about it because they could tell I was supportive. But the ones who still make my heart ache a little were ones I think were most likely gay but didn't even know it themselves.

The first was a married, middle-aged Japanese businessman at the American Language Institute. I did a lesson about gay rights and what it means to be gay. Something in the lesson triggered him, and I think he came up to me for reassurance.

He said, "You can admire men's bodies in the locker room, and even want to touch them without being gay, right?"

My answer was rather offhand, not thinking about his situation at all.

I said, "Maybe. Or you might be gay."

He looked stricken. I wish I had been more sensitive and gentle. I didn't create his feelings, but I hope the realization didn't destroy his life or, if he did decide he was gay, that he found love and a supportive community, even in homophobic Japan.

At City College, I had a Chinese woman student who was a jock, a muscular boyish tennis player with short hair. She looked "butch." She was very close friends with another Chinese student, very pretty and feminine. The butch student would lean over the other woman's desk, her body language and energy indicating deep yearning and attraction.

I didn't want to point out something the tennis player wasn't ready to look at, so all I said to her, privately, was, "If there is ever something uncomfortable or unexpected you'd like to talk about, I'm here."

She looked at me with complete non-comprehension. I hope she found her path to self-awareness, self-acceptance, and love.

Coming Out in the Classroom

I was very afraid to let my students know I was a lesbian. They were new immigrants, some from Catholic countries, most from conservative traditional countries, although a few were more sophisticated city dwellers. It was one of the hard things about being newly lesbian, although I deal with the same issue still at times, that people assume you are heterosexual and you have to decide to come out, avoid, or hide, over and over. I'm a lot more bold and confident about it now, but I still sometimes am scared of judgments, of violence, of negative consequences. There is more acceptance now, but there is still a ton of prejudice.

I remember clearly the first time I talked to my students at City College about this. I wanted to let them know about the annual Lesbian/Gay (as it was called then) Pride Parade in San Francisco in

June. I also felt an obligation as an educator to tell them who I was and start busting their prejudice. My students, by and large, loved me, and I was aware that knowing that someone you love is gay, can really change people's perceptions and stereotypes.

I dressed up and wore lipstick. I looked different enough from my usual style that my students commented on it, which hadn't been my intention; it somehow felt safer to look feminine.

I told them about the parade and about myself and allowed them to ask questions. They were kind of stunned, but had too much respect for teachers to say something mean, even if they thought it.

Exquisitely Different Politeness

At first, I thought some of my students were very rude or behaved oddly. A student who came late, knocked on the door and said "Good morning!" loudly. I thought he was terribly rude to interrupt my lecture and the class. But then other students in my classes did the same thing. So, I asked my students about it. Unlike the U.S., where if you're late you slide in as unobtrusively as possible, in many other countries, you need the teacher's acknowledgement/permission to come in late. I realized they were following a different rule of politeness.

Similarly, when students came to talk to me in my office, they would stay standing and hover rather than sit down. I finally figured out that they were waiting for me to invite them to sit. I began to understand that they were exquisitely polite, but using different cultural rules!

Union Rights!

The faculty were very united at City College and there was a strong union, AFT (American Federation of Teachers). The full-time faculty recognized how unfairly the adjuncts were exploited and supported us for better pay and working conditions. We picketed the Board together, and the union negotiated health benefits and sick leave for us adjuncts. It was a major blessing and miracle to have that.

The Gang's All Here

One of the best things about teaching at City College was the camaraderie among the adjunct instructors. We were all relatively young, we were all exploited, we were all struggling to get by, piecing together work from different schools. We shared tips about teaching shortcuts, difficult student interactions we were struggling with, and which schools were hiring more adjuncts.

And they were an utterly delightful bunch of smart, energetic, innovative, and funny people. We used to get together and support each other, and we also had parties periodically at different people's houses, which were a total blast. It was my first experience of being part of a group like this.

I remember one party at my little cottage in Oakland. I was given a free book at a conference that used existing songs to teach ESL.

And to the tune of "La Cucaracha," the lyrics said, "Do you speak ENGLISH, do you speak ENGLISH, yes-but-just-a-little-bit."

I pulled out my percussion instruments, and everybody took one, and we all sang that ridiculous song together and laughed and laughed and laughed. Carol and Tom, two of the people in that group, fell in love and married. One woman, Laurie, who had previously only dated women, found a boyfriend, asking all the women about birth control options, which as a lesbian she had never needed before. And there were many other small dramas and successes and failures that we supported each other around. And of course, we all had other jobs, constantly changing, constantly hustling to make enough to live on.

Please Take This Job!

Laney College in Oakland was a bit unique, in my experience, with another hilarious non-interview. Two of my adjunct buddies recommended me and I was invited to an interview.

The head of the English department, whose name was Carmen, walked up to me and put her hands together as if she was praying, saying in a pleading tone, "Please take this job."

That was the entire interview. And I taught English and remedial reading and freshman composition there for a few years.

Overworked and Underloved

The worst part of being an adjunct (freeway flyer), was the uncertainty, overwork, and constant commuting. It was like running a marathon all the time. I never knew which classes I would actually teach, because the college administrations could cancel them without notice and didn't pay me anything if they didn't enroll enough students. I was always taking on more work than I could really manage, hoping that the right number of classes would come through. And I still had to prepare for all the classes even if they were later cancelled.

For example, one semester I was working six days a week. On Tuesdays and Thursdays I taught at Laney College in Oakland in the morning, and then went to City College in San Francisco in the afternoon, about an hour and a quarter commute, and then back to Laney at night. Other days, I went to City College and then

Contra Costa College, which was in San Pablo, forty minutes north of Oakland.

I never had Spring Break, because different schools had their vacation in different weeks. And I couldn't afford to take summers off.

One semester, I took on a Saturday class at City College because if another class had canceled I wouldn't earn enough to live on. It was a brutal schedule. If I thought about how long it would be until my next day off, I couldn't function. I became very ill at one point from overwork and stress. And I spent as much time commuting as I did teaching.

During the seven years I was an adjunct, I taught at seven different schools, including City College of San Francisco, Golden Gate University, Laney College in Oakland, Contra Costa College in San Pablo, St. Mary's College in Moraga, Adelante Adult School in Berkeley, and Albany Adult School. I loved teaching, but being an adjunct was an exhausting way to earn a living.

Making Mistakes

One of the concepts from my own healing that I started presenting to students during the first week of each semester was about making mistakes.

I would say to them, "Let's talk for a minute about mistakes." They would look up, startled, because they had never had a teacher broach this topic.

I would continue, "You could sit in class all semester, and never open your mouth to say anything, never write anything, and you wouldn't make any mistakes."

Their eyes would grow very wide and they paid even closer attention to me. "But if you do that, do you think you'd be getting the most out of the class and learning as much as you could?"

Their eyes still very wide, they would shake their heads solemnly.

I would go on, "That's because humans learn by making mistakes. I make mistakes every day. Lots of them. None of us is perfect. I encourage you to make as many mistakes as you can because you'll learn more that way."

They would be amazed and grateful, to put down the burden of shame and perfectionism that they, like most of us, carried. It really set a positive tone for the semester, and I will always be grateful that my own recovery taught me that kind of gentleness so I could pass it on to them. My learning and teaching this continues to help me as well.

Remember/Forget

I taught grammar for almost thirty years. One of the hardest topics for the lower-level students was irregular past verbs. Not the ones that end with "ed" but the ones like "was" and "went" and "taught."

I would explain a bit about the history, that the "ed" ones came from French, while the irregular ones were from Old English and the Germanic origins of our language.

I would tell them, "I can try to give you some rules for them, but basically they are illogical. All you can do is your best to memorize them. And do you know how to do that?" I would ask.

"Study," they would generally answer.

"Yes" I would say, "but here is a tip for how."

Then, I would walk sideways across the entire front of the room, saying, "Remember, forget, remember, forget, remember, forget, and hope you wind up in 'remember' for a quiz or paper or conversation."

I would explain that it is impossible to learn the verbs in one big study session and expect to remember them. They had to study them repeatedly in shorter sessions. I suggested flashcards, study partners, setting time each day. I think that helped the students, but I know it helped me understand how challenging it is to learn and grow, to change our behavior around grammar, emotions, the workplace, recovery!

Living Independently — Berkeley Disabled Activist Style

One of my graduate school colleagues, Brett, had a "gig" at the Center for Independent Living, tutoring disabled Japanese who had come to learn about activism and independent living in Berkeley, which was on the cutting edge of accessibility. He took another job and couldn't continue, so he passed the tutoring on to me, and I had the great gift of meeting all these dedicated activists, fighting for disability rights.

One of the directors of the Center, a woman named Pam, had polio and either walked with crutches or was in a wheelchair depending on how she felt that day. She was the smartest, most energetic person you can imagine. Besides the polio, she had some challenges in the Berkeley community because of being bisexual. She had been in a long-term relationship with a woman during which everyone assumed she was lesbian, even though she knew she wasn't, and when they broke up people felt betrayed or astonished that she was equally interested in dating men.

I also met a woman, Kathy, a Latina lesbian who was blind, and one of the most fearless and talented people I've ever met. She was a drummer and educator, and she traveled all over the world. She wasn't afraid to go anywhere or do anything. Those two women really stretched my ideas of what was possible to do with a so-called disability.

But the reason I was there was to tutor Japanese students. Japan was still very traditional and backwards about disabled people. They were hidden away in their families' homes, sometimes not even allowed to go to school, because disability was considered a shameful secret. I met a number of people who were fighting for disability rights and for accessible environments in Japan. They were all very different from each other.

Dearest Yuho

The one who touched my heart the most, and who later became a dear friend was Yuho. She has osteogenesis imperfecta, otherwise known as glass bones. People with that disability can sometimes walk and sometimes not. Their bones break easily so that they tend to not grow to a normal adult size. Yuho was about as high as your average door knob, and could only walk because she'd had a number of painful surgeries on her legs. She was and is one of the most remarkable women I have ever met. It was such a pleasure to help her learn English, support her in her feminism and activism, and come to know her.

We enjoyed each other and shared our difficulties as well. I'm grateful I realized that we were moving beyond the bounds of tutor and tutee, and allowed our friendship to unfold. I learned a great deal from her about courage and determination and acceptance. We had an attuned, loving connection.

I Love Mexican Food

One of the things I introduced her to was Mexican food, which she had never had before. She came to love it very much and we would often try out different Mexican restaurants. She also met my dear friend Rich, and once the three of us went to see *Alive!* at a women's jazz concert together. Yuho was very impressed with these accomplished women musicians.

I was sad when she went back to Japan, having finished her studies here. She always credits me, including in a book she wrote, with opening her eyes to how strong women could be and helping her be able to communicate effectively in English. We stayed in touch.

One of the other students, named Hiroko, was a thalidomide baby. She had only thighs for legs and very short arms and hands with no thumbs. In spite of that, she was a talented artist. She would hold the pen between two of her fingers and create exquisite, bold, black and white drawings in pen and ink. She had lived at home, sheltered and limited by her parents and coming to Berkeley really opened her up.

English by the Pound

My least favorite of this group was a young man named Takeshi. He was what I came to call my English by the pound student. He didn't want to do any work. He somehow expected if he paid me a certain amount of money, he would learn a certain amount of English; hence, English by the pound. And he felt like he wasn't getting his money's worth. He wanted to spend the money that was his stipend on other things, and I certainly did not want to keep working with someone who wasn't willing to do his part.

My final student was a sweet young woman with cerebral palsy. She was so shy and scared and withdrawn; I felt that more than anything she needed socialization and opportunities to make friends and be with other students. Even though it wasn't in my economic interest, I encouraged the organization to send her to the adult school. We stayed in touch and she really blossomed.

Fashion While Disabled

This same student couldn't handle zippers or buttons, so her clothes choices were dictated by tops and pants she could pull on or pull over her head. A lot of times that meant her clothes didn't match. But when we said goodbye, she gave me a beautiful blue and purple scarf that was absolutely in my style and my colors. Even though she couldn't dress like that for herself, she was very observant and aware of color and style.

The whole clothing issue was interesting with Yuho too. Because she was so small, she tended to wear children's clothes. One time I took her shopping at an upscale children's clothing store and bought her some children-sized suits and jackets that looked professional, but she didn't really care about that at all.

She trusted her personality to triumph over her clothes. Even if she was wearing a ruffled little girl dress, she expected respect as an expert and an adult, and she usually succeeded. One of the areas that she became an activist in and wrote a book about was sexuality for disabled women. The stereotype is that disabled women are asexual or unattractive or undeserving of a rich sexual life, and she did a lot of work to bust that myth and that stereotype. And she had a number of lovers herself!

Psychic and Nightclub Entertainer

Teaching at Albany Adult School was fascinating and challenging in a totally different way. I taught the beginning class (just above literacy). The program wasn't well-designed and it was frustrating to have to use their materials, but the students were delightful. They were immigrants from all over the world who spoke Chinese, Japanese, Arabic, Farsi, Spanish, Vietnamese, Russian, Hindi or Polish, but almost no English.

Most of the time, I felt like a cross between a psychic and a night club entertainer. The students desperately wanted to communicate with me, but their English was severely limited and inadequate. I strained every intuitive part of me to understand.

I tried to make classes interesting and engaging and have them practice (hence the night club MC asking questions of the audience routine), and some of it seemed to help some of them, but it was slow and limited in those circumstances. My art skills also improved as I would draw objects and actions on the board to explain what I was talking about.

But the potlucks were a bountiful display of cuisines from around the world! A number of them had earned their living working in the kitchens of different restaurants, and/or had special family recipes, and when we had a party, the spread of food was truly awesome. I tasted many new dishes I'd never heard of before.

English from Mars

One of the English writing classes I taught at Laney College had a deaf student in it, so they brought in an interpreter. And then two more deaf students joined because the interpreter was already in place. It was really challenging to figure out how to teach them English when they couldn't hear a word I said. I had taught ESL for a while at that point but I had never seen anything like these deaf students' writing. It was like they were from Mars! Their syntax was so distorted it overwhelmed me.

Interestingly enough, of the three of them, the deaf student from Thailand was the best writer in English. Part of the problem was that the other two hadn't grown up in an environment that supported the best learning for deaf students. They didn't have a good program to teach them ASL (American Sign Language) or teach them to read and write in English, and they were really behind and struggling. One of them was a beautiful young woman with blue eyes, golden-brown skin, and very curly hair, a lesbian I later found out, who wanted to be an actor. I encouraged her, and the rest of them too, to read as much as possible in English because that way she would start absorbing the vocabulary and the syntax even though she never heard it spoken.

English Teacher as Sexual Fantasy

When I had a split-shift at City College of San Francisco, I often went to dinner at a Chinese restaurant adjacent to campus. It was too much for me to bring lunch and dinner, especially during the time I didn't have a car. One time, when the restaurant was crowded, I shared a table with two young men (early twenties while I was late twenties) who were students at the College. One of them, it became quickly apparent, had a fantasy about making love to an English teacher! It was odd and uncomfortable, and I had a tiny taste of what celebrities experience. He wasn't interested in me or who I was at all. He didn't actually see me. It was just that I was reasonably young and attractive, and I could be the vehicle for his fantasy. He really tried to get me to go out with him.

The (Mild) Flirt

Sometimes my male students also had crushes on me. They were all adults, and while I did not cross the line with them, I did enjoy the attention and the energy. I was single and longing for love myself. I found it affirming that they found me desirable, hoping it meant someone else would as well.

Students as My Teachers

But in general, I simply loved and enjoyed my students. And they taught me so much about their cultures. I learned about food, about holidays such as Moon Day and Ramadan. And through conversations and their writings I learned a lot more about the gifts and pressures of growing up in traditional families. As I had seen also in Mexico, they felt much more impelled to follow their families' wishes and felt more a part of their families than I did.

Jewish and Chinese Cultural Affinity

One particular affinity I hadn't realized until I worked with a number of Chinese students was how similar Jewish and Chinese culture were in some ways — particularly, the emphasis on food — pushing food, having more than enough food, food as love. Their attitude that it is worth sacrificing anything to gain a good education was exactly the same. And my students' Chinese families were big on guilt. That was part of my upbringing as well.

Before this cultural education, I hadn't known that Chinese are sometimes called the Jews of Asia, because they migrated to a number of different Asian countries. I had a number of students from Vietnam, but learned that there were two distinct groups; the ethnic Vietnamese, and the ethnic Chinese who were sometimes treated as second class citizens in Vietnam, and who spoke Chinese (generally Mandarin) as well as Vietnamese.

I had one student who was ethnically Chinese, and spoke Chinese, but was herself from Argentina, and she bonded with the other Spanish-speaking students far more than the Chinese ones.

Every once in a while, a student or former student, would invite me home to meet their family and have dinner. I occasionally said yes, but I generally felt very uncomfortable. I remember thinking I had to entertain them by talking nonstop, which I'm sure they found as exhausting as I did.

I deeply offended the family of one Iranian woman at Albany Adult School who actually couldn't speak more than a few words of English, when her son called me and invited me to dinner and I declined. I felt unable to struggle through an evening with her limited English, but he clearly felt insulted. In an icy tone, he said, "I see. I won't trouble you further then."

Chapter Nine

Life and Death in the '80s

My platonic soulmate, my best friend, Rich Boehnke died from AIDS in 1988, when an AIDS diagnosis was pretty much a death sentence. He and I met when I was in graduate school to get my M.A. in Teaching English to Speakers of Other Languages (TESOL). He was also a student at SFSU, although we didn't meet there.

My mentor teacher at the American Language Institute was studying Middle Eastern drumming, and told me about her class where the teacher, Mary Ellen Donald, let you rent to buy a drum; and didn't charge very much. It sounded a good way to me to try and keep the rhythm going when I couldn't dance because of a hip injury, so I started taking lessons.

Rich was in my first drum class. We started out as drum buddies and then started growing closer and closer. He had recently moved to San Francisco from Eugene, Oregon which was a small town at that point, and come out as a gay man.

We had a kind of platonic romance. We weren't interested in each other as romantic/sexual partners, but everyone who met us thought we were in love. Our connection was shining and palpable. We were both single, and spent a lot of time together. We did drumming gigs together, we went out dancing together, we shared our fears and our history and our hopes for the future. We hugged each other a lot and even took naps together.

Moving down to San Francisco from Eugene, Rich was like a kid in a candy shop; or really, a young adult set free in a sexual wonderland. He met people, felt attraction, made friends, had sex, and gloried in his freedom. No one knew then about AIDS. He contracted the AIDS virus from a folk dancing friend of his, and all too quickly started feeling sick, along with so many other gay men in San Francisco.

We're Not in Kansas Anymore

While we were close friends, I would frequently hang out with him in the Castro, a gay mecca at that time. One year on New Year's Day, we went to the huge retro Castro Theater together and saw *The Wizard of Oz*. I had never fully appreciated the gay subtext until I saw the movie with a whole audience full of gay men.

When the cowardly lion talked about being a sissy, everyone cheered. And when Glenda the Good appeared, everyone said "Oooooh Glenda" with a gay wave, and instead of a fairy princess/witch, I saw her as a drag queen in full regalia.

When Dorothy said, "I don't think we're in Kansas anymore," everyone who had come from homophobic small towns in Kansas and all over the country, cheered and rejoiced at their freedom. I had a completely new understanding of the movie.

It makes me sad still to think that most of the lovely, joy-filled men in that big audience likely died of AIDS, for which there was little effective treatment and no cure, and a lot of discrimination and obstacles to having treatment. Some men did survive the epidemic, but they lost friend after friend. Most of my friends other than Rich at this time were women, but I lost other friends and acquaintances — my teacher buddy Gaetano Bandaera, other adjunct faculty I worked with at City College of SF, friends of friends, writers I knew.

The Heartbreak of AIDS

When Rich started having symptoms, I was heartbroken.

There was so much going on at that time. Rich had found a steady boyfriend named Joe, who didn't like me very well. And as Rich became sicker and sicker, Joe acted as a gatekeeper who really tried to prevent me from seeing Rich and spending time with him.

I tried, mistakenly, to *make* him let me see Rich, even though I had no power to do that and it made it actually much harder for me to spend time with Rich. I wish I had begged humbly instead, but I didn't know how. And Rich, who did love me but was also very codependent, told me repeatedly that I was the most important person in his life. That isn't what he told Joe however, so I asserted myself in a way that wasn't in line with the reality of Rich's choices and priorities. I still regret that because of my problematic relationship with Joe, I didn't go to Rich's thirtieth birthday party, which was his last ever.

There was a lot of sweetness in going through this dying process with him. It was my first experience of losing someone I deeply cared for. And the Goddess was a big source of support.

At one point in meditation with the Goddess, I asked her, "Goddess, is Rich going to die?"

Her calm response was "Of course he's going to die. So are you. So is everyone."

I said, hands on hips, "Goddess, you know that's not what I meant!" But it did help me gain some perspective nonetheless. None of us get out of this alive.

Rich and I talked openly about his dying and laughed together about past lives we imagined we'd had together. I was able to do a beautiful visualization for him in the hospital once, imagining angels at the four corners of his bed, creating a canopy of light and protection over him. He said afterwards that he had the best sleep that night he'd ever had in the hospital.

He was in and out of the hospital many times. As long as he was alive and present, we could grieve and love together, which was comforting. For quite a while, there was hope that some treatment or other might help him; but in the end, everything failed.

He had dementia and didn't recognize anyone. It was like a wounded non-comprehending animal was trapped behind his eyes — there was no trace of the energetic, debonair, witty, charismatic Rich I had known and loved. The day before he died, I was going to San Francisco on BART to visit him. And the Goddess gave me this beautiful channeling:

His Spirit Is Cloaked in Shining Light

Rich's soul will leave his body soon.
Mourn his passing, grieve his loss, but despair not for him.
His spirit is cloaked in shining light.
Pain, anguish, fear have left him as he leaves his body.
He moves in deepening splendor and bliss, filled with unbounded joy.
He is ready, my child, he is called, he goes.
And none, not even love, can call him back.
But never fear the love you have given him; it has been love well spent.
It will deepen his joy and yours.
For only love can pass through the boundary 'tween the quick and
the dead, only love can he still feel as he moves on.
For oh beloved, the glory of death is very real.
True peace, hearts ease, and rest are his for as long as he needs them,
until he is ready once again to take up the battle and return to life.

I have remembered this channeling all these years because it is beautiful and comforting to me.

While Rich was in the last days of his dying, with fortunate or unfortunate timing, my friend Yuho and her friend Sh'aom arrived from Japan. It was a great comfort to have Yuho there, but I couldn't focus on entertaining them or being very present or hospitable.

The day after they arrived, Rich died. And my grief and desolation were overwhelming. I couldn't imagine how my life would continue without my best friend. I had no sweetheart, no full-time job, and losing him was a huge blow. And for him to die at the age of thirty with so much life and creativity yet to come was utterly unfair and deeply sad.

My grief felt endless. It kept growing. There would be huge waves of grief that I would have to ride out. And I noticed that sometimes when I thought I should be grieving, I felt hollow and numb, and then something would trigger the grief and it would well up hugely at times that didn't feel appropriate.

Once I had gone to The Women's Building in SF to see a two-part original movie, a lesbian soap opera. I happened to see Part Two first and, on another evening, went to see Part One with another friend. It was sold out, and we weren't able to find two seats together. I had no idea that in this first part, one of the major characters dies of AIDS. In the middle of the theater, surrounded by strangers, seeing a painfully thin man on his death bed, I started sobbing and sobbing. And the woman sitting next to me, who I didn't know, put her arm around me to comfort me because she knew what I was going through and why I was crying.

The beautiful channeling from the Goddess helped me know that he was happy and free, but it couldn't make up for the grief and loss. This person who had been extremely important in my life was gone.

Chapter Ten

Turning Toward Japan

After Rich died, Yuho was my best surviving friend. So, that summer I decided to go visit her in Kunitachi, Japan, a suburb of sorts of Tokyo.

Take a Drive on the Wild Side

When she and a friend picked me up at the airport, I had my very first cultural shock. The steering wheel of the Toyota was on the right side of the car! I thought I knew all about Japanese cars, because I had had a Datsun 510, and then a Toyota Tercel, but I didn't know Japan used the British driving system and switched the steering wheels in the factories for cars bound for the U.S.A.

In my surprise and confusion, I blurted out, "Why are you driving on that side?"

Her friend was insulted at my perceived cultural arrogance, as if I thought everyone should drive the way Americans do and said, bristling, "Why don't you drive on our side?"

In that moment, I was the ignorant Westerner who gave offense without meaning to.

Yuho was very kind and generous to me, and set up all kinds of things for us to do. In many ways, it was profound and wonderful visit. And at the same time, I was also deeply grieving the loss of Rich and very uncertain about what was going to happen next in my life. I cried every night, which couldn't have been easy for her, but it was comforting to have someone there while I grieved.

Illiterate Gaijin

It was an odd and humbling experience to spend time in the place where, not only did I not speak the language, and was a foreigner (Gaijin), but I was illiterate, because I couldn't read Japanese (Kanji) lettering either. Unlike Spanish or Italian or even French, where I could puzzle out the meaning of words and read the names of streets, I had the experience of not being able to read at all. Because of my understanding of linguistics, I did have a sense of how to analyze verbal language patterns.

I was able to understand question markers, and started picking up some vocabulary. I probably learned seventy-five words and phrases while I was there. Many people in Japan speak some English, and were very kind and patient with me.

Because Yuho was connected to many progressive movements, I met a lot of interesting rebels and free thinkers and independent women. I learned that when women married in Japan, they lost any legal connection to their biological families. So many more forward-thinking women lived with partners without marrying. Yuho also took me to beautiful museums where I saw traditional Japanese art.

Harvey Milk with Subtitles

She wanted to see the documentary *The Times of Harvey Milk*, which was playing at an alternative theater. I had already seen it in San Francisco, but was willing to see it again. Seeing the film with a completely Japanese audience and with Japanese subtitles was quite a different experience.

Yuho would go off and do things related to her activism and her work, and sometimes if another friend wasn't available or if I was tired, I would just stay in her small apartment. I never answered the phone because I couldn't speak Japanese, but Yuho and I had a special signal; she would call and ring once, hang up, and then ring back and I would know it was safe to pick up.

A Fukushima Accent

Yuho received a lot of phone calls, and as I heard her answer them over and over I picked up what she said and how she said it.

One time when I knew she was calling, I answered the phone "Mooshi moosh," with exactly her intonation pattern.

There was a dead silence on the phone and then she started laughing uproariously. "You said that with a Fukushima accent!," with more laughter.

I hadn't known this previously, but Yuho had a regional (Fukushima) accent, and I had reproduced it exactly. So that opened up another fascinating conversation about regional accents in Japan. Most people when they came to Tokyo, the big city, dropped their provincial accents but Yuho had defiantly kept hers.

Another really interesting thing about the Japanese language was that men's Japanese and women's Japanese were very different. Men's Japanese was forceful and direct, while women's language was sweet, quiet and deferential, with a lot more words expressing politeness. Yuho was only about two-and-a-half feet tall, but she had made a conscious decision to use men's Japanese because of the power it expressed. It was mind-boggling to watch all these taller women deferring to her because of the language choices she made.

Wheelchair Warrior

Yuho had a lot of challenges as a disabled woman and had also been abused by doctors and others as a child. But by the time I went to visit her in Japan, she was absolutely fearless. Japan had a great train system, but at that time most of the stations were not wheelchair accessible. You had to climb several flights of stairs to reach the train platform. Yuho wasn't about to let that stop her! She would flag down young men or women (strangers) and ask them to carry her heavy electric wheelchair up the stairs so she and I could take the train. And, repeatedly, it worked for her and she would be carried like a queen up the stairs. I was in awe!

I also met a friend of hers, Tracy, who was a lesbian from Australia. She said she connected more easily with Japanese folks than she did with the Americans, because the Americans assumed her culture was like theirs when in fact Australian culture in some ways was very different. As I learned in classes about cultural differences, there are many unspoken rules that govern communication. For example, Australians have somewhat different styles for how to get to know someone, especially how to respond to self-disclosure. Americans tend to share a self-disclosing statement in return, while Australians tend to ask follow-up questions instead. Japanese people, unlike the Americans, would assume she is a foreigner, and not have such high expectations that she would communicate "correctly" even though she spoke Japanese quite well.

Gender Bending on a Big Stage

I had a conventional tour guidebook to Japan and Tokyo which I had bought before I went. I saw in the guide that there was a *Takarazuka* theater, part of an old tradition similar to *Kabuki*, but where all the parts were played by women. I told Yuho I'd really like her to take me there. She didn't understand why, because in Japan this type of theater is the province of bored middle-aged housewives and giggly young school girls, not feminists or serious adults, but I begged her to take me anyway, and she did.

This was in the 1980s, and it was a truly marvelous experience to be in a huge mainstream theater filled with screaming fans, where every single role was played by women. In the lobby, there were fan photos with autographs and memorabilia for sale featuring the "butch" and "femme" actors. The night I went they were doing two different pieces.

One was a musical version of *The Tale of Genji,* the novel written by Lady Murasaki Shikibu in the early years of the eleventh century, generally credited as the first novel ever. I couldn't understand a word of the musical, of course, but the samurai costumes were dazzling and the singing was great, and the romances between the women, the ones cross-dressing as Samurais and ones in gorgeous kimonos, were outstanding!

The other piece that evening was sort of a cross between *Saturday Night Live* and Elvis Presley, all glittery dances and mushy romantic duets. The butch women had short hair, but a lot of makeup as well. They were the ones that the school girls screamed for the most.

I said to Yuho, "This is amazing! You don't understand what this means to me as a lesbian to see this in a mainstream theater."

She was smart enough and open enough to move beyond her prejudices about it and understand a bit of what it meant to me.

Guacamole Culture Clash

We went to a Mexican restaurant in Tokyo that Yuho had found. We went with some of her other friends, none of whom had had Mexican food before. The restaurant was very inviting, with white washed walls and brightly colored pink and sky-blue pottery in the shape of animals.

We all ordered mixed platters and when the food arrived, it smelled like Mexican food, but the presentation was utterly Japanese.

There was a small wooden tray with a tiny metal plate of shredded chicken, a small plate with a tiny melon ball scoop of guacamole, and another tiny melon ball scoop of refried beans, and a separate plate with a few tortillas, all elegantly laid out.

Yuho's friends exclaimed, "How are we going to eat all this food?" Yuho and I looked at each other and laughed uproariously, remembering the huge overflowing oval platters of beans and rice and salad and chicken and cheese and guacamole that we had at Mexican restaurants in Berkeley.

When I tried the food, it tasted exactly right. It was as good as any Mexican food I had had in the U.S., so I asked the waitress where the chef was from. It turned out he was East Indian, which is why he understood about spices! The contrast between the very Japanese presentation and the very Mexican flavors was an absolutely funny example of culture clash.

Healing Center in Japan

I stayed at *Youjo-en*, a macrobiotic healing center in Japan, and experienced an acupuncture treatment there. We visited a cave that you could go in to see crystals, but even though they said it was wheelchair accessible, it wasn't, so I didn't see much of it. But at the entrance to the cave was a bas relief of Kuan Yin which was a lovely thing to see.

Where Am I?

Many of the streets in Tokyo and Kunitachi had no street signs. People would draw little maps for each other to help them find addresses. I found a recovery meeting in English for expatriates, and someone drew me a map. It involved leaving the right station at the correct exit, walking past a store with a big TV display on top, turning right past a police station. I took the wrong exit from the station, but eventually managed to find the meeting. It was great to attend a meeting in Japan with other recovering people.

The Lost Beauty of Fukushima

Yuho and her boyfriend took me to Fukushima to visit her family. It was the most beautiful and pastoral farm community before the nuclear power plant disaster. I remember in particular one peach orchard we went past, where the owner had lovingly tied up each individual peach on each tree in a little white net to keep them safe and whole.

We went to the beautiful Five Colors Lake, Goshiki Numa, which was a local Japanese tourist destination. Its water was the brightest distinctive turquoise color because of some special plants that grew in the water. You could take little rowboats out on the lake; it was the most peaceful, beautiful place you can imagine.

Now we think first of the nuclear disaster when we think of Fukushima, and it made my heart ache to see images of all the poisoning and destruction on the news. It may never be a safe beautiful place for agriculture again.

A Thousand Kuan Yins
and Other Manifestations of Spirit

At Yuho's family's house, whenever they received a gift of food, they put it on an altar and clapped their hands to get the attention of the ancestors. Many people in Japan were Buddhist, but they also practiced Shintoism, ancestor worship, with shrines and other offerings. The whole spiritual and religious aspect of Japan was pretty remarkable to me.

Kyoto, City of Spirit

Kyoto is one of the spiritual centers of Japan. With Yuho, I visited a place called *The Hall of the Thousand Kuan Yins*. There were many statues of Kuan Yin, on risers like a heavenly choir. The cumulative effect of seeing all these goddesses together in one place was overwhelming, especially for me, as I had loved Kuan Yin, the Goddess of Mercy and Compassion, for a long time. My heart filled with emanations of the Goddess.

There were also many shrines to unborn children, from miscarriage or abortion. Some of them were made of large stones placed on each other in the shape of people who wore something like chefs hats on their "heads" that I didn't understand. Others were more elaborate with tiny shoes and toys as well as incense and flowers. I thought it was lovely to have a place where people could grieve the loss of their children and the choices they had felt were the best ones to make.

While we were in Kyoto, Yuho heard that her father was ill and she went back to Fukushima to visit him. She left me in Kyoto with a friend of hers who had the same disability she did. He was a very kind man, and had a car, but he hardly spoke any English at all, which was a bit daunting and challenging.

He asked me where I wanted to go first, and I said "please take me to a bookstore where I can buy an English-Japanese phrasebook!"

I couldn't really communicate much even with the phrasebook, but at least I could say some phrases and point to others so we could talk about practical survival issues! The bookstore was huge and had an entire floor of books in English.

I bought a book about Japanese language which talked about the sexism embedded in many phrases, like "wife in a box," i.e. housewife, which I thought evocative, especially in light of my mother's experience, and "office flower," for decorative women at work.

Tri-Lingual

While I was traveling alone, I also went to visit another former student of mine, Hisako, the artist who had been a thalidomide baby, in Yamaguchi prefecture.

Hisako also sang in a musical group, and she told me she wanted to have a party where she invited all her singing friends to meet me. She was warm and welcoming, but she'd forgotten most of her English, and it was exhausting trying to converse with her. I had to speak English so simply and carefully, with so many repetitions and misunderstandings, that I didn't even feel like I was speaking my native language.

When she mentioned in passing that she had a cousin, an architect, who was of Japanese descent but lived in Mexico and was in Japan on a visit, I begged Hisako to invite her to the party. I know Hisako didn't understand why I wanted her there, since she wouldn't know any of Hisako's singing friends, but my Spanish was so much better than these peoples' English that I wanted a chance to talk without working extremely hard to communicate.

When her cousin came in to the party, we started talking and talking and talking in Spanish. It was such a relief! I have never felt more fluent in Spanish than I did talking to her after the severely restricted English and great patience I had to use to convey anything to people with whom I really didn't share a common language.

It was funny though, because she didn't speak any English, and no one else but she and I spoke Spanish, so I kept getting mixed up and trying to talk to everybody in Spanish or with her in English. It was still a lot more fun than if she hadn't been there.

It was also beautiful to see Hisako, who had been trapped at home due to the cultural and family shame about disability, coming out of her shell, much more comfortable in herself and out in the world with her friends. And now, her family was supporting her doing that. She gave me a book of beautiful art and prose she had made and published. I couldn't read it at all, but I could look at her drawings!

Yuho also set up an interview for me with a Japanese journalist about my life and my ESL experiences. She sent me the newspaper clipping afterwards but of course I couldn't understand a word of it — only see that there was a picture of me in it.

The Postcard-Perfect Hills of Japan

Before I visited Japan, I thought of it as a crowded urban environment. And indeed, Tokyo was like that to the nth degree. In Shinjuku, the entertainment district, there were always so many people that it constantly looked like a huge theater had finished a performance and the audience was pouring out. Housing was an issue too. People often had to commute to work two hours or more by train because it was so hard to find housing.

Old-fashioned apartments didn't have baths, and people went to the public bath houses, but more modern homes had baths. By our standards, they were tiny, sort of like the recent tiny house movement. Yuho's had one 10x12 room with a sliding closet to put the bedding in at night, a tiny narrow kitchen with a miniature refrigerator and stove, and a small bathroom. This was pretty typical.

But what I didn't realize until traveling around Japan by train or car, was how big, tree-covered, and beautiful the countryside was. There were long stretches of lush, emerald-green, rolling hills with no signs of human habitation at all. They looked exactly like some of the traditional Japanese murals and paintings, no change in centuries. Looking at Japan on a map, it is a tiny country, but it didn't feel like that in gorgeous, spacious nature.

Are We There Yet?

Years later, Yuho had a daughter, Umi, and when she was four, Yuho, Sh'aom, and she came to visit. When we were taking them to San Francisco, little Umi, who spoke no English, kept asking the same question over and over. We asked Sh'aom what she was saying.

Sh'aom explained, in her slightly formal English, "She is inquiring about when we will arrive at our destination."

My sweetheart and I started laughing, and simultaneously said, "Are we there yet?" recognizing the explanation as the classic kid question when traveling. I learned it wasn't just American children who said that!

I Am Enough

Yuho's English was still quite eccentric when they visited us.

I remember at dinner one day, after we had all finished our first helping of food, I asked her, "Would you like some more?"

She replied, "I am enough."

I know she meant, "I've had enough food," but I loved her answer! She is indeed enough and so am I, and as I have walked my own spiritual path, I have come to believe it more and more!

Looking for Love in a Lot of Wrong Places

Before and after going to Japan, I longed for love — family love, friendship love, and romantic love. Yet, I still had a fundamental fear that I wasn't lovable. I think my criteria for a romantic partner before recovery was someone who was somewhat attractive and willing to pay me a bit of attention. If they said they found me attractive or that they loved me, that was enough. I had no idea who or what I actually wanted.

Despite my work on co-dependence, I still acted as if I had to be satisfied with crumbs, that an unsatisfying relationship was the best I could expect. Because of these beliefs, over and over I picked people who were not emotionally available, who couldn't really love me. Stephanie was the first, followed by Alana and Pam, both adult children of alcoholics and abuse survivors, and others. My dear friend Rich and I were far more intimate and loving, but of course as a gay man he wasn't available as a romantic partner, nor was I interested in him in that way.

My Fervent Prayer

The most powerful experience of the entire trip, which completely changed my life, was a visit to a temple that a friend of Yuho's took me to. There you could buy a piece of wood with a ribbon on it, write a prayer on the wood, and hang it on a prayer tree. Many Japanese people wrote prayers and drank holy water which they dipped from the well. I was the only Gaijin there, but I didn't let that stop me. I bought a piece of wood, and wrote an impassioned heartfelt prayer, in English of course, to the Goddess.

"Dear Goddess, I really need my life to change. I can't bear to go back home to my same life. Please help me find love and work."

I knew I couldn't make my life change, but, in that holy place, after all my grief about Rich and all my work on myself, I was truly ready and open to change. And that heartfelt prayer of desperation was completely and miraculously answered in every way!

This prayer and the trip to Japan were a major turning point. Within two weeks of my return, I was hired as a full-time, tenure-track, ESL professor at a community college, after having looked for a position for two years. Within four months, I met the love of my life, after waiting for seven years, all thanks to the Goddess's intervention.

It all happened at once —
a 20-year mashup of
love, tenure, darkness, and death.

My life during the 20 years from 1989 to 2009, was a complicated mixture of finding enduring true love, joyfully attaining and despairingly keeping a full-time, tenured teaching job, and showing up and grieving for a lot of illness and death. I'm going to start with love . . . .

Chapter Eleven

Finding True Love at Last

I lived in the Berkeley/Oakland area for sixteen years. When I finally found a full-time teaching job and moved to Carquenas, I left behind most of my support system. I was very much alone and still single, but hopeful this might be a fresh start for finding romance.

I continued taking action to find my true love. In my channeling and journaling, the Goddess was telling me that she (my beloved) was on her way, that she was coming soon, that it was all going to unfold, but I was growing very impatient and frustrated. I had several false alarms where I met someone and thought she was "the one," then quickly realized she wasn't.

Love in the Vineyard?

Soon after I'd moved, I went to a dance in San Francisco and met a woman in my recovery program. We really hit it off, and after the dance, made a date to go to a movie together. Soon after that, she came up to visit me in my new home. We had a picnic in a vineyard near St. Helena, which I thought was very romantic, and as we were leaving the vineyard, she put her arm around me. I was sure that this was the beginning of a beautiful relationship.

And then, as she was driving me back to my cottage, she suddenly said to me, "You know, when I get romantically involved with someone, I want them to meet you."

I felt stabbed through the heart. I could hardly process what I was hearing. I thought *we* were getting romantically involved! But clearly, she had a different view of the matter. I do think she was giving me mixed signals, but nonetheless, there I was with another huge disappointment with a new person I'd pinned my hopes and expectations on. I said goodbye somehow, and walked inside my cottage feeling devastated.

Haranguing the Goddess

Then I let the Goddess really have it! She'd promised me true love, and I'd been waiting far too long.

I said, "Ok, Goddess, I get it. I've been single two and a half years, and maybe you want me to be single another two and a half years or more. And if that's what you want, I know that that's what's going to happen. I cannot control this process. I don't think it is at all fair or right, but here I am.

"I could go to every event for single lesbians in the Bay Area, and it doesn't mean I'll find my true love. I can write the best personal ad in the world (this was before Internet dating) and it doesn't mean I'll find her. I can work a spiritual 12-step program around my codependency and strive to become a much healthier and saner person who attracts another healthy sane person, but this doesn't guarantee I'll find her either.

"I can be good and kind, and try to have a happy life alone, but it doesn't guarantee anything. I can take a red candle and a white candle and set them six feet apart and meditate on the relationship I want every night and move the candles one inch closer every night, and it doesn't mean she will come my way. (I did all this).

"I'm NOT happy about it, but I get that it's up to you. I've tried everything I know to control the process and it isn't working. It's clearly your decision. But I'm telling you right now that *I want a girlfriend and I want her now*! So, I'm putting in my request."

How I Met My Basherte (Fated Beloved)

Four weeks later, I met Linda at a housewarming party in Carquenas and we have been together ever since.

I had hung my prayer on the temple prayer tree in Kyoto in July 1989, and by the end of August I had a full-time tenure-track job. Then in January 1990 I met my true love. Sometimes the Goddess works quickly (at last)!

Living in Carquenas, I felt very isolated. It wasn't like the vibrant progressive artistic lesbian community that I had been part of in Berkeley and Oakland. There was one woman, a lesbian named Shawna, who everyone seemed to know. It was as if she were THE public lesbian for making connections in Carquenas County.

I met her at an open informal Friday night event for lesbians, and she invited me to a housewarming party she was having the next day. I almost didn't go, because I was so tired of feeling vulnerable and putting myself out there to meet new people and not really connecting with anyone.

When I feel that way, it's reflected in my process of deciding what to wear, dating back to my childhood as I wrote about earlier. When I feel scared or nervous, I think I'm fat or ugly, and everything I think of wearing feels wrong — too dressed up, or not dressed up enough. I *have* to be dressed exactly like the other people there to fit in. Otherwise, if my clothes look different from the other people there and I didn't intuit correctly what to wear, I am convinced I am wrong and bad. I almost gave up going because my entire bed was covered with rejected items from my wardrobe, and I still wasn't dressed.

Finally, I asked myself, don't you want to meet people? You can show up and then leave whenever you want. I put on some clothes and went to the housewarming. Two tall athletic women came in together, and I assumed they were a couple, thinking, "Oh, too bad," because I thought they were both very attractive. I happened to sit down next to one of them, on an ottoman because it was the only seat left. Her name was Linda Jones, and it turned out she was also in recovery. I very sincerely and innocently asked for her phone number, saying that I needed people to make program calls with up here. She gladly gave it to me. Not being very familiar with the area, I didn't realize that Santa Rosa, where she lived, was an hour away, about as far as Oakland.

Linda's part of this same story is also very beautiful. The other tall woman she came to the party with, also called Linda, was her good friend and ex-girlfriend. By the way, lesbians are unusually good at staying friends with their exes, and years after they broke up, the other Linda was like her sister or her best friend. She also happens to be psychic.

As they were driving to the housewarming, my Linda told me later, the other Linda said to her, "You are going to meet the love of your life at the party."

Linda said, "I wasn't sure what to think. But Linda's been right about many things in the past. I couldn't totally discount it."

And there I was.

As she tells it, "You sat down next to me, and you were so beautiful, and when I told you I'd had surgery six weeks before and was in early recovery from that, you put your hand on my arm with so much kindness that I was deeply touched."

A First Date

Linda called me the next week, telling me she was going to "be in the area" and did I want to meet for lunch. I didn't know that she was actually going to drive from Sonoma, where she was picking up her paycheck, to see me. I dressed up as much as I thought I could get away with, since she didn't know how I usually dress for work, and we went to lunch.

I thought she was attractive and kind but a bit codependent. It seemed like she was falling in love with me without even knowing me, which I thought was a warning sign, similar to dysfunctional relationships in my past. I didn't know she could read energy and see inside people.

The next week we went for a walk, and as we were walking, I heard an inner voice say loud and clear and sure in my ear, "She's the one."

"The one what??? What are you talking about?!" I responded. But I soon figured it out.

Holding Hands

After lunch and another walk, our first real date was for dinner and a movie. We agreed to meet at an open house for the new office of a chiropractor we both knew in Santa Rosa. I arrived there first, very nervous. I saw her walk across the parking lot, looking so tall, handsome, and totally cool/hot in a black leather jacket, which I found out later she had borrowed from her same friend Linda.

The panicky thought flashed across my whole being, "Oh God, I am totally attracted to her! What do I do now?"

We stayed at the event briefly, and then went to Linda's house for dinner, as we had previously arranged. I followed her in my car rather than letting her drive me, still being cautious about becoming involved too quickly. She took tremendous pains to make a delicious dinner that accommodated my food allergies! I was touched and impressed.

Then I was worried she was going to put the moves on me far too soon, but instead, she handed me the movie section of the newspaper, "What would you like to see? Please pick something."

We picked *The Music Box*, which is an excellent but grim drama about a woman finding out her father was a Nazi war criminal. Not exactly an ideal "date night" movie! But we connected anyway. At one point, Linda put her hand on the arm of my chair, clearly wanting to hold hands.

I was all in my own head, wanting to do things differently, my brain buzzing with anxious questions. "Is it too soon? Will I be sending the wrong message and jumping off a love-cliff again?"

Finally, a different part of my brain said, "Look. It's Saturday night. You are out on a date with someone you are very attracted to. You get to hold hands!"

After the movie, we went back to her apartment and started kissing on the couch. It was sweet and delicious! The only problem was, the jacket Linda had borrowed smelled very strongly of her friend's girlfriend's perfume, so we had to wrap Linda up in a towel to avoid triggering my allergies.

Finally, she walked me out to my car. The windshield was completely frosted over, and she ended up driving me to my friends' Lisa's and Venus' house, where I was spending the night. The next day, Lisa drove me back to pick up my car, and I knocked on the door to say hi to Linda. I didn't leave until we had had another very hot make-out session!

I told Linda bluntly, "if you want me to spend the night, you are going to have to get rid of all the perfumes and scented products on your vanity."

I couldn't tolerate being around any fragrances because of my multiple chemical sensitivities. Her motivation was high, and she did get rid of them. It turned out they were starting to bother her as well, so it was a good move, not only for our relationship, but for her health as well.

No U-Haul This Time

One of the classic jokes about lesbians is, "What do lesbians bring to a first date?" Answer: "A U-Haul," so we can move in together.

We are notorious for thinking we are in love immediately. I actually wrote a song about this well before I met Linda. In three verses, it summarized many dysfunctional lesbian relationships: falling instantly in love, moving in, merging and being inseparable, making love non-stop, starting to fight, breaking up, looking for someone new.

When Linda and I first got together, we didn't have to worry about merging or spending all our time together, because I was working full-time during the day Monday through Friday and she was working full-time on the night shift as a nurse and only had every third weekend off.

I remember when she finally had a weekend off and we were going to spend it together. As it turned out, I had menstrual cramps and abdominal cramps both, and I sat on the closed toilet lid in her bathroom sobbing, so disappointed that we couldn't have the romantic weekend I had anticipated. She came to find me, very concerned, and I cried to her about my disappointment and said, "What are we gonna do this weekend if I'm not feeling well?"

She put her arms around me and said, "It'll be ok. We can talk and relax. There doesn't have to be a big agenda if you're not feeling well."

If I hadn't started falling in love with her already, I would have at that moment. She was kindness itself.

Romantic Valentine's Day

We started dating in January, so Valentine's Day came a few weeks later.

Linda has the soul of a romantic. On Valentine's Day, we agreed to have dinner together at my house. She used the key I'd given to her to come in, and set up a whole Valentine's table, including a huge bright red Mylar heart-shaped balloon, a card, and a heart-shaped ring box of red satin.

She was sitting on my couch all dressed up, with a black bolero jacket and a bolo tie. I walked into the room, and I was overwhelmed. No one had ever taken such special and romantic care of me before. I was a little concerned about the ring box, because it was far too early for rings, but when I opened it up, it was a plastic humorous ring! She had also made and brought dinner for me. It was a very special evening of tenderness and passion! And because of the work I'd done on myself, I believed I deserved it.

Worth the Wait — Thanks, Goddess!

I had been so very angry at the Goddess for her promises that my true love was on the way but never seemed to arrive. In total, with false starts and short awful relationships with dysfunctional people, I waited for almost ten years, which I still think is a very long time. But I can say now that Linda was absolutely worth the wait. And without that long lag time, which I filled with recovery and therapy, I wouldn't have had as much sanity, self-love, or communication skills to bring to our relationship.

I frequently let the Goddess know how grateful I am that She brought Linda and me together; and Linda feels the same way. She is the imperfect, amazing love of my life that I feared I would never find but met at the perfect time. We both agree that if we had met when we were younger, we would have lacked the skills to sustain a healthy relationship despite our deep attraction to each other.

The Illuminating Olive

Part of the miracle is that I am able to have the loving sane relationship that my parents never modeled. A visit to a restaurant with my parents in 1989 illuminates my parents' marriage, and what my childhood had taught me about relationships and life.

My mother's attitude in general was that since she was married to my father, and whatever he did would impact her, it was her right to control and manage his life, and tell him what to do, particularly about health and nutritional issues. It takes two to make a dysfunctional agreement like this, and my father with some grumbling, pretty much let her run this.

My parents had come up to visit me from Southern California, and we all went out to dinner at a Mexican restaurant. At that time, I wasn't eating olives, so I asked them if one of them would like mine. They didn't want it, but the fact of my asking made my mother realize that my father's olive had disappeared, and therefore he must have eaten it in defiance of her regimen.

"Did you eat that olive?" she thundered at him.

My father replied in a pitiful whimpering voice, "It was just a little olive."

My mother then launched into a full-blown self-righteous lecture.

"How could you?! Don't you know how bad the salt is for you? How could you do that to me!?"

It was all I could do to keep my composure and not laugh in the face of this major battle over a tiny olive. Yet in many ways, this was a metaphor for ongoing aspects of my childhood.

There were no boundaries, psychic, physical, or emotional. Anything my mother thought was hers was hers and we all had to go along. I didn't understand the trap she felt herself in, constrained and forced to stay home and take care of us by social conventions, when it was the last thing in the world she wanted to do. She did it with as much love as she could muster through her frustration.

There was nothing she knew or saw that let her know, in the 1950s, that she could choose her career, that she could let others care for her children, that she deserved to feel fulfilled.

Nonetheless, it was an awful way to grow up. Anything I did or failed to do could potentially impact her so dramatically and totally that it didn't feel safe to make any move or to even think an independent thought. I recovered a memory in therapy of feeling psychically smothered, unable to breathe.

I told my beloved Linda about all this, and the olive story became a touchstone for us of how we did not want to communicate or behave toward each other.

I Married My Mother!

After Linda and I had been living together for a while, and the first shiny pink bubble of love had settled down a bit, I began to see, with astonished horror, that in some ways Linda was a lot like my mother. Her family background, with many children fighting for attention and of being ignored as a girl compared to the attention paid to the boys in the family, was very similar.

They both had "rageaholic" fathers and a fear of not doing things right and being abused. I was shocked and dismayed to realize Linda was controlling and judgmental: a perfectionist very much like my mother. She triggered some of the negative feelings I had from my childhood — that I was never good enough, that nothing I did in the house was done well enough. It felt like the rules were a moving target and I could never get it right, so I was the target instead!

At first, I wasn't sure if we would be able to work out this issue. I never ever wanted to live with my mother again! It felt like reliving a nightmare I thought I'd escaped from. But though Linda's background was similar, her way of dealing with problems and differences was, thankfully, very different. She wanted to communicate, to speak her truth, and she also knew how to listen deeply and understand my perspective.

She was completely willing, once she did understand, to look at her part, acknowledge her contribution to a fight or problem, and work to change her behavior and thinking that were faulty or mean. And I too, was different. I didn't believe I deserved abuse anymore. I was willing to speak up, to set limits, and to look at my own part without taking the whole issue on as my burden. Our process, and Linda's generous willingness, made me love her and appreciate her even more.

Crimes against Windows

When we could laugh at some of these issues and our childish out of control behavior, humor became another sweet tool to work through disagreements and let go. A burst of inspiration brought me the "Crimes" series. Instead of crimes against humanity, we struggled with Linda's perfectionism and judgement, which led to *Crimes against Windows*, *Crimes against Dishes*, and *Crimes against Laundry*.

If I didn't put the blinds up or down on the window, or open or close the windows when she thought it was the right time, she would be very angry with me and yell at me for doing it wrong. Similarly, if my dishwashing wasn't up to her standards, or I didn't place the dishes in exactly the right spots in the dish drainer to promote maximum air exposure according to her criteria, she would act affronted and lecture me on the proper (her) way to do it. If I didn't hang the clothes or fold laundry the way she believed correct, she would redo it and instruct me how to do it correctly in a thoroughly condescending tone.

Initially, this would completely trigger me emotionally. I would react with major anger and defensiveness, and we would have screaming fights. I did inner work with little Lorry to remind her that Linda wasn't my mother, and affirm that my little one was okay and didn't have to take on Linda's judgments. But it was hard work!

But if I could call Linda on a "crime," instead of reacting defensively and letting all my negative self-talk from my childhood be triggered, we could move through incidents much more quickly and return to harmony.

The Long Path to Immediate Forgiveness

I wrote a blog post about one screaming fight we had in the kitchen, squabbling like four-year-olds over vegetables. We resolved it within ten minutes because neither of us wanted to hold on to anger.

In our early days, when we lost our tempers, one of us, more often me, would storm off in a huff. We would sleep separately and sometimes take days to forgive each other. It was tiring and made us both very sad. We talked about how we had all these golden tendrils of love and connection between us, and when we were angry or in resentment some of the tendrils broke off, and then we had to rebuild the network.

We still struggle at times with some of these triggers and differences. But I know from my long recovery work that there are no perfect human beings. If I were with someone else, we might have the same set of issues or perhaps different ones. Part of being in a human relationship, I know now, is fighting and struggling and having problems. It is the beautiful way Linda and I deal with disagreements, which has allowed us to stay together, growing deeper in love.

My Father's Admonition

Eventually I came out to my parents and they met Linda. They were fairly accepting, though a bit of homophobia still peeked through at times. My mother loved having a nurse join the family — almost as good as a doctor. I knew my father accepted us because of the way he admonished me when we were walking around Spring Lake one day, a few yards ahead of Linda and my mother.

He said to me, with heavy emotion, and virtual finger shaking, "Be sure you don't blow it with Linda! Don't make any mistakes!"

I nodded solemnly at the time, but with secret amusement. It was such a negative view of relationships, and, yet, he would have said the same thing if I were with a man, so it was acceptance of a sort.

From Momentary Matrimony to Lawfully Wedded Bliss

Until very recently, marriage for lesbians was not an easy path. In 1990 when my beloved wife and I first fell in love, it seemed utterly impossible that we would ever get to be legally married no matter how committed we were or how much we wanted it. Things began to shift with Lambda Legal Defense Fund, the National Coalition for Lesbian Rights, and Evan Wolfson's *Freedom to Marry* project. Some gay and lesbian groups took up the cause of marriage as a very traditional human need and a radical concept at the same time.

Not everyone in the LGBTQI (lesbian, gay, bisexual, transgender, queer, intersex) community embraced it. Marriage has such a mixed history, with its link to the patriarchy, to women held as domestic prisoners or owned as property, as well as other ways that marriage impeded women's agency and independence, as I wrote about earlier. But nonetheless, many of us wanted the option. Finding Linda, and knowing she was my besherte, my fated beloved, I wanted to be legally connected to her.

One Thousand One Hundred Thirty-Eight Rights and Responsibilities

I learned that there were over 1,138 rights and responsibilities connected to marriage, most of which Linda and I couldn't replicate no matter how many legal documents we prepared and signed. The right to be next of kin, to visit each other in the hospital, to make medical decisions for each other, to inherit, to have access to each other's pensions, and many other areas were not guaranteed. The longer we were together, the more we longed to make a legal and spiritual commitment and have our relationship seen and honored.

Momentary Matrimony

Our first attempt at marriage was a booth at the San Francisco Pride Parade called "momentary matrimony," which was raising money for the Gay Men's Chorus. The gay man running the booth would marry you and take a Polaroid picture of you under an arch of rainbow-colored balloons to commemorate your five minute marriage. Linda and I did it, and it was the first step of a very, very, long journey.

Several years later, the Sonoma County Pride Celebration offered a commitment ceremony, en masse, for couples who wanted to be joined together. We did that several years, and one time our photo was in the local paper.

Periodically, I would ask Linda to marry me but for a while she wasn't sure. Then she was. And not knowing if it would ever be legal, we decided to have a big ceremony anyway and make our commitment to each other public.

I Am My Beloved's and My Beloved is Mine

We wanted to have a wedding and make our vows, though there was a frustration and a bitterness that we couldn't make it legal. A heterosexual couple could meet and marry on a reality show, and they would immediately have all these rights that were denied to committed same-sex couples like us who had been together for years. But there was also a lot of joy in our process, as well as the stress most people feel when planning a wedding.

We took over a year to plan everything, and paid as we went, so we didn't debt to have a big beautiful wedding.

Our rings came to us first. We were up in Mendocino for a short vacation and the fine jewelry store up there, *Old Gold*, had beautiful 18-carat gold bands with diamonds that we both loved. We ordered them. It was far and away the most either of us had ever spent on jewelry, but it was worth it.

We bought and read books about planning weddings. The most practical one, complete with checklists, was called *The Working*

Woman's Wedding Planner. Another was humorous and useful, called *The Lesbian and Gay Guide to Getting Married,* which had sections on how to find same-sex cake toppers and how to deal with homophobic relatives.

We also found books to help us create our own ceremony. One was a book about unconventional wedding ritual elements, one was a description of actual different lesbian weddings. Actually, a lesbian anthropologist, Ellen Lewin, contacted us and wanted to include our wedding in her book, *Recognizing Ourselves,* so we said yes. She used pseudonyms, so as "Cynthia Kelly" and "Alisa Rosenberg," our wedding became part of history!

We also used a booklet from a party planning store, *Nancy's Fancies,* about venues and other wedding elements. And we found a beautiful home in Guerneville whose owner at the time hosted and catered weddings, with a garden, a redwood grove, a deck for dancing. It was miraculously affordable.

Hundreds of Petty Decisions

One of hardest aspects of planning the wedding was how many small decisions we had to make. For example, if we wanted the front row of chairs reserved for immediate family, we had to decide how to do it. And if we decided on ribbons to block off the rows, we had to pick the color or there wouldn't be ribbons. And if we wanted food, we had to pick it. And if we wanted a DJ, we had to find one. And if we wanted to wear clothes (ha), we had to decide if we wanted traditional dresses, suits, more casual dresses. Everyone goes through a lot of this when they marry, but in 1995, two women getting married had a lot less tradition to rely on!

Crafting Our Ceremony

I had been in a Goddess circle group in which we took turns planning rituals. I understood that crafting rituals was a lot like lesson planning, so I knew a bit about how to put different pieces together. We looked at many beautiful ritual elements, but we had to set a limit so the ceremony wouldn't feel cluttered. And, we wanted to incorporate all our cultures and spirituality, which meant it had to be a Jewish (me), Celtic, Czech, (Linda) pagan, 12 Step (both of us) wedding. And we did it!

I went to the library at Sonoma State University and did research on the microfiche (Internet research wasn't common then) about Czech wedding customs. Most of the ones the anthropologists described seemed very archaic or not at all appropriate for us, but I did, after exhaustive research, find two elements we could use. Bridesmaids were called *druszicki,* and they used rosemary for remembrance in the ceremonies. We had a book with Celtic prayers and another with pagan rituals. We had friends who could be priestesses and others who could be druszickis, drummer friends, including Linda F. and Kathy, and a guitarist friend, Lisa. We had also been inspired by the Friends (Quaker) wedding of Carol and Kenny we had attended, so we had an artist make a beautiful combination signing piece and *ketubah* (Jewish wedding contract).

My parents, my sister and brother-in-law, and my three-month old niece Lillian all came, as did Linda's mother Vi and sister Joy. Linda's brothers, who loved her, were swayed by their very fundamentalist ministers not to come because the ministers said it would be a sin to attend. And my mother wildly threatened that if I invited my extended family, her siblings and my cousins, she wouldn't come, so I didn't invite them. I found out only after her death that she had never revealed to any relatives that I had come out as a lesbian nor that my sister had converted to Christianity. She was afraid of being shamed and judged.

The Wedding Day

On the day of the wedding, we both had a hard time transitioning from wedding planners to brides. We are both such competent people, that we didn't realize we needed more help to let go and be present.

Linda had put her makeup in my makeup bag and I couldn't find my lipstick. I had a (mercifully brief) total meltdown. And at the beginning of the ceremony, I was focused on empty chairs that should have been moved instead of being present.

Linda's best friend, Linda, the same one who told Linda she'd meet the love of her life (me) at the housewarming party, reminded us right before the ceremony, "Remember," she said, "it is a ceremony, not a performance." That helped!

Despite the challenges, it was a beautiful ceremony that moved everyone to tears. Because we had to work hard for it and decide consciously to wed, when we two mature women stood up and declared our love, it was with deep conviction and full knowledge. And the Goddess' spiritual energy was clearly present.

Lisa played guitar as we walked in. The priestesses called in the Four Directions, traditionally a part of pagan ceremonies. We had a *huppah*, a canopy traditional to Jewish weddings, decorated with ribbons, flowers, and sprigs of rosemary (traditionally part of Czech weddings). Our drummer friends played at dramatic moments.

We did a pagan/Celtic version of the *Sheva Brachot*, the traditional Jewish Seven Blessings. We fed each other and drank from a goblet saying, "May you never hunger, may you never thirst," and received a blessing of Brigit, the Celtic Goddess. We smashed two wineglasses. And we made our vows, partially adapted from traditional wedding vows with a 12 Step slogan thrown in:

"I promise to love, honor, and cherish you. To stand by you through good times and hard times, in sickness and in health, one day at a time, for this life and beyond, as the Goddess wills."

And when we exchanged rings, we each said,

"With my body I worship you, with this ring I wed you and pledge my faithful love." (I had read this vow in a Dorothy Sayers book when Harriet Vane wed Lord Peter Whimsey).

Everyone was crying by the end. I think our straight friends were even more touched than our gay friends. After the ceremony, we had wonderful food and dancing to a DJ on the big deck.

The Power of Vows

Even though it wasn't legal, making our vows in front of everyone we knew deepened our commitment to each other. I thought I loved Linda completely, but I loved her even more after the ceremony. One of the things the Goddess prompted me to say to her, which became one of our touchstone sayings, was "I love you as much as one human being can love another. But the Goddess loves us far, far more."

Lesbian Poster Couple

In 2000, very conservative groups in California put Proposition 22 on the ballot. It proposed, "Only marriage between a man and a woman is valid and recognized in California."

It was a preemptive strike designed to prevent same-sex couples from ever being able to marry legally in California. Linda and

I became very involved in the campaign to stop it. I happened to be on sabbatical, which freed up my time. One way we helped was setting up speaking engagements and being speakers.

I called it being the *poster couple* — here we are, the charming, normal, healthy lesbian couple in love, who want the same right to get married and have all the legal rights and protections that heterosexual couples take for granted. Linda and I wrote a "duet" speech together, which was quite effective.

We included one of Linda's stories about her four brothers, and how she had been to each of their weddings, more than one wedding for two of her brothers. Whenever we said that, the audience laughed, but Linda started waiting for the laugh, and I, having an intuitive sense of comic timing, told her she had to act oblivious and pretend she wasn't expecting it. We spoke at synagogues and churches, and I did one for the local Democratic Club that Linda wasn't able to attend because of work.

We worked with interesting people — lesbian activists, savvy gay and lesbian political operatives, like the wonderful Maddy Hirshfield, progressive heterosexual allies, and the first transgender couple I ever met.

Diane was a math teacher at Santa Rose Junior College and had been a man before transitioning while still at the school. His/her wife, Ann, had a hard time with the transition, but stuck with her, and they stayed together, one of the first couples who did that when one transitioned. Later, I had them come speak several times about transgender issues and their story at the community college.

We also met a lesbian couple, both doctors, who with their young daughter moved down to Guatemala for a year to run a rural medical clinic and train medics and midwives. For a while, I read their blog, and their experiences were heart-wrenching and heart-warming. They felt so very useful and fulfilled that they stayed for years and their daughter grew up there, completely bilingual.

Proposition 22 passed, and it wasn't until 2008 that same-sex couples, even briefly, won the right to marry. It was a sad disappointment to lose the vote, and meant Linda and I still couldn't be legally married, but I do believe that campaign planted seeds of awareness and activist practice that helped in 2008 in California and 2013, nationally.

Ann and Diane and other people we met on the campaign were also active with school and school board issues, wanting more education about LGBTQI issues included in K–12 classes; and more safety in schools for LGBTQI youth who were bullied and committed suicide at far higher than average rates.

In the Santa Rosa School District, part of the school board held an open forum, inviting a published homophobe to speak. He was pretty out there, also claiming the Nazis had been gay.

A lot of us turned up to protest. The audience was about half LGBTQI people and supporters, and half right-wing homophobes. The most dramatic moment was when the speaker claimed that gays were recruiting their children. The progressive half of the audience burst into spontaneous and raucous laughter, while the other half nodded in somber satisfaction and indignantly told us to hush.

It really felt like we were in different universes, and theirs was imaginary. We *were* gay and knew none of us were recruiting anyone. It was an old stereotype from the '50s that wasn't true then or now. But these fearful, credulous people would rather believe that any children of theirs who were gay had been recruited rather than deal with it as a natural, human way of being. If they had been willing to talk to us, we could have reassured them, but that wasn't what they wanted.

Legally Married at Last (Sort Of)

Lesbians and gays were continuing to make progress toward legal marriage. In June 2008, we won the right to marry in California. Linda and I were among the first in line at the Sonoma County Courthouse on June 16 at 5 P.M., the first day and time any of us could acquire marriage licenses.

The line was long, the crowd ecstatic. People brought flowers and little wedding favors; journalists snapped photos and interviewed couples.

When it was our turn to talk with the clerk, we choked up. I said, "We never thought we'd actually be able to do this!" The clerk was truly moved; her eyes filled with tears, and we all cried a little.

At first, we intended to get married at the County Courthouse, because after all, we had had a wedding in 1995. But it felt so important to be legal at last that we decided to put together a simple wedding.

We took over a year to plan the first wedding. The second one, we put together in a few weeks, starting as soon as the Courts refused to stay implementation of the decision that we could marry. We were married at our friends' Jenny's and Weston's beautiful house. They had an exquisite yard and deck and pool.

Riding in the Goddess's Limousine

This time, I was determined to stay serene and present and really enjoy the wedding. We planned out the entire wedding and the sequence of events. We invited all our friends. We invited family too, but no one could make it to a second wedding. We hired a caterer, and my friend Floralee made the wedding cake. We chose simple summer dresses. My synagogue bandmate Rose played viola. We had a *huppah* again, and our good friend Linda ordered a minister's card online and officiated. We made the same vows we had earlier. But we had paperwork for the first time, which made it feel real!

And I did most of the pre-planning, but this time I gave the whole schedule and who was doing what to my friend Cate, and let her be the wedding manager. We had one role this time on our wedding day — to be the brides! We even asked a friend, Moira, to be our handmaiden and help us get dressed.

A friend of mine from one of the 12 Step meetings used to say, "At any time, we have a choice. We can drive the old clunker of self-will or ride in the Goddess's limousine." Because I had more recovery and spiritual connection than I had had in 1995, I was able to "stay in the limousine" almost all day. Linda "stepped out" into self-will briefly about the music and the wine, but I didn't let that stop me. And she came back in the "limousine" too. It wasn't perfect, but a beautiful day.

And my old boyfriend Alan and his wife Patricia, who feel like family, were there, which was special. Our dear friends mica and Angelica got lost, but made it there just in time to help hold up the *huppah*. We had wonderful food and dancing, followed by a pool party.

Filing Seven Tax Returns

Although being recognized as married in California felt wonderful, and we started referring to each other proudly as "my wife," legally it actually made our lives more complicated. The federal government didn't recognize our marriage, but then had passed a law recognizing community property. So, we had to file two single tax returns for the feds and a joint tax return in California, but the CA return is based on the federal return, so our accountant had to mock up a joint federal tax return first. Then we had to file more returns because of the community property issue. It was murky and uncomfortable. And as Ruth Bader Ginsberg later said, it felt like a "skim milk" marriage, a thin version of marriage with the "fat," i.e. most rights and responsibilities, missing. It wasn't the "whole milk" marriage of heterosexual couples.

Are We Still Married?

Then on Election Day in November that same year, homophobic Proposition 8 passed. The window of opportunity had closed and same-sex partners could no longer marry. Despite lawsuits and mass protests, the State Supreme Court upheld the amendment. And it was up to the Court to decide if those of us who married between June and October would be "grandfathered" in or not. I remember sitting in a meeting at 9 A.M. that morning, Tuesday, May 26, 2009, not knowing if we would still be married at 10 A.M. after the decision was announced. It was an awful feeling to know our rights could be taken away so arbitrarily. But we stayed married, and in 2013, our marriage was "upgraded" to full federal status.

Endless I-5

Since Linda's and my family both lived in Southern California, we drove down there many times for weddings, holidays, illnesses, and ultimately deaths.

Interstate 5 is the quickest way to drive down and the most boring. It feels like flat, straight roads go on forever, with little of interest to break up the landscape. Irrigated fields in the Central Valley, small clusters of gas stations and fast food places at intervals, trying to hang on and stay awake until the next break, the next cup of coffee. And unless you speed recklessly, even the fast way is an eight-hour drive.

This Is a Test

In the movie *L.A. Story* with Steve Martin, one of the magical realism elements is that a particular electronic freeway sign sends him messages and gives him advice. One time when Linda and I were driving down to San Diego for her sister Joy's wedding, we had car trouble and then were stuck in horrible L.A. traffic. We were late and impatient, and traffic had come to a full stop.

We saw one of those electronic freeway signs which said, "This is a test."

We both began to laugh, accepting the sign's message as encouraging us to slow down, trust, be patient.

Chapter Twelve

Death

I am so grateful that I had my beloved Linda and a strong connection to the Goddess as we navigated the illness and death of her father, my father, my mother, her mother. Our mothers died within a year of each other, so that was a lot of grief and mixed emotions to deal with.

Apart from our feelings for our mothers, when they died there was no one left to stand between us and our death. Of course, none of us know how long we have, but in general we expect the older generation to go first; and now they were gone. I felt unprotected from my own mortality. It was a hollow, somewhat fearful feeling, even though I knew my soul would always be safe with the Divine.

Fathers

Linda's father had been an abusive alcoholic, and she was still dealing with the anger and grief from her childhood and his controlling, rageful, presence. She was supposed to feel grief, but I think she actually felt more relief. I only met him once, so I was more detached, focused on supporting Linda and all her feelings.

When my father was dying, the situation was different. I loved him and knew he loved me, but he was depressed and cut off from his feelings for most of my childhood and unable to be emotionally present as a parent. I didn't actually know him well. I did a lot of inner work to understand that he had done the best he could.

He became sicker and weaker very gradually. We went down to visit him for his birthday, November 9, when he was weak but relatively alert. He seemed accepting of the impending end of his life, and very happy that my mom had at last relaxed her (well intentioned) rigid control of his diet and he could eat pizza again and whatever else he chose.

I had some time alone to talk with him. I asked some questions about his life and my childhood, a final opportunity to share and listen, to be closer to him.

He told me, "You're mentally lazy, just like me."

It hurt to hear him say that, and to know he believed that. One of the worst insults of my childhood was to be called "lazy." It was almost as bad as the ultimate insult — to be "selfish." It was also one of the worst messages from my own inner critic.

I know, as I wrote earlier, that my perfectionism and fear of making mistakes paralyzed me and stopped me from taking action or completing projects; and perhaps that is what he was referring to, but when he made that comment, it hadn't been true for many years. He still saw me as that tormented little girl, not the relatively self-loving, proactive adult I had become. That insult has some power left to hurt me. It was such a deep pervasive message of my childhood — that I was never enough, that I was a disappointment, that I never achieved enough.

I wanted to talk to him about this, and even wrote a letter to him about it, but I never sent it because he moved so quickly into the final stages of dying.

Vigil at My Father's Deathbed

It was a miracle that I was present at my father's death. I knew he was getting closer to dying, and I wanted to go down to Los Angeles again, but my sister really didn't want me to. She was being protective I guess, and thought it would be too much stress for him and for my mother; but he was my father too, and he was dying.

Finally, Linda and I hastily packed up the car and went, against my sister's wishes. Linda didn't tell me until later, but her psychic friend Linda, who had predicted our relationship, told her we had to hurry or we wouldn't arrive in time to say goodbye.

We made it. My father, Henry, was literally on his deathbed. But when I came in to the bedroom, he recognized me and said, "Lorry," with a sweet smile on his face. The doctors had stopped all the medications that were keeping him alive but not really helping him anymore, so it was only a matter of time.

My mother, in some denial, was spending all her time in the kitchen with a care coordinator, arranging caregivers for the next few weeks, which Linda and I knew wouldn't be needed.

I said, "Mom, why don't you go and sit with him for a while and leave this for now?"

"No, no," she said, "I need to do this now."

I guess she couldn't bear the thought that he would die soon. So, sadly, she wasn't by his side when he died. Linda and I were there at the moment he passed.

And I spoke out loud to him, "Dad, it's all ok. Just go to the light." I hope it helped his spirit to hear that.

He died on Christmas Eve, 1995.

My poor mother was grief-stricken when he died. She took his hand and stroked his head, crying and screaming, "Don't leave me Henry, please don't leave me."

In their later years, they had become true companions, and her grief was huge.

The mortuary people came to take him away. He was to be cremated, but my mom didn't want to do anything with the ashes, so they just carted him off. It was terrible to see his empty flopping body leaving.

Comfort of Yahrzeit

One good thing Linda and I did during this awful period was to go to the gift shop of a local synagogue and buy a *Yahrzeit* (years end) candle holder and candle. It was a Jewish tradition to light a candle on the anniversary of someone's death. My mother actually lit it every year she was alive, even though she was agnostic. It seemed to comfort her a little; otherwise, she was inconsolable.

I couldn't understand why she didn't want a memorial service, or to sit Shiva, (traditional Jewish mourning period), or do anything to mark my father's passing, except have a gathering of friends at an open house. Maybe she was afraid of breaking down in front of other people; I'm really not sure.

My sister and brother-in-law took care of the food. I bought flowers, and provided the only ritual element. I gathered up all the photos I could find of my dad at different stages of his life; a photo when he was a boy with his sister, Rose; a photo of him in uniform when he went into the service during World War II; his and my mom's wedding picture; him holding his granddaughter, Lillian, when she was a baby. I found frames and set up the photos on shelves and end tables and put flowers next to them. It comforted me, if no one else, to acknowledge him in that way at the gathering.

My mother had a lot of (self-willed) inner strength, and after a while she found ways to go on and enjoy her life, although she always missed him.

Wedding Picture — Toulouse-Lautrec Style

When I was looking for picture frames for the photos of my Dad, I found a photo of Linda and me at our first wedding, face down in a drawer. It really hurt that she had it hidden away instead of displaying it with the other family photos. I didn't say a word about it then, because it was a much smaller issue than what she was going through. She had newly lost her husband, and my job was to support her.

But some months later, I did talk to her about it and tell her that it hurt. She was very defensive and blamed it on our picture being "too big." We didn't talk about it anymore, but the next time we came down, she had a cut down version of photo displayed. She had cropped it so we were cut off at the thigh, both of us looking like we had extremely short legs, similar to those of the French artist Toulouse-Lautrec. It was ugly and awkward. I showed it to Linda and we both had to laugh (so we wouldn't cry).

Vi and Fran

While Linda's mother Vi and my mother Fran were both still healthy, they met once at my fiftieth birthday party; and to Linda's and my surprise, they bonded with each other. You couldn't imagine two more different women from their generation.

My mother was a Jewish agnostic, well-educated and articulate, with a Master's degree. She was a career woman and school psychologist who often expressed superiority and judgment about people who didn't have much education. Vi was quite Christian and spiritual, had only a high school education, a homemaker who had never held an outside job.

The one thing they truly had in common, was the ingrained belief, part of the brainwashing of women of their generation, that it wasn't okay to assert yourself or ask for what you wanted; that all you could do was be indirect, passive-aggressive, manipulative and a victim.

And, even though she was often drugged up and barely present, Vi presented as a good, agreeable listener; and my mom loved being heard and having her opinions agreed with! I would never have predicted their companionable conversation. My mother asked after Vi several times before she became ill.

My Mother Chooses Her Path to Death

My mother lived at home and died at home. She was able to manage her own life with help from caregivers until the very end. She had colon cancer and surgery and some good years; thanks to Linda in part, who helped her "escape" from the hospital when they still wanted to keep her there for more and more tests.

But then, about eight years later, her cancer came back, and it was the beginning of her end. Until her last few days, she was still reading the newspaper and commenting on current events. It was her body that gave out, not her brain.

She was willing to fight and try new procedures as long as her doctor thought there was a chance of healing and recovery. But when he told her it was now only about prolonging her life a bit with no chance of healing, she let go and wanted to go home to die.

You *Want* Her To Die!

My sister and I were in conflict about all this. She accused me of wanting my mother to die because I accepted the inevitability of her death and wanted her to die peacefully with palliative care rather than in an ICU with constant, painful interventions. I knew that people in hospice care sometimes lived longer than those receiving the more invasive interventions because the pain was managed and they could relax. My sister didn't agree. She wanted every intervention possible to keep my mother alive.

When my sister screamed at me "You want our mother to die!" I ran out of the waiting room sobbing.

Linda hadn't driven down from Santa Rosa yet, so I was all alone. I sobbed all through the hospital and then went to find the chaplain, who happened to be a young rabbi that day. He didn't really know how to help me, but it was a little better than not having anyone.

When my mom was still in the hospital, she, like my dad earlier, talked about me in disparaging terms. "You are so lazy. I don't know why you get things wrong or don't finish anything."

It really hurt, but this time, I was determined to talk to her about it while I had the chance. I asked the nurse to leave the room.

Then I told Fran, "Mom, your opinion of me isn't true now, and it wasn't true when I was a child either. I want you to take it back."

She didn't really apologize, but I felt better that I had the chance to speak up and set the record straight, at least for myself. I hadn't had the opportunity to do it with my father, but I seized my chance with Fran.

When my mom decided to leave the hospital and go home, I rode with her in the ambulance and started, with Linda's help, to arrange hospice and nursing help for her. My mom was hoping that she would feel better when she returned home, but after the initial relief, she quickly realized that being home would not save her from dying.

Linda and I were there constantly to help her and give her oral morphine in the middle of the night. My sister was there for a while, but she could only take so much time off from work. She asked us how long it would be until Fran died, but of course we didn't know. Finally, she had to go home to Sacramento, where she was living and working. She had been the one to visit with our mother almost every week for years, while I only came down to visit in person a couple of times a year; so it was my turn. And, fortunately, I wasn't afraid to look her death in the eye.

Saying Goodbye

In her last days, my mother finally stopped her judgements of me. Basically, she stopped talking. She was still aware and so sweet. When I did something to help her she would wordlessly pat my cheek and smile.

One beautiful moment was when her dear friend Lorraine B. came to visit. They had met each other through the secular Jewish community, and Lorraine was her platonic soulmate, even though she was too busy to be an ongoing presence in my mom's life as Fran would have liked.

But when Lorraine walked into her bedroom, even though Fran hadn't said anything for several days, she sat up and embraced Lorraine with pure and total joy, calling her by name. It was utterly touching. I'm glad that she and Lorraine had a chance to say goodbye.

The for-profit hospice company didn't provide the support they had promised, so the last few days were intense and horribly exhausting. My mom was ready to die in her spirit, but I saw how her body, how her very cells, clung to life with a persistence and vitality I could never have imagined. We talked to her about journeying toward the light, and gradually, her whole being let go and she died.

Linda, who is psychic, saw Fran's spirit pause at the doorway to the light and glance back at us before leaving. It was sad but also a relief that her pain and weakness were gone. One of the hospice nurses came then and we helped her wash and prepare my mother's body for cremation.

Fran's Spirit Flies Free

The next day in meditation I saw and felt her spirit, filled with joy, flitting freely around the universe.

She said, with incredulous gladness, "I never knew it could be like this. I never knew I could be so happy!"

I was very happy for her and glad to get this message. And, at the same time, I was disappointed that she didn't apologize for all the shit she put me through! Not one word about me, no thanks, no apology! But I quickly put that aside and was grateful she was healed and free and reunited with Henry and her other loved ones.

A Beloved Member of Her Community

Before and after Fran died, many of her friends and community members called to see how she was. They were devastated when I told them she had passed. Some burst into tears, and many of them shared what a good, kind friend she had been; how well she listened to them and supported them, and what good advice she had given.

I was bewildered at first, and jealous of their positive experience of her. They seemed to be talking about a different person than the judgmental, intrusive mother I had known. But then I realized that her same energy, spread out over forty people, would feel quite different from when she obsessively focused only on my sister and me. I could accept that.

Remembering and Honoring the Dead

The next phase of my struggle with my sister was about having a memorial service. Like my mother with my father's death, my sister didn't want to have anything public; no memorial service, or public acknowledgment of any kind.

When my father died, I deferred to my mother's wishes, but Fran was my mom as well as as my sister's, and I wanted a ceremony.

Also, she had an entire community of people who loved her and wanted a chance to honor her and say goodbye.

I tried to talk with my sister about it, but she was adamant in her refusal. I wish I had been able to handle it better and insist with more love and include her more, but at the time I didn't know how to do it or how to be more open in my process. I don't know exactly why she felt that way, but she was and is a very private person, so perhaps she felt too vulnerable to have grief in public.

So, I went ahead and planned a memorial by myself. I called Fran's rabbi, arranged a time and the use of the synagogue, bought food, and wrote a eulogy. I invited everyone and told my sister what I'd done and invited her to the memorial. She was very unhappy about my doing it. She did come with her husband and daughter, but her reproachful, angry, grief-filled eyes stared at me. I knew I was the only one in the family who wanted a memorial, but it felt important to me to have that.

The service was lovely. The rabbi had known my mother well, and she spoke kind, true words about her. I gave the eulogy and other people shared too. My mother had loved chocolate, and I found a gourmet brand of chocolate called Fran's and bought some bars to include with the food.

My Deep Unexpected Grief

I had done a lot of healing work on my relationship with mother. I had let go of resentments and forgiven her, realizing on a deep level that she truly had done the best she could with the skills and knowledge she had. Although I still had self-hateful messages that echoed some of my experiences with her as a child, I didn't have unfinished business with her. I was healing and growing up again in a healthier and saner way, and the Goddess had become the unconditionally and completely loving mother I had longed for but never felt I had with Fran.

Honestly, I didn't and don't miss her. Because of her worry and judgments, she could never listen to me or support me without wanting me to do or be something different or telling me that what I did, thought, and said was wrong.

She criticized and worried about my weight, my hair, my clothes, my career choices and pretty much everything I did. I loved her, but I always had to protect myself from her criticism and disaster predictions; and be very careful about what I told her about my life, or what I said in response to her stories and comments.

She would ask my advice repeatedly about her own life and then, if I offered a suggestion, say "Yes, but . . . this is why it is wrong, stupid, or won't work."

Finally, I learned to say only, "That's sounds challenging, but I'm sure you'll figure it out."

Once I returned home after the memorial service, I was surprised by the depth of my grief. I felt stricken, like heavy stones were weighing down my heart. I could barely function at work or at home, and it went on for days and weeks.

We weren't close, but she was my mother. She had carried me in her body for nine months and raised me as best she could. She had been one of my biggest and most difficult teachers since I was born. Losing her was one of the hardest events of my life.

About six months after she died, I joined a hospice grief group. I learned about all the different ways people respond to grief and loss, including rage. That helped me understand my sister's behavior better. And, it was comforting to be with others who were grieving.

One of the weeks, we each took a turn to do a "show and tell" in which we shared whatever we wanted to about our loss and our lost loved one. I showed pictures of Fran and talked about her life and accomplishments. I read the eulogy I had given, and also talked about the not so nice parts that I didn't put in the eulogy but have talked about here. It was another layer of healing and detaching. After that, my grief gradually lessened and my heart grew lighter again.

Chapter Thirteen

College of Darkness

*Note: *The names of the town and college, and the names of most people in this section, have been changed or shortened to protect my peace of mind.*

I dreamed I was back at Carquenas Community College.

In the dream, our offices were dorm rooms. I woke up suddenly in the middle of the night and knew two things — the building was on fire, and I was the only one remaining in it. The people in charge had forgotten me when they implemented the evacuation plan.

I got out of bed and looked at the door. It was locked with a double deadbolt, no doorknob or key. Terrified I thought, "I'm trapped; I'm going to die here." But when I put my hand up and touched the door, it opened. So did the door at the entrance to the stairwell and the one at the bottom of the stairs. I made it safely out of the building.

Later in the dream, I met with the head of the school to complain about what had happened, and how they had abandoned me. She looked at me as if I were insane, and began to calmly and reasonably justify their actions, indicating that I was the one with the problem and that they hadn't done anything wrong.

This dream, which I had six months after I left the College, accurately reflects how I felt working there for twenty years. I endured and survived the workplace injury called mobbing, a kind of mass bullying with participation, or at least collusion, by management.

When I first learned the term mobbing, after most of this abuse had already happened, I sat in my office and sobbed for an hour, in grief at what had happened to me, and in relief that there was a name for it, and I wasn't alone.

You have to understand that I was a skillful and hard-working professor. I earned consistently good evaluations from my students and the adjunct instructors I supervised. I always finished reports on time, led some committees (including the College Budget Committee and the Diversity Task Force), and contributed to many others. I organized cultural events at the College, did outreach to the community, served as a consultant to colleagues in other departments about how to serve their ESL students, and spent extra time with my own students. My innovations were often adopted by others, although I was rarely if ever given credit.

But in the dysfunctional stew that was this workplace, my skills, hard work, and creativity themselves were threatening. Because these qualities were combined with my minority status (progressive, Jewish, lesbian, woman) and my willingness to stand up for principles and against injustice towards other minorities, I became a target.

The ordeals during the time I was at Carquenas Community College made it perhaps the darkest period of my life. I'm grateful for all the support I had from Linda, from my 12 Step programs, from therapists, and from friends. But nonetheless, my whole being, my entire sense of self-worth, were under assault and attack; and it went on and on.

Although there were challenges throughout my twenty years there, the final six years were a nightmare of fear, shame, PTSD, and emotional battery. It all reinforced and validated the worst messages of my childhood — that I was worthless, that I would never be good enough, that nothing I did was right, that I had no value except for what I did. And if someone criticized me or my actions, then I wasn't lovable or worthy of respect and kindness, but all alone in a sea of hostile people.

How I Got the Job from Hell

When I recommitted myself to ESL and decided I was really going to go for a full-time job, even if it meant relocating, it was a whole process of sharpening my resume, then finding and applying for job openings. Several times I made it to the second interview but wasn't hired.

I almost didn't go on the interview at Carquenas because it was scheduled for the day after I returned from Japan. They hadn't contacted me via phone, only sent a "snail mail" letter, which I happened to open in my huge stack of mail right after I came back.

I panicked and called them and asked if there was any way to reschedule it, but they said no, it was this or nothing.

I thought, "I've worked hard and long for these interviews and to land a new job, so I'll go. I can rest after that."

I found some pantyhose and a copy of my resume and looked up directions and went up to the interview; and Carquenas ended up being the college that hired me. I was too tired and jet-lagged to be nervous, so I'm sure that helped.

A Very Brief Honeymoon in 1989

I was ecstatic to finally have a full-time tenure-track job after seven years of being a freeway flyer.

The head of HR told me later there had been some uncertainty about hiring me because they thought I was too "big city" for this small-town environment; and they didn't think I would fit in. I found out later that "big city" is often code for "Jewish." And concern about "fit" often disguises a desire to hire people exactly like them instead of seeing the value of diversity.

So, there I was — newly hired, thrilled and excited, naively thinking that now I would belong and have supportive colleagues in a forward-thinking environment. Being an adjunct, or 'freeway flyer', had been very hard. I was running around to many schools. I was overworking because I was afraid there wouldn't be enough work or that classes would cancel. I never really had time to do anything thoroughly. I was always scrambling to start the semester, to finish the semester, to plan lessons, to deliver lessons, to grade tests and essays, to turn in grades, to teach, to do the very best I could for my students with inadequate time and never enough money.

And I was grateful to finally be paid decently, to have benefits and summers off, and once I attained tenure, to have job security.

When I first started meeting people there, everyone was cordial and welcoming. I remember sitting in my brand-new office the first week feeling tremendous joy. I was truly a professional and a professor! I had my own office! I had status, a permanent school, a true career. I had arrived! Now, I thought, I could really spend all the time I needed to lovingly craft lessons and become the best teacher I could be. It was the fulfillment of a deep longing.

Little did I know that I would have to use every trick I had learned as an adjunct to prepare for classes quickly and teach effectively with all the other responsibilities that were thrust on me. Nor, innocent and straightforward, did I understand the malice, mediocrity, and pettiness which are all too often part of academia.

The one advantage to being an underpaid and exploited adjunct faculty, which I hadn't fully appreciated at the time, was that I slid by a lot of the politics. I'm sure that other schools I worked at as a part-time adjunct were dysfunctional too, but I didn't have to deal with it. I was tired all the time, commuting and teaching, going to an occasional department meeting, and doing my best, always on the move. But, I steered clear of the venomous snake pit that many academic institutions are.

My pure joy only lasted a few weeks. There was a dissonance from almost the very beginning. My first semester, I created an expanded schedule for the next semester's ESL classes, and right away the acting VP of Instruction, told me there wasn't any classroom space to add new ESL classes. I was baffled and bewildered. They had hired me, paying me quite a bit of money for a full-time job plus benefits, to expand and strengthen the ESL program; and to better serve the (mostly Mexican) immigrant students. But here they were, immediately denying me the practical tools and logistical support I needed to fulfill the mission I was hired for.

Nevertheless, I kept working on the schedule and proposing creative ways to add classes; and was finally able to secure rooms.

In retrospect, that was a small example of the way my entire career there would be. Over and over, they paid lip service to ESL students, to diversity, to making things better, but when it came down to the practicalities, no one wanted to give resources, space, or time. Almost no one wanted anything to change at all.

Even worse, there was active hostility and discouragement about change. Even now, it's hard to write about all this. The cruelty, the indifference, the disconnect between what they said and what they did confused and frustrated me. And, I was trying to manage everything with self-will, because my relationship with the Divine hadn't yet become a sustaining part of my daily personal and work life.

Benevolent Division Chairs Shielded Me

I didn't feel the full effects of these negative attitudes and behaviors for the first seven years I was there, because I was protected by my Division chairs.

Dolores, the Division Chair during my first year, had an odd mixture of beliefs. She generally behaved in a very kind and inclusive way, and had a dear friend at the College, Arthur, who was an openly gay man. But at the same time, in a separate compartment of her beliefs, she was a very traditional Catholic who told me she believed unequivocally that homosexuals were going to hell. I certainly didn't feel safe to come out to her.

At the end of that first year, Dolores retired, and I was sad to see her go despite our differences, because she had no malice and was supportive of my academic work. Fortunately, Rich took over as Division Chair for the next six years. He had been on my hiring committee and was my ally and supporter for many years.

Fifties Time Warp (Again)

Dolores wasn't the only prejudiced person at the College. The head of the criminal justice division at the College pulled me aside my first week there and told me in a low tone, "Just so you know, Carquenas is in a 1950s time warp."

"Really?" I said, not quite believing him.

But I learned very quickly that he was absolutely right. Carquenas was very much like Downey had been when I grew up there in the 1950s and 1960s. It wasn't a safe place for a progressive Jewish lesbian who talked to the Goddess. I felt lonely and stifled, not safe to talk about who I really was.

Having come out in the San Francisco Bay Area, I had never before experienced what it was like to be closeted, though I had read and heard about it. I never ever want to feel that way again.

When you're keeping a big secret, you can't be open with people, you can't relax, and so of course it's harder to make connections. I did know of a few lesbians who lived locally, and tried to reach out to them. That was another rude awakening. Again, because I came out in the San Francisco Bay Area, I thought all lesbians were politically progressive, artistic, spiritually aware — sophisticated citizens of the world.

But the lesbians I met were very much like the people there who weren't lesbians — politically conservative and with limited experience of a wider world. I didn't feel very comfortable with them either. I could be open about my sexuality, but they didn't understand much of anything else about me, especially my being Jewish and progressive.

Student Disconnect

I also had a big challenge I had not anticipated because the students were very different from my ESL students in San Francisco and the East Bay. All the students I'd had before at the community college level at other schools, had a high school education or some college in their own countries and languages. When I started at Carquenas, I didn't understand that most of the students there were very poor immigrants who hadn't had much opportunity for education in Mexico, or whatever country they had come from.

And the ESL program at the College wasn't well designed to serve the students. Before I was hired, the program seemed to be going through the motions in a perfunctory way, teaching students a little bit but not holding them accountable for anything.

I frustrated the students and shamed them at first, unintentionally, by having expectations of them that were completely unrealistic. I didn't realize that they couldn't do what I asked in terms of homework or writing and grammar, because they lacked context, background, and understanding of the concepts.

A few of them complained about me to the VP of Student Affairs. I can't imagine a worse way to address this important issue than what he did. He didn't tell me there were complaints. He didn't tell me he was meeting with some of my students. He didn't talk to me afterwards about what the students said or let me respond or share my perspective or ask questions. He didn't work with me to understand what had gone wrong and how to fix it; or help me work with the students. He didn't meet with me at all. Instead, I heard through gossip that a meeting was happening and that he had invited other administrators as well. He held the meeting during our class time without informing me or even all the students, so some of them were with me for class and some went to the meeting. I was publicly criticized without any fair or balanced process at all.

My Expectations Shift

Rich was able to protest how this had been mishandled and protect me from any escalation. I was hurt and angry, but I wanted the students to be successful and for me to be the teacher they needed. Determined to find answers, I took a hard look at what was missing; the students needed explicit instruction in college success skills. So, I redesigned the curriculum to incorporate basic study skills: time management, step-by-step concept building, a process for learning and remembering, and strategies to study for tests. None of these skills had even been mentioned in my TESOL master's degree training, but I researched this and learned on my own how to teach this. I began to include these skills in every ESL class I taught, and made sure my adjunct faculty did the same.

I still held students to high academic standards, but because I was supporting them and helping them gain the skills they needed, they saw me as an ally, even when I was tough on them academically. As I learned to understand them and meet them where they were, I could see my students at the College were every bit as wonderful and dedicated as the ESL students I'd had earlier; and we began to love and appreciate each other. As I healed myself in recovery, it was easier and easier to find the balance of strict accountability, but with warm support.

Belated Appreciation

Lila had been one of the leaders of this student movement, and had expressed rage and resentment against me. Years later, she finished her education and was hired as support staff in the EOP (Economic Opportunity) program at the College. I ran into her on campus one day, and she apologized to me. She told me how much she appreciated now what I had tried to do to help the students succeed, and how much she had learned from me without realizing it.

Full-Out Assault and Maddening Petty Microagressions

The attacks I experienced intermittently were a crazy-making mixture of petty insults, subtle acts of exclusion, microaggression, and full-out assault. For a while, Rich protected me from some of the worst impacts, but even he couldn't prevent it all. Over time, I saw subtle or blatant expressions of racism, misogyny, and hatred of LGBTQI people, tolerated or ignored, as long as it was expressed by the favored people in authority, mostly older white men and a smaller group of women whom I called the icy blonde coterie. At the same time, any mistake, no matter how small on the part of newer, younger Black, Latinx, Asian faculty or, occasionally, white women, was pounced on as proof that we didn't belong there. When Rich stopped being Division Chair, I was exposed to the full force of the malice and dysfunction on and off for years.

Microaggressions, microinsults, and microassaults, tend to be smaller, more subtle aspects of mobbing, but quite hurtful cumulatively. Here is one that stuck in my mind: At a Division meeting, people were asking about a website for free graphics. I had found one, and even though I was mostly keeping quiet in meetings by this time, it seemed safe enough for me to write the website on the board so everyone could use it. The next day Kathy, one of the faculty, sent an email to every single person in the Division, about sixty people altogether, which said Lorraine wrote down the website wrong and here is the right web address. I double-checked, and I had written the right address on the board. I wanted to answer back — you wrote it wrong not me! But it was a lose/lose situation. If I sent an email to everyone correcting her, I seemed petty and hysterical.

If I said nothing, it fueled the narrative that I was incompetent. If this had been the only time something like this happened, it truly wouldn't have been a big deal. But small slights and insults like this happened over and over. They frustrated me deeply and wore me down. I was smart, effective, innovative, and outspoken, but in the wrong "package." If I had been a white man, these qualities wouldn't have been seen as nearly as much of a threat to the status quo.

The general bigger assault pattern, which repeated over and over was: Administration or faculty would make outrageous accusations against me or attempt egregious denials of resources. I would challenge it and fight it, and eventually it would be dealt with or cleaned up. One big theme was malicious gossip against me — that I was difficult, pushy, that I lied, that I was crazy, that people didn't want to work with me. This kind of false gossip, as I later learned, is one of the hallmarks of mobbing.

My personnel file in particular was like a revolving door, with lies and accusations added, then my documentation challenging the lies, then the offensive material being removed. The President of the College put a personal letter of apology in my file after one of these lying campaigns. But nothing changed. I didn't yet have enough self-love or spiritual support to brush all these false criticisms off. Of course, that kind of situation is horrible for anyone, no matter how sane or loving. This kind of abuse was intermittent the entire time I was there, but certain situations were especially malicious.

Agatha Hates Me from the Very Beginning

The new Division Chair, Agatha, decided that how I handled ESL curriculum development and changes was proof that I was an incompetent slacker/liar. It gave her the excuse she wanted to make my life a living hell from then on. It didn't matter to her that I had done exactly what Dolores, the previous Division Chair had requested, renumbering some existing courses and adding new ones; nor that I was absolutely willing to make any changes Agatha wanted that would work academically. No, I had broken her (invisible) rule, and I was her enemy forever, to be conquered and broken. Here are some of the actions she took to undermine and discredit me, alone and with her co-conspirators, since she spread her lies about me to the whole division.

Honesty Is the Enemy

Agatha and the new English Department Chair, Emmeline, took away developmental English classes I'd been teaching without notifying me, setting me up to be abusively screamed at by Emmeline when I asked what had happened and why she hadn't let me know that she didn't want me to teach for her.

A Boldfaced Lie

Agatha told the VP of Instruction that I had hired teachers as adjunct faculty without clearing them with her, which would have been a huge breach. Fortunately, as part of my CYA (cover your ass) thorough documentation, I had saved a copy of the memo I sent Agatha, with her scrawled response giving me permission to go ahead with the hiring. I brought a copy to the meeting with her and the VP. Agatha didn't acknowledge or apologize for her "mistake." She hated me more for showing her up.

The Star Chamber Evaluation

Each faculty member had to go through an evaluation process every three years. I had always before easily received very satisfactory ratings, but Agatha was determined to give me a bad evaluation. If I was given an unsatisfactory rating and didn't bring it up to satisfactory by *her* standards, the College might be able to start proceedings to fire me, even though I had tenure. This unsatisfactory rating would also have put me under her thumb and completely in her power.

To perpetrate this, the biased evaluation team, Agatha and the other members, hand-selected their allies and gathered anonymous, malicious feedback against me. With no names, specifics, objective data or documentation, all they had were anonymous general statements that these people didn't like me or think I was doing a good job. The evaluation team ignored all the positive specific comments from the adjunct faculty I supervised, and the glowing appreciation from my students and some colleagues. Nothing I said, nothing anyone wrote on my behalf, could penetrate their determination to blame me.

There Is No Law against Being Stupid or Cruel

But the one thing I could do and I did do was refuse to sign off on the evaluation form. Agatha thought she could badger and intimidate me into signing my name, but even though I felt afraid and vulnerable, I absolutely refused. Without my signature, they couldn't go forward.

Instead, Agatha brought my evaluation to the VP of Instruction, who hadn't a clue how to deal with the situation. Instead of doing her job and looking objectively at what was happening, she hired an outside administrator to go around the campus and ask everybody if I was difficult to work with. A few of them said I was difficult, or they didn't like working with me, but there was nothing specific to point to.

The Academic Senate, the local union, and HR refused to help me, but I appealed to the state level of the union and they hired an attorney specializing in discrimination to assist me. The very first thing she said to me when I walked into her office was, "You have to understand, there is no law against being stupid or cruel." This was blunt, but absolutely true.

It took eighteen months for a process that should only have lasted three months, but I finally found my way to a satisfactory evaluation and was able to have all the inflammatory and offensive material removed from my file. But this took a devastating toll on my physical and emotional well-being. I had drawn much of my self-esteem from my work, and I was baffled and deeply wounded by the virulence of this unwarranted and malicious attack against me. The most frightening part was that the truth didn't matter, that the lack of evidence for my "crimes" didn't matter, that nothing I said or did made any difference. They were determined to find me "guilty." I was far from the only target, though one of the few white ones. Sometimes I was an ally to others who were targeted, which made me more of a target too.

Sometimes I was attacked for my strengths, such as presenting a lucid report that could be a model for others, having a screwdriver on my Swiss army knife to help with the language lab assembly when the male lab tech didn't have one (and glared at me in hatred when I produced mine), or standing up for a Black faculty member, a Black instructional assistant, or a Filipina history professor under attack for trying to add more progressive curriculum; or my closest colleague, Marlene, an Afro-Caribbean, Puerto Rican woman, who was even more of a target than I was.

Diversity Efforts Hit a Wall, Time after Time

The College included Diversity issues as a key mission (this was years before DEI, Diversity, Equity, Inclusion, Belonging, were the preferred descriptive terms). A small group of us started a diversity committee, dedicated to making the mission statement a reality. We worked hard and diligently, but our efforts were stonewalled. They sometimes even backfired and made us bigger targets. Here are a couple of examples.

White Men Want to Keep Writing History

Jane was a new Black and Filipina professor in the Social Studies Department who didn't yet have tenure. Her Division Chair asked her to create a new class about the history of the Philippines, which she did, accurately including topics about U.S. colonization and hegemony in the curriculum. Our small group of diversity advocates heard that the Curriculum Committee was not going to approve the class, so we all went to the meeting. Although Jane's Division

Chair should have presented the class proposal with her, she was too frightened of this group to stand with her, and Jane was left to face the wrath of the favored bullies alone. Because of our intervention and our questions, they ended up approving the class, a victory. But then the committee members met secretly and changed the rules to close the Curriculum Committee meetings, which had always been open to anyone, so we could never protest a decision of theirs again. No one in the Administration was concerned about this change.

Diversity Trainer Becomes a Target

The Diversity Committee also wrote a proposal and gained funding to bring an internationally known diversity and intercultural communication expert to the campus to do trainings. Marlene and I took a leadership role in making this happen. We had such high hopes that this would change the campus climate, but we were naive to think that one training, no matter how astounding, would bring about the change toward equity and inclusion we longed for. We did succeed in bringing her on campus. She said afterwards that it was the most hostile, oppositional school she had ever been to. Unlike her experience at most colleges she had consulted and spoken at, none of the high-up administrators would meet with her. Faculty and staff refused to participate fully in the trainings.

Attacked for Being an Advocate

Often, I was attacked for advocacy actions for my immigrant ESL students as well. Most of the faculty thought that any resources to help these students meant less for their departments and routinely opposed it.

The horror continued after Agatha left as Division Chair. The new Division Chair was an ex-military Major and current Spanish teacher named Pedro. From my observation, he basically hated women unless they were very feminine and compliant. He definitely hated lesbians, and he hated me in particular for being outspoken and thinking I had a right to be treated with respect as the ESL expert I was. Although he didn't say this to me directly, one of the counselors, who was Black and on the Diversity Committee, told me he overheard Pedro, Thomas, and others using insulting language about me as a lesbian.

A Turning Point:
From Powerless Rage to Forgiveness

I walked out of my office one day after yet another egregious injustice, the details of which I can't recall. But I clearly remember walking into the building lobby filled with a blind and fiery rage. For a fleeting moment, I passionately hated every single person there and wished them ill.

I shocked myself with the power of this overwhelming anger! I never wanted to be consumed with hate! It terrified me that I felt so desperate and enraged and out of control. I knew then that I had to work on forgiveness and letting go, or my heart would shatter into a thousand bitter pieces and I might never recover. I began to pray for these horrible people. I did that every day for five years.

Forgiveness Is a Gift for Me

I didn't pray to forgive them because I thought what they did was right. I did it for me and for my own well-being. My initial prayer said:

Grant these people (each one listed by name) everything I want for myself, including spiritual, emotional, and physical healing, transformation, and enlightenment, because they really need it! Grant them love, prosperity, peace, acceptance, success, an open heart and mind. And grant that I may release bitterness, rage, resentment, grief, shame, and blame, so I may let go, forgive, and be free.

I had learned about forgiveness in my 12 Step programs and praying for my oppressors at the college in this way was the catalyst for later including forgiveness work in all my conflict resolution teaching and coaching.

Saying that prayer every day, though I didn't at all mean it at first, helped me. It softened my bitterness and resentment. And gradually, over time, I found some compassion for the people I was praying for.

What they did to me and others was horrible, but I came to understand that they felt as if they were fighting for their very survival. The very idea of change, and the possible loss of unearned privilege, which I represented, were so terrifying to them that they felt justified in doing anything to stop it and me. I was a change agent and therefore their archenemy. The names on my prayer list changed, as some people retired and new ones with the same attitudes took their places, but the need for forgiveness remained.

The Hijacked Language Lab

The school badly needed a language laboratory. When an opportunity came to land a Title III grant and create a lab, I put in hundreds of unpaid hours to secure the grant, figure out the best lab configuration, select a lab management system and other hardware and software, design the physical layout; and then teach myself how to use the new software and teach it to other instructors. Everyone was quite willing for me to be responsible for this, and I doubt the lab would have become a reality without my work, but I was never given credit or acknowledgement for it. The grant was supposed to help underrepresented students, and criteria specifically mentioned ESL, but once we had the lab, no one from the granting agency followed up to make sure the lab was serving the students it was intended for.

An additional serious problem was that the language lab technician had no training in the new software. It was frustrating because the students needed assistance when they were working independently in the lab. The VP and other administrators ignored my complaint that he needed training. I wasn't his supervisor, and he wasn't open to taking help from me.

When I did offer software training for the ESL and Languages Department, he and Pedro sat in the back with contemptuous smirks on their faces. They openly scoffed at the idea that I, a woman, and not a technician, could have taught myself the software and how to use it. They weren't willing to accept my hard work and knowledge.

Finally, I asked the VP of Instruction to make sure that Thomas received training or, as a last resort, that he be transferred and have someone else be our lab tech who would learn the software and be able to assist the students. But, the issue was framed by Human Resources and the Administration as a personality clash. I insisted it was an issue of competence and job performance. The head of Human Resources decided she would hold a mandatory "mediation" to deal with this. At the so called "mediation," I was targeted and publicly chastised by the lab tech, my Division Chair, the head of HR, and the union representative who was supposed to be supporting me. No one was there to intervene, to make sure the process was fair and balanced and civil, or to be an ally for me. They took turns venting and verbally attacking me, saying how horrible and wrong I was in every way. I desperately wanted to leave the meeting, but feared they would have said I was "uncooperative." It was a star chamber again, mob rule, and I walked out shaking and completely devastated.

This Can't Be What a Mediation Is

The horrific mob "mediation" eventually showed me a way out of the nightmare. During the meeting, I thought, "This can't be what a mediation is. There must be better ways to resolve conflict."

A fellow ESL teacher at another college told me about a Conflict Resolution certificate program at Sonoma State University and a class starting soon called *Gender and Conflict.* I took it, and I started taking all the classes for the program while I was still a professor at Carquenas. I loved those classes and they ended up lighting the way to a new career.

A Year of Deepest Darkness

My last year there was pure hell. I was working toward another career, but this was the only way I had to earn a living in the present. I felt beleaguered, surrounded by enemies, beaten down. Even Marlene and I were no longer close. I realized that while she wanted and appreciated my listening ear, my support, and perspective, she was not able or willing to be present for me in return. I was systematically stripped of any say in the functioning of the lab, and time and resources for the lab were redirected to the Spanish and French departments instead. We only used the lab a few semesters before it was basically taken away from us, which broke my heart. It was a sad loss for my students and our hopes to strengthen the ESL program.

Invisible Woman

I did what all the literature I read said to do if you were being mobbed but weren't ready or able to leave. I kept my head down, I did my work, I hid in my office, I documented everything, I withdrew from any leadership positions, and I basically didn't talk to anyone. I started therapy to help me with the PTSD and broken-heartedness I was already experiencing.

My Friends Fear for Me

Everybody who cared about me, my beloved Linda, dear friends, my therapist, and program comrades, were worried about me. They witnessed the horrible negative impact on my body, mind, and spirit, of being in this place day after day where I was under assault. My therapist said it was as if I was driving into a prison every day and then coming home; then with dread and grief, doing it again the next day.

At Least I Wear Pink

My poor inner child, little Lorry, could hardly bear it. Since I wouldn't leave, the only thing she asked was that I wear pink every day when I went there. My whole last year I wore a pink top or a pink scarf or sweater every single day. But nothing was enough to keep me safe or ok there. And it took little Lorry quite a while to forgive me for what she went through.

My Fears Kept Me Stuck

I was terrified to leave for an uncertain future. I had worked long and hard to have tenure, to have a secure teaching job with benefits. But it became clearer and clearer that I had to get out, or my spirit would not survive intact. I knew I was also at risk for physical symptoms and illness because of the stress and hostility I experienced on a daily basis.

During this time, I had a Goddess Can, a coffee can into which I put messages to the Divine. I wrote note after pleading note, "Please get me out of here." "Please show me the path to leave. I can't take it anymore."

Plotting My Escape

In 2008, I obtained my Conflict Resolution certificate. Sonoma State offered me a very part-time job teaching in the program starting 2009 because people were retiring and they knew I had a lot of college level teaching experience.

I started making a plan to leave. I had the one class to teach at Sonoma State and I also applied to be an adjunct faculty member in ESL at Santa Rosa Junior College. They hired me and gave me a contract for a class.

But when I proposed cutting down to 80% at Carquenas, which I was legally allowed to do, the acting VP of Instruction, a member of the mob, wouldn't let me cut the number of classes I taught unless I stopped being Program Coordinator. I knew without a doubt that if I gave that position up and was no longer able to set my own teaching schedule, they would screw me. They would make up some reason and insist I be there weekends and evenings and it would be worse than working there full-time mostly during the day.

My Mother Vs. the Goddess

I knew I had to leave completely, without the transition to part-time I had hoped for, but I was scared. The final clear decision came one day when I was walking on campus.

I heard a voice say strongly, "You must never ever leave a secure job. Even if it kills you, you have to stay."

And I thought, "Whose voice is that?" I knew instantly, it was my mother's voice, child of the Depression that she was.

I asked myself, "What would the Goddess say instead?"

I knew she would say, "I love you, and I will always take care of you. Your soul and well-being are more important than the job."

I Choose the Goddess

I had a stark choice. I could listen to my mother's voice or I could listen to the Goddess. I made a whole chart with two columns: What the Goddess Said versus My Mother's Opinions.

I found the courage, trust, and self-love to choose the Goddess's voice and actively began to plan my escape.

Three Crucial Letters

As part of my healing and saying goodbye, I wrote three crucial letters; not to send but solely for my spirit and healing.

College as Dysfunctional Boyfriend

I wrote one as if the College were a dysfunctional boyfriend I had broken up with.

"You said you loved me. You've apologized for your behavior many times and promised me repeatedly you would change and treat me better. But none of that is true. You've shown me over and over that you're lying, that you won't change. I'm through with you and your abuse! I'll still be polite

*to you if I meet you on campus, but I will not be fooled
again! I don't believe what you say, and I deserve better."*

My Darling Baby Lab

The second letter I wrote was to the ESL language laboratory. I wrote
it as if the lab were a child that I had lost custody of.

My darling baby lab,

*It was no accident you were born. You were conceived in
love. I planned carefully for you. I worked very hard to
birth you and nurture you. I wanted you to grow and
flourish with warm support.*

*But they've taken you away from me, and there is nothing
I can do to help you or protect you. I have to let you go,
and I'm so sorry that I can't be there for you while you
grow up.*

Goodbye, my darling.

Thank You for All You Did

The third letter I wrote was after I had officially submitted my resig-
nation but was still finishing my last semester at the College. The VP
of Instruction sent me a stiff formulaic three-sentence letter thanking me for my (unspecified) service. Instead of feeling bitter and
unappreciated, I wrote the letter to myself that I knew I deserved,
thanking me for all the gifts I gave to the College.

I know I made many mistakes while I was there, and nothing
I did brought any long-term changes at Carquenas. The ESL depart-

ment diminished to the former level after I left and there was no one to advocate for it. The toxic culture didn't shift; I heard from several people at the College who were mobbed in the same way years after I left. Nonetheless, I can feel good about the positive difference I made in many people's lives while I was there, and claim my accomplishments in the face of toxic hostility and opposition.

Here is the letter I wrote for myself:

May 26, 2009

Dear Professor Segal,

I know we far from appreciated you properly while you were working at Carquenas Community College. But I can't let you leave without sincerely and thoroughly acknowledging and expressing my appreciation of your outstanding dedication and service to the college in many areas.

First, your teaching. You have become one of the best teachers I ever had the pleasure of observing and working with. Your unique combination of expertise, creativity and playfulness, innovation, original and thoughtful curriculum, helped the students learn not only English, but life skills, college success skills, critical thinking and analysis skills, intercultural competencies, and a conscious awareness of American society and cutting edge social and political issues.

Because all these elements have been coupled with your genuine, heartfelt, caring approach to your students, your classroom has been a safe and inspiring place for students to take risks, learn, and grow.

Second, your work as Program Coordinator has been outstanding in many ways. In an extension of your stellar teaching skills, you have mentored and inspired many adjunct faculty, observing them in the classroom, giving supportive, insightful feedback on how they can improve as teachers, generously sharing materials, inspiring them to take risks and try new approaches, and giving them the space and the support to develop their own teaching styles.

You also supported their professional growth by getting funding for projects and including them, such as your work in developing the new low-level grammar/writing class and student learning outcomes. You shielded them from some of the worst college dysfunction and advocated for their needs as adjuncts, such as petitioning for office hours and pay raises for them.

You taught yourself how to run the department smoothly and efficiently, dealing with problems with flexibility and the courage to make difficult decisions. You advocated for your ESL students and their needs at hundreds of meetings, as well as creating and teaching workshops about how college instructors in other departments, especially nursing, could understand and serve their ESL students better.

Third, your contributions to the soul of the institution, in the face of unremitting opposition and hostility are worthy of the deepest respect and admiration. You worked hundreds of extra hours alone, or with small groups, or on committees, to get the college to look at its prejudice and discrimination, to get us the training we needed to change ourselves and to change college protocols for hiring, for assisting black, Latino, and Asian students, for supporting new Black, Latino, and Asian employees, and in general making this a safe egalitarian place that honored difference and respected achievement, not similarity and in-group status.

The special program you created and secured approval for, so undocumented students could attend academic ESL classes, benefited many who would otherwise not have continued their education beyond the adult schools.

With great personal courage, you stood up in difficult and frightening situations for people who were targets of racism on the campus, including Marlene, Hiroko, Jane, Edward, and others.

Unfortunately, you paid a huge price for your work in these areas and were yourself discriminated against, scapegoated, abused, and mobbed.

I want to apologize for the horrific, hostile, and utterly unfair treatment you received, particularly in the malicious evaluation process with Agatha, and all the injustice, abuse and stupidity about your excellent work in creating an ESL lab.

You never received the appreciation and acknowledgement you deserved for the lab, or the status and authority you should have received. Your courage in standing up for yourself and others with almost no support and in the face of so much hostility and opposition is worthy of a medal of valor.

I understand why you are leaving the college, but it is with great regret and shame that I see you go. You have been such a force for good, for positive change on the campus, such a model of outstanding achievement, clarity, courage, and progress. You have been too good for us. You have shown us our mediocrity, our stupidity, our cowardice, our lack of vision, our lack of compassion or open-mindedness. We could not bear the mirror you held up to us, preferring to see you as the problem rather than try to change.

You are once again showing great courage in leaving and I commend you for choosing life, for choosing a leap of faith rather than hanging on to the known, the safe, the miserable, as we always do.

Thank you for trying. Thank you for your courage and integrity. Even though you won't be at the college to see it, I believe your accomplishments will make a difference eventually. You will leave a huge hole at the college that will be very difficult to fill.

All your skills and abilities will be tremendous assets to you in your new career. I know you will be very successful financially and in every other way, and I wish you all the appreciation and respect that you well deserve, but never received here.

Sincerely,

Carquenas Community College

I wrote that letter and I claim it as mine! I'm grateful and proud I could own it and give myself the praise and acknowledgement and apology that were my due and which helped me move on!

Escape!

Once I truly decided to leave, I went to CalSTRS (California State Teachers Retirement System) and filled out all the retirement papers. I was lucky that they had a (now defunct) early retirement program. I don't think the retirement counselor had ever dealt with anyone like me.

I sat in his office crying uncontrollably, saying "I don't wanna leave. I'm not ready to leave, but I have to."

There were tears all over every page I signed. It was such a hard choice. I was terrified, but it was right.

I gave official written notice to the College and to Pedro. When I saw him after he had received the letter, he smirked at me and said, "Well, you're full of surprises aren't you?"

And that was all he ever said to me about it.

I Leave with Integrity

I left everything in my department in as good shape as I possibly could. Pedro knew I could've left things in a huge mess, with classes unstaffed and papers in chaos. There would've been no consequences because I was on the way out, and in a way, it would have been "justified" because of how they treated me.

He was clearly bewildered at my efforts to leave the department in an orderly way. But I wanted to leave professionally and in integrity, for myself and for the students, not for the school. So, I staffed all the classes, I triaged all my papers, I gave the important ones for running the department to the only other full-time person, who would have to take over as coordinator. I gathered the teaching materials and papers I wanted to take home, and I recycled the rest.

Before I left, I took one other action: I made amends for my part in negative interactions with people there. This came directly from step nine of my 12 Step programs. I learned in my programs that I don't have to take the whole responsibility, or believe the other person was right, but I do need to look at my share, no matter how small, and "clean up my side of the street." I didn't want to hold on to blame or rage.

So, I apologized to one teacher who had been a friend until she became Agatha's ally, for not explaining to her why I withdrew from our friendship.

I apologized to the other full-time ESL teacher, for my part in trying to "make" him respect me and do what I thought was right.

I apologized to Marlene for having expectations that she couldn't meet.

And, I apologized to Thomas. I was scared of him and felt intimidated, so my sponsor and I agreed that I could make written amends to him rather than verbal. After I loaded up my car for the last time and was ready to drive off the campus forever, I stuck a letter to him in the intercampus mail, apologizing for not understanding him and for trying to make him do things he wasn't able to do.

And I left. And I've never gone back. And I've never regretted it.

Chapter Fourteen

Out of the Cruelest Darkness into Light, Joy, and Right Livelihood

Even though writing or talking about my time at Carquenas can still bring up some grief, I see now that this great darkness was an important part of the path that led me to the deep joy of right livelihood. I can't regret what happened. It was horrific and I don't wish it on anybody; yet, it was a launching platform for my beautiful new career.

Grateful Even for the Darkness

Through this dark journey, as the Goddess promised, I found work that I am truly meant to do on the planet. Doing my conflict transformation work with love and care is a source of deep satisfaction and boundless joy. I am always growing and learning, knowing that I am in the right place doing the right thing, making a small contribution to *Tikkun Olam* (Hebrew expression for the repair and healing of the world).

Though I was battered and wounded from my time at Carquenas, it led me to work I am meant to do.

But finding my path didn't mean instant success. My business has been the next humbling teacher for me about acceptance, surrender, and aligning my will with the Divine. I have had many miracles and now have a lot of gratitude, but the path and timeline were not at all what I had in mind!

Goddess Is My Employer

I read a quote from a philosopher, Frederick Buechner, that offered a vision that inspired and guided me. He said, "The place God calls you to is the place where your deep gladness and the world's deep hunger meet."

I prayed to find a new career, a new calling, where that gladness and need would meet, and I found it in the conflict transformation field. But finding my path didn't mean instant success. My business has been the next hubmling teacher for me about acceptance, surrender, and aligning my will with the Divine. I have had many miracles and now have a lot of gratitude, but the path and timeline were not at all what I had in mind!

Self-Willing a Business (Ha!)

When I first left the community college in June 2009, it wasn't enough for my perfectionism that I was saving my soul and my life, I was still judging myself by my critical mother and other negative influences, and had a need to *prove* I deserved to leave.

The proof, I believed, was in showing how very hard I worked, and using my self-will to *make* business success happen. The proof I craved was quantity — how many articles I wrote and published, how many clients hired me, how many teaching opportunities I had, how many hours I worked, and, most of all, how much money I made.

Some of this is a pitfall of people like me who, smart, determined, and innovative, have had success as creative problem solvers. I really thought that if I learned enough and worked hard enough, I could figure out how to *make* my business more viable, how to market, how to reach and enroll more clients.

A Steep Business Learning Curve

Since I knew nothing about creating or running or marketing a business, I took many steps to fill in the gaps.

The biggest single investment I made was a pricy year-long marketing and business development program. It involved four intense classes, mastermind groups, individual coaching, and homework assignments. I was a diligent student, doing everything I could to learn and grow. I tried so hard to learn their techniques and implement them. And, for a while, I was seen as a star student. I had some success with opportunities for giving presentations and then attracting attendees to a free initial consult, but when I took the class on selling, and how to actually enroll clients, I not only didn't have success but was in tears after every class session.

I Tried Everything I Could Think Of

I gave at least twenty-five presentations at community, professional, and business groups, and did over thirty free consultations in a row without enrolling any clients at all. I also created a website and have been (happily) writing a blog for thirteen years. I started a newsletter and an e-mailing list. I looked for and found opportunities to be a featured or guest blogger on other websites. I took classes in SEO and tried every networking opportunity I could find at least once.

I did informational interviews with people I thought might have referrals or suggestions for me. I collaborated on workshops. I taught classes at Sonoma State and invited my professional students to think of me as a resource.

Crashing and Burning, Again

A few years later, I took another five-month class that seemed promising, claiming to use a spiritual approach to help me learn skills to attract more clients and money. Some of it was valuable, but when I reached the "sacred selling" conversation, in which we were supposed to actually enroll clients, I crashed and burned again. I couldn't even practice without choking. I was enraged and devastated when I realized I had stalled and failed at the exact same point that I had in my year-long program seven years before.

There was something about trying to sell, especially using someone else's "proven" techniques that just short-circuited me. I could intellectually understand the process, but I couldn't do it without feeling like a hypocrite. When I talk to people who have conflict and communication issues, I can easily come from love and offer support and insight, but not when I'm trying to sell.

Crying Out in Despair

I reached a point, more than a few times, of total frustration and despair. The Goddess kept telling me She had a plan, that it was all unfolding in exactly the right way and time. But I thought She was lying! I cried for a whole month every day grieving the loss of my vision and my hope. I had poured all my heart and effort and energy and money and time and willingness to learn into my business for several years and had virtually nothing to show for it.

My business is fueled by my desire to be of service, to bring my gift to the world and move the world toward something I know it needs: peace and healing and the resolution of conflict. But I realized loud and clear that nothing I was doing was working — not my hard work, not my willingness to learn, not my creative problem-solving, not my self-will, not my passionate love for the work or my skill at doing the work. I couldn't make myself believe I was good enough at helping people. And, I couldn't muscle through the gap between my skills and my (lack of) success.

I realized that I had to surrender, but I didn't know how and I didn't know what it meant to let go.

I would surrender a little bit, and immediately think, "Did I surrender enough? Will it work now?" I hadn't really let go at all. I wanted to control my business still through surrender.

My Inner Separation
Between Money and the Sacred

Finally, I realized that something about my own relationship with money was getting in my way. So, I backed off the external foot work, and did a bunch of internal spiritual work. I worked the 12 Steps again with my business and money sponsor, specifically about my inner separation between money and the sacred and my addiction to overwork. We came up with questions and then I wrote answers, some channeled from the Goddess. Here is some of what She said:

> ***My dearest child,***
>
> *You have done so much work in many areas to heal the false beliefs and the wounds of your childhood and earlier adulthood. Your fears and false beliefs about money are your next challenge, one I know you will meet with my guidance and all the tools and support you already have.*
>
> *Listen to me now, my dearest, and believe. I am love and I am abundance. I am money and I am miracles. I am the Source of all that is good, and that*

good includes money. It is not separate or evil, it is a tool and a jewel of life.

You deserve a prosperous life, filled with love, purpose, and more than enough money. I want this for you. I will grant you this. All you need do is trust as much as you can each day. Strengthen your faith muscle every day. Do the footwork with gentleness and ease, knowing that I am keeping you safe and nothing can harm you while you are in my care, as you are always.

Your fears and worries are those of a small child, who sees something she doesn't understand and turns it to monsters under her bed. The only monsters are your distorted thoughts, dearest, I hold them and you with gentle love and kindness, soothing your every fear. All is well, my dearest, you are safe, and whole, and good, and protected, and loved, in this and every moment.

Give me all your fears and worries, let me heal them for you. Miracles are here, miracles are coming. There is enough money and love. There are enough clients just for you, and they will find you, and you will find them to great mutual joy, healing, and money, which are all part of the same whole.

Around overwork:

My darling child,

Stop overworking. Yes, stop. Yes, you. Yes, right now. You don't need to prove anything to me. I am working on your behalf to bring you all good, and I won't work any harder or faster because you are overworking. That is not how this process unfolds. You are not meant to be frantic and exhausted. You are not meant to feel totally responsible and take all this on.

Simply take some actions, dearest. Pray, meditate, and surrender. Do your small part and let go. All is unfolding more beautifully than you can possibly imagine. I've got you safe, and all you want will come to you in far better ways than you can foresee and in delicious abundance. You are on the path. Savor it. Trust. Hold on to me and let go of the rest, especially overwork.

It Is Still Hard to Surrender

Even with these direct loving messages, and lots of evidence that they are true, I have still found it difficult to let go of control in this area. The Divine brought me my beloved wife and a path out of Carquenas Community College, but I didn't want to surrender my business and business success. I wanted to micromanage everything!

But, since I was getting nowhere, I decided to try, to give Her all my fear and doubt, all my willful longing, all my resistance, my impatience, my scarcity thinking, my shame and self-blame, my belief that I'm supposed to suffer and overwork, and, instead, *to humbly ask, to trust, to do footwork, to go gently, and to surrender all outcomes, all transformations to the Divine.* To act as if I believe in Her miracles and Her plan.

Healing My Ancestors Around Money and Trauma

I also worked with a somatic therapist and uncovered ancestral trauma around money. Recent studies in epigenetics have shown that traumatic events can be passed on via DNA to descendants. The underlying message I absorbed, linked to my ancestors' experiences of antisemitism and fleeing pogroms (genocidal attacks on Jews), seems to be:

"You must do everything you can to accumulate as many financial resources as possible. But no matter how much money you have, it is never enough to keep you safe. It could all be taken away from you at any moment and you will have to flee again."

My wonderful somatic therapist, Jen, suggested I go back three generations to heal my ancestors and myself. With Jen's help, and with additional self-guided visualizations, I ended up going back nine generations to heal that trauma. I imagined meeting three generations of my ancestral mothers. I created a safe place for them to rest with a campfire. I welcomed them, wrapped them in blankets, washed their feet and hands and gave them soup.

Then, I asked if any of my ancestors were willing to go back further generations. Three of them volunteered, and that is how I was able to work on healing nine generations of my ancestors. It was powerful and helpful.

I really thought I would have an easier time enrolling and charging clients and receiving abundance. But like other approaches I'd tried, it didn't bring in more work or ease around money.

A True Miracle

But then I realized that I had had a true miracle.

Some new clients who needed help with bullying found me through my website and my blog posts, especially one I wrote called *The Injury of Mobbing in the Workplace*. A piece I had written about my own experiences being bullied in the workplace was finally, after a six-year delay, published in a book called, *Stand Up, Speak Out Against Workplace Bullying: Your Guide to Survival and Victory Through 23 Real Life Testimonies*. I spoke at a conference and gave other presentations and workshops about bullying issues.

Previously, I would do my best to help people who came to me with these issues, but I hadn't done much outreach, because when I would hear their stories or share mine, it would set off my PTSD and I would start to feel shaky and fearful.

But, with these new clients and speaking engagements, I wasn't getting triggered! I couldn't figure out why. I knew time and distance alone are not sufficient to heal these wounds.

So I asked myself, "Why am I more healed? What changed?"

And I realized with astonishment that it was the healing work I had done around money and my ancestral trauma that made the difference.

A Blinding Revelatory Light

This was like a blinding light. I have been freed to a large extent from the trauma of my toxic bullying workplace. But I hadn't even known I was working on it when I dealt with those spiritual issues around money! I thought the point was to bring me clients and prosperity.

But clearly, the Goddess wanted me to heal around my trauma and PTSD from Carquenas as well. The trauma my ancestors had experienced, which affected my attitudes toward charging for my services and believing in my skills as a coach and trainer, had worsened during my experiences at the College. And it was all healed at once by the spiritual work on money.

Her Plan

I knew with certainty that this had not been my plan, that I hadn't had a clue about this outcome. This was *Her* plan, and it was better than mine, beautiful and helpful and awesome. I thought, "If She has a plan around my healing that I don't know about, then maybe she really does have a plan for my business and how it is going to unfold."

I began, humbly, to trust and hope and surrender on a deeper level; to worry less about it all. I could gratefully focus on all the gifts and miracles that I do have in my life.

Messages from the Goddess Along the Way

I am blessed that because of all the spiritual work I've done, I can communicate directly with the Goddess. She speaks to me and says many wise, loving things I could never think of with my conscious brain.

Here are some more of my favorite messages/images from Her.

What Do You Have To Lose by Trusting Me?

Before I could even sit still and meditate, I did walking meditations. In an early one of these visualizations, the Goddess pinned me with Her gaze. Even in my mind's eye, it felt uncomfortable.

She stared intensely into my eyes and asked, "What do you have to lose by trusting me? What do you have to lose by believing I have a plan and am bringing all good things to you at exactly the right time and in exactly the right way?"

I knew immediately that what I had to lose was my fear and worry.

Have I Ever Dropped You Flat?

One time when I was feeling discouraged and frustrated, the Goddess encouraged me to look back over my life.

She asked me, "Have I ever abandoned you? Have I ever dropped you flat?"

"No," I said, "you never have."

"Then why do you think I'd drop you now? I never ever would."

Take My Hand, Look at Me (The Bridge)

Another pair of visualizations involved crossing a bridge. The Goddess was standing right in front of me and behind Her was a narrow, rickety suspension foot bridge made of worn wooden slats. She wanted me to cross the bridge.

She held out her hands to me and said, "Take my hands. Don't look down. Look at me, take the first step."

I did, but I was scared!

I told my somatic therapist about this, and did the same visualization sitting there with her. This time, when I took the first step on the bridge, I saw that, like Indiana Jones stepping out into the abyss in the film, *Indiana Jones and the Last Crusade*, the seemingly rickety bridge was actually surrounded by a rock-solid crystal bridge that was almost invisible. I knew it was completely safe to cross the bridge; that there was absolutely no way I could fall. It was a whole different level of trust.

Hiding Under the Covers

It is good to take right action, but the Goddess has assured me, "I love you every bit as much, even if all you do is hide under the covers all day."

I rarely feel like doing that anymore, but it is wonderful to know that I am loved and cherished unconditionally just for being, not for what I do.

Unhooking Worth from Dollars and Recognition

It has become easier and easier to stop equating my value as a human with the money I earn or the recognition I receive. I still want both, for sure, but the Goddess has told me so many times that all I have to do is put my light and love out in the world, and She will be glad. It doesn't matter to Her if I reach ten people or ten thousand, earn a hundred dollars or a hundred thousand. To Her, it all counts.

My Miraculous Journey — There Are No Dead Ends

As I look back over my life, with all the twists and turns, the seeming dead ends, the periods of terror and misery and frustration, what felt like endless times of waiting for self-acceptance, for true love, for right livelihood, I can see that the Goddess did indeed have a plan for my entire life, far better than any I could come up with.

And every piece of my journey has been essential to creating the immensely satisfying life I have today.

My parents gave me the early gift of books and words. Dealing with my mother's misery and control helps me develop empathy and sensitivity to others, which serves me well as a coach and teacher and friend. Being bullied and mistreated as a child because of being Jewish and different has sensitized me to oppression and prejudice.

Moving to Berkeley opened my mind and heart to the power of feminism and progressive politics, and I began to explore healing and music and the Divine Feminine. My search for a career led me to Mexico and Japan, which expanded and deepened my understanding of the world and different cultures.

Studying and teaching ESL was an ongoing education in life skills and compassionate clarity, about accepting and loving and meeting my students where they were. Years of teaching writing also helped me with my own writing and my writer's block. Running an academic department and supervising adjunct faculty taught me management skills without my realizing it.

My recovery programs lovingly transformed me and strengthened my resilience. I learned to forgive myself and take responsibility for my mistakes without shame.

I began to believe I deserved a good life.

Nothing was wasted. All the years I was unhappily single, I was actually learning how to appreciate and accept myself and others and building good communication skills, so that when I finally did meet Linda, I could love her as the beautiful, imperfect, human being she is.

The young adult I was couldn't have sustained a relationship like that because I couldn't love myself enough or see beyond my own negative feelings and fears. But now my darling wife and I have been living together for over thirty years in steadfast love.

My years working at the College of Darkness, perhaps the most difficult period of my life, taught me about standing up for myself and others in the face of hostile opposition and relentless harsh criticism. I found inner strength I hadn't known I had to fight the good fight, and then, finally, have the courage to walk away.

Experiencing that toxicity was awful, but I see now it was the only way the Goddess could pry me out of a narrow constrictive niche so I could find work that I was meant to do. If the College had been a more positive environment, I would most likely have stayed. It wouldn't have been a tragedy if that had happened, but I would never have known the far deeper joy of fulfilling my soul's purpose with conflict transformation coaching and teaching.

Starting and running my own business triggered my feelings of inadequacy all over again, and I had to surrender my fears around money and success in order to heal at a deeper level. I had started writing a blog purely to attract more clients, but that too, has been a source of satisfaction and a bridge to believing I could write a book.

Being of Service is the Deepest Joy

My dear cousin Laurel said to me recently, "You have more joy than anyone I know."

It is true that I have found a deeper capacity for joy than I ever knew was possible. Over and over, one day at a time, I am learning to turn from the darkness to the light, making a conscious choice each day to stay in the moment as best I can, and to embrace joy, trust, and gratitude, instead of shame, worry, or fear.

When negative feelings do arise, they pass through me far more quickly, and I can reset to peace. Instead of a harsh inner critic that contemptuously tells me everything I write is garbage, I have my adoring inner muse, Bookie, utterly loving and cheering me on.

And, I do keep getting wonderful new clients and opportunities, somehow. I know that I am not in charge or making it happen. Helping people heal around conflict and resentments through coaching and training, fills my heart with joy.

I am a handmaiden of the Goddess, and I use almost everything I ever learned through classes and life experience. I share all my mistakes and life wisdom with my clients and students, and they are grateful to know they don't have to be perfect to make things better. They are inspired by my journey to persist with their own.

In 2019, I created a professional development certificate program in Conflict Management at our local university, Sonoma State. It was a dream come true to take my vision of the best possible foundational program and make it real. I included a week on forgiveness and letting go of resentments, which was particularly satisfying. And the feedback from the students was overwhelmingly positive.

I still attend 12 Step meetings and work my programs of recovery, because I know I need the support and reminders to stay healthy and sane. Gratitude has become effortless.

Just Sit There and Let Me Love You

Recently, the Goddess started saying to me in meditation, "Just sit there and let me love you."

It is becoming easier and easier to let Her do that. And, resting secure in Divine love, guidance, and wisdom, I know that come what may, I am never alone in a hostile world.

We Are All Miracles

I always have hope, and support, and love, and purpose, and a beautiful sustaining path forward. I cannot control what happens next, but one day at a time, I can live a life beyond my wildest imaginings. Not a fantasy of perfection, but a real, beautiful, imperfect life filled with challenges, joy, love, satisfaction, angels, earthworms, and wonder. I wish that for all of you, dear readers. I truly am a miracle. And you are too.

Acknowledgements

I am so grateful to the many people who have guided me, inspired me, and supported me in living through the gifts and difficulties of my life, and in writing this book and getting it out into the world!

Big thanks to wonderful editors and book coaches Ginger Moran, Katherine Dieter, Lisa Tenner, and Meri Furnari. Any errors of grammar or writing are mine and no fault of theirs!

My brilliant marketing and book launch coach, Shayla Raquel, has been invaluable in helping me get the word out in the best ways possible. Judy Baker helped me organize and understand all things media.

The beautiful covers and interior are thanks to Melinda Martin, my inspired book designer.

BAIPA (Bay Area Independent Publishers Association) and all the kind, knowledgeable and talented members made me feel that publishing was possible.

I'm grateful to all the members of Shut Up & Write!, and to Stella Orange and her Show Up and Write group, who gave me places to write in community.

Thanks to marvelous mediator and interviewer Alesa Grace Thompson, and the equally wonderful Colin Rule, Clare Fowler and all the members of the Mediate.com community. Thanks as well to all the amazing conflict management organization, ACR, my professional home.

Appreciation to my cousin Laurel, my sister and her daughter, my other nieces and nephews, my mother and father, and all my other family members and in-laws whose stories are important to my own.

Thank you so much to all the wonderful courageous folks in my recovery programs, past and present, Casey M., Chris B. and Chris K., Bill B., Galen, Earik, Anna, Claude, Kate, and the many, many lovely and loving Tuesday, Friday, and Saturday morning people — you know who you are.

To all the members, past and present, of the beautiful Sistah Boom sisterhood, especially Yolanda Elizabeth Noriega, Bonnie Rosalind, and to Laurie Ann and all the brave women, men, and non-binary people who embraced radical feminism and a better world.

To my dear friends Meri "mica" Furnari, Angelica Chiong, Yuho, Umi, Laurel Etheridge, and Alan Alpert. I am grateful you have shared such important parts of my journey.

Thanks also to all my ESL students and my conflict management students and clients, who have been and continue to be some of my best teachers. Special thanks to Aron Ramirez for his articles about redlining and racial convenants in Downey.

To amazing therapists Ahbi Vernon, Patricia Stenger, and Vipasana Esbjorn-Hargens, who helped me heal and grow.

Thanks to my wonderful wife, always.

And in memory of Selene, Goddess sister; Rich Boehnke, dearest friend; Kay Sato, beautiful musician and spirit; Ricky Sherover-Marcuse, brilliant pioneer in unlearning racism; and Jen Rothman, powerfully loving healer, all of whom died far too soon.

The love, joy, and miracles in my life would never have happened without all of you. May you walk in the sunlight of the spirit always.

About the Author

Lorraine Segal

After surviving the '50s and '60s, as well as twenty years in toxic academia as a tenured professor, Lorraine Segal was inspired to start her own business, *Conflict Remedy*, happily teaching, coaching, blogging, and consulting about workplace conflict transformation. She is addicted to reading novels and enjoys walking and hiking in beautiful Northern California, where she lives with her wife. Her cartoon muse, Bookie, insisted that she write this book.

Leave a Review

If you enjoyed reading *Angels & Earthworms*,
please consider leaving a review on your platform of choice.
Reviews help self-published authors find more readers like you.